BUILDING THE ACADEMIC DEANSHIP
Strategies for Success

Gary S. Krahenbuhl

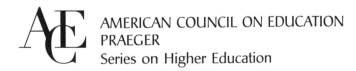

AMERICAN COUNCIL ON EDUCATION
PRAEGER
Series on Higher Education

Library of Congress Cataloging-in-Publication Data

Krahenbuhl, Gary S.
    Building the academic deanship : strategies for success / Gary S. Krahenbuhl.
      p. cm. — (ACE/Praeger series on higher education)
    Includes bibliographical references and index.
    ISBN 0–275–98326–9 (alk. paper)
    1. Deans (Education)—Vocational guidance. I. Title. II. American Council on
Education/Praeger series on higher education.
    LB2341.K73   2004
    378.1'11—dc22   2003068724

British Library Cataloguing in Publication Data is available.

Library of Congress Catalog Card Number: 2003068724
ISBN: 0–275–98326–9

First published in 2004

Praeger Publishers, 88 Post Road West, Westport, CT 06881
An imprint of Greenwood Publishing Group, Inc.
www.praeger.com

Printed in the United States of America

∞™

The paper used in this book complies with the
Permanent Paper Standard issued by the National
Information Standards Organization (Z39.48–1984).

10 9 8 7 6 5 4 3 2 1

Copyright Acknowledgments

The author and publisher gratefully acknowledge permission for use of the following
material:

An edited version of "Faculty Work: The Integration of Faculty Responsibilities and
Institutional Needs" appeared in *Change* 30, no. 6 (November/December 1998), 18–25;
the original manuscript is reprinted as chapter 6 with the permission of Heldref Publications.

"The Ethics of Recruitment and Faculty Appointment" by the Council of Colleges of Arts
and Sciences. Unpublished, issued in Nov. 1992, is reprinted as "Faculty Recruitment Ethics
Statement" (appendix C) with the permission of the Council of Colleges of Arts and
Sciences.

"Professional Guidelines for the Evaluation of Academic Deans" is reprinted (appendix G)
with the permission of the Council of Colleges of Arts and Sciences. Unpublished, issued
in Nov, 1998.

CONTENTS

ACKNOWLEDGMENTS

While the focus of this book is on leadership in higher education, the perspectives offered are drawn from a lifetime of experience. At any point in one's life, all that has come before exerts some influence on the impressions that one forms, the positions that one takes, and the decisions one reaches on the many activities that make up a typical day.

People serve as rich resources in that lifetime of experience. This book, therefore, is the product of the shaping influences of the formative years and of a wonderful career of interaction with special people. It is with deep appreciation and respect that I acknowledge some of the most significant contributors to the enrichment of my life and, both directly and indirectly, to the messages contained in this offering on academic leadership.

To my parents (Orville and Lillian Krahenbuhl) and to my immediate and extended families, I acknowledge the importance of a sound foundation, support, and encouragement. To my wife (Richey), I acknowledge the special love and partnership that keeps life on an even keel, so that major projects can be undertaken. I also wish to acknowledge the scores of teachers and mentors that provided instruction, guidance, and mentoring over many years of formal education.

It was life as an academic and later as an academic administrator that placed me in a position to write this book. I therefore acknowledge the individuals who expressed special confidence in me at each stage of my career, by placing me in ever more responsible positions in higher education: Ed Chui, who hired me to my first university faculty position;

Jim Odenkirk and Deane Richardson, who brought me to the institution that would be my professional home for thirty years; Guido Weigand, who appointed me as department chair; Sam Kirkpatrick, who provided an invaluable learning experience as part of his administrative team (as associate dean); Dick Peck, who asked me to serve as dean and then told people it was "the best appointment he ever made"; and Lattie Coor, who gave me a chance to experience life above the deanship as senior vice president (to coordinate our institution's multiple campuses).

I wish to acknowledge the individuals who shared leadership responsibilities with me during my eleven-year deanship—the assistant and associate deans and development officers who were (at one time or another, some for the entire time) part of my administrative team. Included here are the associate deans (Gretchen Bataille, Dan Brink, Linell Cady, Len Gordon, Nancy Gutierrez, Milt Sommerfeld, Mary Beth Stearns, and Wendy Wilkins), assistant deans (Brice Corder, Gerry Corey, Doug Cornell, Mary Green, and Gwen Stowe), and development officers (Bob Alber, Gina Collins, Jill Demichele, Naomi Goodell, Sandy McKenzie, and Amy Nitsche). It was the exceptional talent of this group that not only helped the college run smoothly but in its collective wisdom was the source of many of the ideas contained in this book.

I wish to acknowledge the broader administrative team at Arizona State University, including the president, campus provosts, vice presidents, Academic Senate leaders, the deans of the other colleges on all of our campuses, and the many department chairs and center directors that were housed in the college. The many councils, task forces, and committees that were led by the individuals in these roles shaped in significant ways the content and perspectives that appear here under my name.

I wish to acknowledge colleague deans from a variety of colleges at other institutions, especially the deans with whom I interacted through the programs offered by the Council of Colleges of Arts and Sciences (CCAS), the Council for the Arts and Sciences in Urban Universities (CASUU), and the PAC 10+2 deans' group. These organizations, featuring "deans helping deans," provided fertile venues for the exchange of ideas about academic leadership. Two past executive directors of CCAS (Dick Hopkins and Ernie Peck) were especially important in providing continuity to the largest of these professional development organizations, as deans moved into and out of their leadership roles.

The first draft of this manuscript was reviewed by over a dozen individuals, who provided invaluable feedback in preparing a revision. I wish to acknowledge the thoughtful suggestions provided by Gretchen Bataille, Bob Bjork, Linell Cady, Bill Covino, Emily Cutrer, Sam Kirkpatrick, Tim

O'Rourke, Ernie Peck, Gwen Stowe, Jerry Thomas, Wendy Wilkins, and Mimi Wolverton. The final version of this book reflects the broad experience and good judgment of these generous people.

Finally, I wish to acknowledge the hundreds of students and faculty who have been part of my higher education experience. The pursuit of ideas through unfettered inquiry is a wonderful way to spend a professional lifetime. I feel privileged to have been able to share my time with so many extraordinary people, who in ways they will never know have enriched my life and contributed to this work.

CHAPTER 1

Introduction

Ansel Adams once said that chance favors the prepared mind.[1] To many casual observers, good fortune seemed the only reasonable explanation for Adams's incredible black-and-white landscape images. Those more closely acquainted with Adams knew that the study, preparation, and patience that characterized his approach to photography were far more responsible than chance for Adams's success.

So it is with the academic deanship. Individuals who succeed in these important roles are not so much the benefactors of chance as they are those who are best prepared in terms of personal attributes, sound habits, essential understandings, and basic skills.

Unlike with many positions, there are no formal professional programs for those seeking positions of academic leadership. There are programs that study academic leadership as an area of inquiry, but most such programs reside in colleges of education, where they attract few enrollees in the form of faculty from other disciplines intending to become deans.

The career track to an academic deanship typically starts with a tenure-track faculty appointment. The resumes of most deans will reveal that they developed strong cumulative records as academics, moving in a timely way through the ranks to become professors at an early age. Most deans are individuals who were called upon to provide leadership as unit heads, directors, or department chairs. Success in such roles often causes colleagues to observe in them qualities of leadership that will be helpful at higher levels, and as a result to encourage such administratively gifted individuals to consider positions with a greater scope of responsibility.

Administrative talent among unit heads does not go unnoticed by those in the upper levels of administration. Often an institution's senior officers will have contributed to the development of those leadership abilities through informal mentoring and organized professional development efforts. Not infrequently, individuals with talent to succeed at the next level are nominated by their supervisors to fill vacant positions for which they are suited.

Few faculty members enter graduate school imagining that they are going to move into administration. Instead, some individuals are selected to serve, and a few of those serve with distinction, discovering that they actually enjoy leadership roles. In the academic culture, however, one is reluctant to make such a confession lest he or she appear to be less than fully committed to academic scholarship. Nevertheless, a few individuals— whether publicly or secretly—find they enjoy such roles and thus look for other opportunities at the ends of their terms as chair, head, or director.

A somewhat smaller number of individuals come to the deanship after a second administrative stop, usually as associate dean. This is a less common route; it is fair to say that most assistant and associate deans never become deans. Whether such a position is a stepping-stone or an administrative dead end depends on the individual and on the scope of responsibility of the position. When the individual serving as associate dean is strong, and if the position both carries significant responsibilities and provides an opportunity for professional growth, there is a very good chance the experience will be career enhancing and lead to administrative appointments at higher levels. This is especially true if the dean and his or her college are highly regarded. It is clearly less true if the dean is seen as bumbling or the institution does not seem to be well run. It is clear, however, that a successful stint as associate dean makes many individuals far more attractive as candidates than they would have been had their experience been limited to heading an academic department or research center. This is especially true for individuals holding nontraditional degrees or coming from disciplines that are not generally seen as being "central" to the college's activities.

Promotions in all fields involve a period of learning. It is difficult to imagine anyone moving to a new leadership position and being fully prepared to perform at the highest levels from the first day. Searches are carried out to identify people who show the most promise of succeeding in the new role. Occasionally searches attract applications from individuals who have already demonstrated success in positions similar to the ones being filled. Moves that appear to be truly lateral—in terms of the span or authority (rank) of the position or the quality of the institution—are often viewed with suspicion by those conducting a search.

The general view seems to be that it is healthy to be driven by the opportunity for advancement in rank but curious (at best) to seek a new administrative position when the span of authority remains unchanged. The suspicion about those seeking lateral moves is that their decisions are being driven by the need or wish to escape their current circumstances rather than by a deep interest in the new opportunity. Lateral moves that feature the opportunity to do a similar job at a better institution are viewed less skeptically, but they are not common, because searches often lean toward individuals coming from institutions that appear to be stronger, not weaker, than the ones seeking new leadership. Nonetheless, when a strong institutional fit exists between the needs of the position being filled and the candidate's previous experiences, a lateral move can be good for both parties.

How does one improve his or her chances for success in the role of dean? One key to success is preparedness. That is the purpose of this book. It is intended to acquaint individuals who are either newly appointed deans or about to become academic deans with the typical challenges that come with such leadership positions. The various sections offer information, observations, and examples that give insight into the role of dean. Attention is given to the review of personal attributes, sound habits, essential understandings, and basic skills that are observed in successful deans and more broadly in successful leaders.

One successful leader who influenced me was Robert Galvin. Galvin, the son of the founder and for many years president, CEO, and chairman of the board of the Motorola, Inc., spent a lifetime wondering about the basis for creative genius. This was important to him because, in its competition for sales and profits, Motorola preferred to invent and develop new products rather than copy others, in order to start with 100 percent of the market share. That percentage would be eroded over time as others entered the competition, but Motorola's corporate preference was to be the first to introduce a new technology. Although Galvin never discovered the nature of creative genius, he regularly urged employees to imagine the possibilities. So encouraged and supported, Motorola employees were responsible for a steady stream of discoveries that contributed to many decades of profitability for the corporation.

Deans lead their own organizations and care deeply about their quality and productivity. Colleges, like corporations, operate in a competitive world, and colleges exist today in a time of great change. Each decision made by a dean slightly reshapes a college and serves either to improve or degrade its competitive advantage. If a college is well led it will become stronger, improving its position on the campus and among those institutions with which it most directly competes. If a college is ineffectively led, it will suffer in the campus competition for support and will be viewed less favorably in external comparisons.

A college will be dynamic if, in part, the dean creates an environment where the people who make up the college—its faculty, students, staff, alumni, and friends—are empowered to imagine the possibilities. This means looking ahead and being optimistic, expecting that the future will be better because of ideas that emerge to be pursued. This means that the dean wants a proactive organization, aggressively shaping its future. The approaches to leadership described in this book emerged over time in an environment that encouraged people to dream. Many of those dreams were realized, much to the benefit of the individuals, to those they served, and to the university.

Nothing that appears in this book should be taken as a prescription. This is not a "how to do it" book. Every setting in higher education has unique features. The people, the delegation of authority, the nature of shared governance, the institutional culture and traditions, the opportunities and challenges all will vary from place to place. What works in one setting is almost never immediately transportable to another setting. A book such as this is successful only if it helps the reader develop a mind better prepared to lead a college. This goal is best achieved by addressing important items across the range of responsibilities carried by deans and by providing conceptual and operational perspectives on how one might approach the many challenges to be faced.

There will be instances where actions that mimic examples provided herein, with some tinkering, will work in the reader's institutional setting. It is equally possible that an illustration provided in this book will stand out as totally unworkable in settings featuring different rules and constraints. Nevertheless, such illustrations can be useful in two ways. First, it is always valuable to see how others have managed a similar challenge. Second, knowledge of an approach that is unworkable may cause one to have greater confidence in a course of action that is different in necessary ways from something appearing on these pages. There is value in considering how various options might play out and then settling on a course of action that one believes will lead to the desired result.

The book is organized into chapters that cover the major areas of a dean's authority and responsibility. The early chapters focus on the process of being selected as dean and settling into the new role. Special attention is given to getting off to a good start.

An entire chapter is devoted to improving the talent level of those who form the administrative team of the college. This treatment may seem extravagant, but experienced deans know all too well that their use of time is driven significantly by the talent of their administrative staff members (associate and assistant deans) and the heads/directors/chairs of the academic units that report to the dean. If these individuals are ineffective, the dean will spend all of his or her time trying to undo problems. If these individuals are effective, the dean can spend time in more productive pursuits, and the college will function much more smoothly.

The longest chapter in the book focuses on the dean and the faculty. This should not be surprising, because in the university hierarchy, the professor is seen as holding academe's most honored place. Since the work of the university is accomplished largely as a result of faculty efforts, a great portion of the dean's job is establishing an effective tone and appropriate processes for recruiting, mentoring, winnowing out or promoting faculty, and supporting their activities. Ineffectiveness in any aspect of faculty management will undermine the college's ability to achieve its goals, because the quality, morale, and productivity of the faculty are central to success.

The chapter on student affairs is not meant to be comprehensive, because most individuals coming into a deanship will have a well-developed acquaintance with student matters, and also because a large portion of the administration of undergraduate student matters is typically handled by a university-wide student affairs office. Student issues that are more often the unique concern of the dean or members of his or her staff are the focus of this chapter.

The chapter on research and creative activities is treated more comprehensively than the chapter on student affairs, because deans often come from disciplines that are vastly different from the disciplines in which they must now lead, in terms of the nature of research and creative activities. A special attempt has been made to touch on such newly emerging issues as the protection of intellectual property rights, licensing and patenting, and the transformation of discoveries into new wealth-producing companies.

The chapter on external affairs and fund-raising assumes only a modest acquaintance with this aspect of the dean's job. Most new deans have no experience in this realm and are not anxious to spend time "begging for money." There are special sections on capital campaigns, raising money through direct solicitation, developing case statements (of college needs), and the creation of external support groups. Advice is also offered on where the dean can turn for personal professional development on this increasingly important role.

In what may seem to be an inordinate amount of space, a chapter is devoted to college events. The hosting of social activities may seem to be an unnecessary excess, but events play a vital role in giving life to a college. They provide occasions to celebrate successes, honor the best and the brightest, say "thank you," have fun together, build new friendships and relationships, and help tell the college's stories. A college with no events can be a sterile place, with no purpose for existing except administrative tidiness.

A final chapter covers a variety of other topics—space and facilities, management trends, legal matters, and many others. The appendix contains numerous resources, keyed to specific text sections, that will offer very useful resource material for the dean.

Anyone looking in this book for theory will be disappointed. Several recent books that are more academic in their orientation are those by Wolverton and Gmelch (2002) and by Wolverton et al. (2001). This book is meant to be practical and enlightening. It is meant to help deans imagine the possibilities in ways that normally come only with years of experience. It is intended to provide a seasoned glimpse of college leadership, so that the reader will gain wisdom—not in the form of easy answers and simple solutions but in the ability to develop deeper, more fully informed perspectives from the first day of the appointment. Chance favors the prepared mind. When it comes to performing effectively, a dean with the knowledge contained in this volume will have chance on his or her side.

NOTE

1. A similar aphorism is attributed to Louis Pasteur, who was quoted as saying, "In the fields of observation, chance favors only the mind that is prepared." Rene Vallery-Radot, *The Life of Pasteur*, trans. R. L. Devonshire (Whitefish, MT: Kessinger Publishing Company, 2003).

CHAPTER

The Selection and Appointment Process

The best deanships may well be the most rewarding administrative positions available in American colleges and universities. Deans typically enjoy significant autonomy. A dean normally has the authority to make a difference. The dean is one step removed from departments but still close enough to stay in touch with, and draw vicarious enjoyment (and inspiration) from, the successes of students and faculty. Unfortunately, many deanships turn out not to be good opportunities. How does one know if a vacant deanship is one to seek or to avoid? This chapter examines some of the important variables to consider in assessing these administrative opportunities, indicating how they will influence aspects of the deanship. The chapter closes with a discussion of compensation for deans.

HOW THE POSITION BECAME VACANT

A good thing to learn early in any search process is how the position came to be vacant. The factors that led to the vacancy can make a position more or less attractive. The presence of negative factors (that remain unchanged) does not necessarily make a position unattractive to pursue, but it may. In the search process the sophisticated candidate will discover these factors and assess how to succeed in spite of them. If negative factors appear to be handicapping in nature, likely to endure, and potentially difficult to overcome, the wise candidate might well leave this vacancy to others.

Potentially Problematic Reasons for the Vacancy

There are many potentially problematic reasons why a position has become vacant. These include such conditions as a dysfunctional state in the college, an intrusive higher administration, a provost who is difficult to work for, high rates of turnover at the presidential and provost levels, severe budget difficulties, or a situation in which the former dean was either terminated or resigned. One should be wary of any deanship that becomes available under such conditions. The university and its location might be very attractive, but the prospects for success in a position should be the overriding concern for any potential candidate.

Healthy Reasons for the Vacancy

There are many healthy reasons why deanships become vacant. In cases where the previous dean has been successful and has, after an appropriate period of stewardship, moved on to another position, there are usually fewer reasons to be wary. In these situations the conditions for success should exist, and the major concern is that expectations are sometimes difficult to meet when the outgoing dean was popular. When the vacancy has occurred for healthy reasons the new dean will be able to build on the solid base of support from below and from above. It is also very helpful to have a budget that is adequate for the college's mission, as well as the flexibility to use that budget in creative ways. One hoping to become a dean should look for such conditions, because they increase immeasurably the chances for success.

NATURE OF THE SEARCH

Searches for deanships play out in many ways. Search processes reveal a great deal about an institution, and they influence to a significant degree how the new dean is received. In the typical search the Vice President for Academic Affairs (or provost) appoints an overly large committee and designates as chair someone who is believed to be trusted by both the faculty and the administration and who is capable of moving the search process along at a reasonable pace.

The Search as Recruitment or Screening

There are two extremes in how colleges and universities handle their administrative searches. At one extreme, the institution makes every decision with an eye toward building the enthusiasm of the candidates, so that at the end of the search the favored candidate will be inclined to accept the offer. This is a search that focuses on recruitment. At the other extreme, the institution makes every decision with the goal of separating candidates as to their desirability. This is a search that focuses on screening, or the elimination of candidates from pools. Searches of the latter type seldom encourage a candidate about an institution and often cause sophisticated candidates to withdraw. The culture of an institution is partially revealed by its search habits; therefore, the process itself will provide the candidate with insight about the character of the place. In general, institutions that are more mature and confident will have processes featuring the recruitment approach, while younger and less confident institutions come up with processes featuring elements that are uncomfortable for both the institution and the candidate, although they do serve to provide a more secure basis for making a decision.

Search Firms

Searches for deans occasionally use the services of professional search firms. This is done for a variety of reasons. Most commonly, institutions hope that the firm will help to attract a strong pool of applicants. Such firms can also be helpful in doing discreet background checks and in keeping candidates in the pool. This is especially true in states with sunshine laws, because the search firm can keep candidates' identities from being revealed until very late in the search process. When search firms are involved, interested candidates can improve their chances of being considered if they ask those who are serving as their references to contact, and have personal conversations with, the firm's individuals assigned to handle the search. Search firms might be expected to be neutral and objective about candidates, but they have the ability to influence perceptions about candidates, and they often do, most typically in decisions about who should be advanced to an interview list.

Candidate Attractiveness

How does one position him or herself to be attractive in a search? The first consideration is one's fit with the published criteria. If the required qualifications are not met, an application will be futile. If the required qualifications are met or exceeded and the preferred qualities and qualifications are present in the applicant's record, an application will be considered, and its attractiveness will depend its competitiveness with the records of other candidates in the pool. A strong letter of application that calls attention to how one's record meets or exceeds each required and desired qualification is a good first step in being considered for inclusion on short lists (for reference checks and interviews). A strong letter of nomination is also a very effective way to get strong and positive statements on the record early in the process. Finally, it is important to arrange one's curriculum vitae so that the important administrative elements are featured. Academics often make the mistake of using a resume made up largely of lists of publications, presentations, grants, awards, and other items so important to defining one's place in the discipline. While these items are important in helping the screening committee to determine a candidate's academic productivity, they tend to be less important than evidence of administrative experience and promise, which need to be featured.

Scope of the Search

Some searches for dean are internal to the institution, some are limited to external candidates, and others are open to any candidate, whether internal or external. The open search is most common, followed by the internal search and the external-only search. In searching for opportunities, an external individual should attempt to use contacts in his or her discipline to discover if there are strong or popular internal candidates. It is sometimes the case that the likely appointment is known and that the external search is being conducted to legitimize the internal candidate as someone who was selected in a national search. If this appears to be the case, there is little use in spending the time and emotional energy that goes into a search and interview process, unless one will be happy with nothing more than the experience gained.

The selection of a dean through an internal search usually suggests that the institution is generally content with itself and with the college. It also means the candidate knows—better than an external candidate could ever know—the culture of the organization and the people who make up its membership. This is probably the most comfortable way to move into a deanship. He or she knows the institution, and its members know him or her. There will be surprises both ways, but typically each side knows what it is getting. In such appointments, the expectation is for things to remain largely as they have been. This is not necessarily the case, as there can be significant stylistic and philosophical differences between individuals, even though the new dean is a product of the existing culture.

Selection of a dean through an external search usually means that the institution has a more aggressive change agenda and is hoping the individual selected will bring good ideas from his or her former institution(s) for implementation at his or her new home. In such searches, the recruiting institution will often lean toward appointing someone from a place it considers more prestigious and who can move the institution forward more rapidly than an internal candidate would.

Satisfaction with the Process

Search complications are common. Many agendas play out in a typical search, and various sorts of naughtiness can be exhibited. It is not uncommon for faculty members to want the new dean to come from their discipline, because they imagine it will lead to an understanding of their condition and perhaps even favored treatment. It may also mean the addition of a new faculty member in their unit (the new dean), which may be viewed as either favorable or unfavorable, for reasons often having little to do with the credentials.

When the search has not gone smoothly, the resulting appointment is often not fully accepted. This means the new dean will come in under less than ideal conditions. If the successful candidate knows that the search process has been criticized and that significant groups oppose the recommendation, it would be wise to learn everything possible about the situation before accepting an offer.

Someone moving to another institution as dean typically wants to be a tenured professor in the appropriate unit. Some colleges and universities time the question badly and treat this as a process entirely separate from the search. It is not uncommon, when the process is decoupled, for the successful candidate to be degraded by a review of his or her suitability for tenure. This is extremely unfortunate for the candidate and reveals a good deal about the character of an institution. It is better to integrate the two processes, so the issue of "tenurability" is known before short lists are constructed.

AUTHORITY OF THE POSITION

In considering the attractiveness of the position, a candidate for any deanship should determine what authorities are vested in it. If there is any lack of clarity, the candidate should attempt to learn with precision what authority resides in the office before the appointment is made. One should also see if the authority vested in deans is uniform across campus. When a college is in troubled times a Vice President for Academic Affairs or provost sometimes selectively removes authority from one college but not another. If this has been the case, it would be a good idea to get the authority returned to the college as a condition of appointment.

A CHANGE AGENT

It is not uncommon for the university conducting the search to have an action agenda for the new dean. The nature of such an agenda is sometimes revealed in the position description and is almost certainly shared with the candidates during interviews. Typically, the university is trying to make progress in certain areas and is dependent on the college for success. In this case the new dean will come in with a specific charge, a set of expectations about what is to be accomplished. When this is the case, and especially where there is going to be resistance to the changes that are contemplated, the new dean will want assurances about support from above, knowing that the role of a change agent almost certainly comes with opponents, who can become detractors. The question that must be answered to the candidate's satisfaction is this: Can the dean make a difference of the sort expected, given existing structural, budgetary, and environmental constraints? Unless the answer seems to be "yes," taking such a position would be very risky.

DEANS' COMPENSATION

In a typical search, the position description and advertisement for a deanship will say nothing more about compensation than that terms will be "competitive" or "commensurate with training and experience." These are encouraging phrases, but in reality local circumstances and institutional practices result in an enormous range of appointment conditions that are deemed to be consistent with these published assertions.

Take deans' salaries as an example. The range of salaries for academic deans is surveyed annually by the College and University Professional Association for Human Resources, which reports it by institution type (doctoral, master's, and baccalaureate) in *The Chronicle of Higher Education*. In 2002–2003, the median salary for academic deans ranged from a low of $50,266 to a high of $157,000, excluding deanships encompassing medicine and law. (The complete table is available on the *Chronicle* website, at chronicle.com/weekly/v49/i31/31a03801.htm.) Salary variation around these median figures is large. Deans in large universities and prestigious private institutions will often draw annual salaries that rival those of many university presidents. In each case, whether the salary is high or low within the range, it is probably viewed as "competitive" by those extending the offer.

As salary is where the compensation package usually begins, it is good to find some benchmarks against which an offer can be compared. Published data like those provided in the report cited above are most useful as a starting point. Median salaries for the type of institution one is considering can be determined. One can also see how deans in different academic areas compare. (For example, deans of engineering usually are more highly paid than deans of colleges of humanities.) Some better benchmarks will be the salaries of other current deans (if the figures are in the public record) at the hiring institution, or of deans of similar units at similar institutions.

How the salary package is structured will also vary among institutions. Some places set an academic-year salary (usually considered to be nine months, but sometimes ten) and then add a summer supplement. Many institutions will offer a fiscal-year (twelve-month) salary that includes paid vacation. Another common practice is to set a base academic salary and add an administrative stipend that ends if the individual leaves the deanship. Whatever the practice may be, it is important to understand the basis for the total figure and (1) the portion of salary that is eligible for raises during the deanship and (2) the portion that is retained following completion of the deanship.

There are many things to consider in addition to salary. The list below represents an attempt to be inclusive. A small number of the best deanships will include nearly all of these items, but most will include only a few.

In addition to the normal benefits available to all members of the faculty (such as medical, dental, life insurance, and retirement), deans often are able to negotiate an automobile allowance, club memberships, contributions to a tax-sheltered annuity or deferred compensation plan, and a discretionary account for entertainment expenses. (This latter item is critical to fund-raising.) Other items for consideration may include appointments to corporate boards, predetermined paid administrative leave after a period of service, and legal liability protection while serving in the administrative role.

"Negotiation" may be too strong a word for some items of importance, but there should be clarity on a number of other issues. Expectations about the level of research or teaching to be carried out by the dean should be clear. Many deans attempt to remain active in all areas of scholarship, but few are successful in maintaining their academic scholarship at pre-dean levels of productivity. Some institutions expect their deans to be full-time administrators and hold no expectations for continuing scholarly contributions. One should know what is expected and be willing to embrace those conditions or decline the offer.

Other important items are the conditions of the appointment, including the term and term renewal or extension; duties, responsibilities, and authority; forms of evaluation and salary adjustment; rules regarding paid consulting; and limits on outside income from honoraria.

If the search is external, there should be provision for moving expenses, to include one's household, office, and laboratory (in some circumstances). There should also be a commitment to provide appropriate computers, printers, high-speed Internet connections, and fax machines at one's home and office. Some sort of portable device for communicating while traveling is also often provided.

In negotiating an offer, it is important to understand the culture of compensation of the hiring institution. What would seem to be a normal request at many places would be considered extraordinary, even inappropriate, at others. As a general rule, institutions that see their deans as professional administrators and part of the senior leadership team construct more elaborate packages. When the dean is seen as someone who is rotating though the position and will return to the faculty, the compensation package is usually more limited. Asking about the many items identified above will help the candidate assess the type of institution he or she will be joining.

Should deans negotiate for things in addition to personal items, such as a "dowry" for the college? The answer to this question is best answered by learning whether or not the institution has well-established and principle-driven practices for making budget decisions. If a place is known as one that does not connect its budget decisions to its priorities and makes decisions that seem to be driven by patronage, one should either decline the offer of an appointment or accept one only after securing a commitment of resources to achieve certain agreed-upon goals. If, on the other hand, the institution has a history of sound budget decision making, then it is probably best to accept an otherwise attractive offer and trust that the institution will respond the best it can and as fairly as possible to your prospective college's needs.

In summary, the conditions under which the vacancy has been created and under which the position will be filled can be important to the attractiveness of a position and to the likelihood of success for the individual eventually selected to fill it. The wise candidate makes inquiries to learn all he or she can about the reasons why a position is vacant and remains attentive to the search process as it plays out. Constraints to progress should be known and understood. It is a mistake to ignore such important information or fail to use it in one's decision process. It may seem far-fetched, but some deanships are doomed to fail by things that are apparent before the position is filled.

If the search turns in one's direction, and discussions about the contours of an offer begin, then the candidate should prepare him- or herself by assembling benchmark data and developing a list of items to be negotiated. Compensation packages for deans cover an enormous range, so the candidate will have to decide which items are "deal breakers" and which ones are luxuries but not necessities. The culture of the hiring institution is probably the best guide as to which items are typically included in the package. In the end, to accept an offer, the candidate should be excited about the opportunity and satisfied that a competitive offer (for the setting) has been extended. The excitement of a new challenge is then realized.

CHAPTER 3

On Being Appointed as Dean

The newly appointed dean has (or certainly should have) many things on his or her mind. This chapter is meant to suggest some "dos" and don'ts" as one gets ready to move into the new role. This chapter will provide information that will help a new dean, review items that will command his or her attention, and then conclude by discussing some common mistakes to avoid.

There are a number of things one can do to improve his or her readiness to assume the position of dean. This section reviews some factors that are almost universally recognized by experienced deans as being important to a good start.

LEARNING ABOUT BEING DEAN

One of the best steps that an individual who is newly appointed to the position of dean can take is to attend one or more of the "new dean" seminars that are offered annually. In the arts and sciences, the Council of Colleges of Arts and Sciences (CCAS) offers each summer one of the best seminars. It features current successful deans as speakers and covers many important topics, ranging from budget to personnel and fund-raising. These seminars provide ample opportunities for questions and discussion, so that the attendee can not only learn from the general advice provided but also get answers from experienced individuals about questions specific to his or her new setting.

In academic areas outside of the liberal arts and sciences, some of the sponsors of these seminars include the American Conference of Academic Deans (ACAD), the Council of Graduate Schools (CGS), the Engineering Development Forum (EDF), the American Bar Association (ABA), the International Council of Fine Arts Deans (ICFAD), the University Continuing Education Association (UCEA), the American Association of Colleges of Nursing, and the Consortium on Institutional Cooperation (CIC). When possible, it is best to attend such workshops with individuals coming from similar institutions and carrying similar responsibilities. In addition to learning about specific challenges facing those in academic administration, attending these meetings will help the new dean develop a network of colleagues who can be called upon for advice in all manner of circumstances. Experienced deans find such contacts invaluable.

There are also seminars for deans, not specifically new deans. These seminars typically focus on two or three timely issues that are being faced by deans everywhere. The issues are almost certainly going to be important to the new dean. What is especially useful in these seminars is that one begins to learn how experienced and successful deans see things and think about the world of higher education. The deans' views are different from those of chairs or heads and are on occasion quite different from views held by faculty members. Part of being successful as dean is to see things from an expanded perspective. These seminars provide an opportunity for developing this capacity.

Deanships come with expectations about fund-raising. Most people coming into such positions have little or no experience in this area. An organization that puts on excellent programs for deans and their development officers is the Council for Advancement and Support of Education (CASE). CASE offers two- or three-day seminars featuring experienced and successful deans, development officers, volunteers, and alumni groups. These seminars can be incredibly valuable to the new dean, especially one with limited experience who is inheriting significant new responsibilities in the fund-raising area.

In addition to seminars, there are a number of books on the market that address the unique interests of subsets of deans. Deans of professional schools or colleges are referred to Austin et al. (1997). Those seeking a lighthearted look at the deanship will enjoy the book by Martin (1988). Finally, *The University: An Owner's Manual,* by Rosovsky (1990), provides a very traditional look at university life through the eyes of a dean.

ROLES THE DEAN MUST PLAY

After serving as dean for a number of years I was asked to give a talk on the subject of roles the dean must play. I had never given this much thought but agreed to make the presentation. After a review of my calendar (which covered several years) and some reflection, I was surprised by the list that emerged. Most people imagine that the job of the dean is to administer the college and provide stewardship for its intellectual domain. What follows, however, are general thoughts that reveal a good deal about the many roles the dean must play if he or she is to be an effective leader. What are the roles, and why are they important? Anyone who is interested in becoming a dean should be ready to engage in the roles that are described in the next few pages.

Chief Administrative Officer

The dean is the individual who carries both the authority and the responsibility for the operation of the college as an organized unit of the broader institution. The authorities that reside in the office of the dean are vested in the president by a governing board and delegated to the college level. The areas of authority and responsibility that are vested in deans are normally substantial. This means that they are greater than the faculty might prefer but somewhat less than is probably desirable. As chief administrative officer, the dean is responsible for managing the affairs of the college and its many dimensions, including personnel, budget, academic programs, facilities and space, student affairs, development—the list goes on and on. Many people have written about the qualities of successful leaders and managers. Some of the qualities that appear on most lists appear below. Each of these qualities is important.

1. Competence (it is difficult to be effective if one is incompetent)
2. Honesty (no one's memory is good enough to be otherwise)
3. Vision (a dean has to be able to imagine the possibilities)
4. Decisiveness (leaders have to make decisions in a timely way)
5. Communication (shortcomings here are very handicapping)
6. Empathy (this will lead to more humane decisions)
7. Balance (emotional, intellectual, behavioral; moderation applies especially to deans)
8. Humor (don't treat things lightly but have fun and create an atmosphere for those around you that is upbeat and happy)
9. Delegation (fail here, and the work of the college will grind to a halt)

10. Optimism (it is hard for an organization to be more optimistic than its leader)

11. Inspiration (seeing what others fail to see is a gift few have; settle for lifting others to greater success)

12. Role Model (the dean might cut his or her own budget first, teach a freshman seminar each semester, be a leader in deans' professional organizations, and be a good university citizen).

Search committees, of course, are always looking for candidates who exhibit each of these traits, but search processes seldom reveal much about their presence or absence in candidates. As dean or as one who aspires to be dean, work to establish these attributes as part of your character. To the extent you succeed, you will have a sound personal foundation for being an effective dean.

Chief Academic Officer

The dean is the guardian of the academic philosophy, standards, and programs of the college. With the advice of faculty, the dean works to ensure that the college's requirements, majors, and course offerings have intellectual integrity and contemporary relevance. As knowledge unfolds and contexts change, academic offerings must keep pace with change. The dean oversees this steady evolution, trying to balance (a) the security and comfort offered by tradition with (b) the pressures to feature cutting-edge knowledge of immediate practical utility. Colleges and universities, being conservative in nature, tend to take great care in testing ideas before adding them to the canon of a discipline. The dean helps to guide that part of the process that shapes the college's academic offerings.

Chief Development Officer

The dean may have a development staff, but in the end it is the dean who is responsible for the success or failure of a college's fund-raising efforts. The development staff can handle most of the detail, but it is the dean who must effectively connect with donors and friends. It is only through the relationships of donors with deans that significant gifts to the college will be secured.

Chief Communication Officer

Who tells the college's story? Who decides what the story is? Who articulates the vision of what the college is and what it might be? The dean, working with members of his or her staff and with university personnel involved in media relations, should decide on some high-priority messages that he or she wishes to get across to the public. Stories are then developed that convey these messages and reinforce the impressions one hopes to create about the college.

Other newsworthy items will occur, and these should be called to the attention of the media. It is a mistake, however, to limit news coverage to the items that come up in almost random fashion and for which there is probably no predictable or coherent message. Many stories can be developed that are compelling in nature and serve to illustrate such things as the college's (a) care for undergraduates, (b) contributions to economic development, (c) involvement in the community, (d) commitment to the preparation of teachers, (e) efforts to improve the college preparedness of underrepresented groups, or (f) any other worthy activity that contributes to the greater good.

Chief Adjudicator of Differences

Aggrieved individuals need avenues of relief, or they fester, fret, and agitate in ways that torment their spirit and poison the atmosphere around them. Most campuses have all sorts of mechanisms for review. It is good for the dean to familiarize him- or herself with these formal mechanisms, because the aggrieved individual can often be directed to a review body that is appropriate to hear and make recommendations about the claim. At times the recommendations of such bodies will come to the dean. He or she should review the facts of the case and decide whether or not to resolve the case by taking the recommended action.

There will be times when the dean believes that the recommended actions are inappropriate. In such cases it is wise to communicate with the members of the recommending body, so that they understand which aspects of their recommendation will not be followed, and why. Often, the dean can honestly say that if he or she viewed the matter from the faculty perspective, his or her recommendation would be identical to the one forwarded by the committee. The dean has a slightly different perspective, however, and this different perspective causes a somewhat altered set of actions to seem more appropriate. Often a faculty committee will understand such differences and endorse the altered action. Sometimes they will disagree (reasonable people can disagree), but they will appreciate being informed about why the dean's actions deviate from their recommendation.

Often people seeking an audience with the dean have conflicts with their immediate supervisors or are dealing with issues for which there are no apparent formal mechanisms of review. The dean may then feel compelled to review the matter personally. When this occurs, the first thing to remember is that there is no reason to believe that the first version of the story conveys the facts of the case completely and correctly. The dean should take good notes and verify with the individual bringing the complaint the accuracy of what he or she has noted. If the issues are complex, one might ask for something in writing. The individual bringing the complaint should be told that all other relevant individuals will be asked for their versions of the facts and that every effort will be made to understand all aspects and perspectives of the case before a decision is made about how to adjudicate the matter.

It is usually best to proceed using a nonadversarial approach, by which the rules for admitting evidence are far less constraining and confrontational. In seeking to find the best course of action, it is good practice to attempt to find the path that maximizes the good and minimizes the drawbacks that will come with the resolution selected. When this is accomplished the decisions normally stand up to further grievances and litigation. Furthermore, decisions reached with this goal in mind normally resolve the problem in a way that is fairest to all concerned.

Chief Morale Officer

The dean sets the tone for the college. If the dean is constantly complaining about the college's circumstances, there is almost no chance that morale will be good. Even in the bleakest of times there will be numerous good stories to tell about the accomplishments of students, members of the faculty, research groups, departments, and perhaps even the entire college. Call attention to the much success and good work that is being accomplished in spite of the difficulties. Be optimistic about the future.

It is important to remember that the public's investment in education is substantial and that this investment is a statement of optimism about the future. There is an ancient Chinese proverb: "If planning one year ahead, plant grain; if planning ten years ahead, plant trees; if planning fifty years ahead, educate the people." The public's investment in education reflects a belief in our ability to build a better future through education. In this country, we see education as providing the individual with access to opportunity and contributing to the foundations of our democratic society. An educational leader, the dean in this case, must be optimistic about the future in order to provide effective leadership.

Principal Steward

The stewardship of the college falls to all of its members, but it is the dean who is seen as holding ultimate responsibility for the affairs of the college. The dean is charged with ensuring that the support provided by education's many sponsors is employed in appropriate ways. The dean is expected to honor and uphold important academic traditions. The dean is the chief defender of academic freedom. As the chief steward of the college the dean must manage, supervise, administer, and guide the activities of the college. The range of responsibilities carried by the dean has financial, intellectual, operational, functional, organizational, and legal dimensions. Effective stewardship means that each dimension is handled thoughtfully and effectively, whether or not anyone is looking.

Lead Mentor

We live in an imperfect world. People err. What happens when mistakes are made is crucial to an organization. Obviously, proactive steps should always be taken to avoid difficulties. Furthermore, when errors occur, the dean should not be bashful about calling attention to the difficulty, showing disappointment over what has happened, gently scolding the individuals involved, and providing guidance on how such problems should be handled, including an explanation for why another action would have been preferable. It is only through such attention and feedback that people learn and improve their ability to make good decisions. Such interventions should not be public; they should be handled individually, in private. The dean must serve as a mentor if significant organizational development is to occur.

Master of Ceremonies

Chapter 10 reviews the important of events to the life of the college. Someone has to serve as the host or the master of ceremonies at such events. When a college puts on events, the individual to whom such responsibilities normally fall is the dean. It is important to spend time preparing for these events. The dean should be familiar with the flow of the program, should know enough about other individuals involved to make accurate introductions and provide necessary recognitions, and be prepared to make remarks appropriate to the occasion. The dean's preparedness and performance will significantly influence the success of the event.

RELATIONSHIPS WITH THE UPPER ADMINISTRATION

A dean's effectiveness (or lack thereof) depends heavily on the quality of his or her relationships with members of the upper administration. Most important here, of course, is the position to which the dean reports—usually a Vice President for Academic Affairs or provost. Also important are all of the staff members who make up that individual's administrative team. (It is common for such senior executives to have assistants or associates attending to the budget, personnel, academic programs, research and graduate education, and facilities and space.) The dean and members of his or her staff should work to cultivate healthy working relationships with each such individual on whom they must rely.

A new dean should recognize little can be said that is universal when it comes to academic vice presidents or provosts. Each one will have his or her own personality, possess institutionally specific authorities and responsibilities, and operate with a unique administrative style. The dean should assess each of the specifics of personal nature, habit and practice, and scope of authority. If the vice president or provost does not make it clear how he or she wants to have things done, the dean should ask. The dean should feel free to make suggestions about process for consideration, but such suggestions are best made in private rather than in public settings.

Presidents and provosts dislike being surprised by news of any kind, but they especially do not like being caught off guard by something that may develop into a negative news story for the university. It is critical for deans to inform those above them in the chain of command about newsworthy items. When the event or issue is likely to be controversial or in all probability will require some sort of university response, the university leadership should be alerted and provided with a briefing that identifies the issue, the key individuals involved, the key facts, and one's best assessment of the status and directions of the case. A university spokesperson is often designated to comment on the matter for the media. This responsibility may fall to the dean, but if so, professionals in legal affairs and external affairs should coach her/him before responding. At many institutions the spokesperson on all matters is the Vice President for External Affairs.

In well-run organizations, written job descriptions spell out the specifics of each position and the ground rules regarding performance reviews and the extension or termination of administrative appointments. It is not unheard of, however, for reviews of deans to be handled in capricious ways; therefore, a statement on professional guidelines for the evaluation of academic deans can be useful in improving a university's administrative review practices. A copy of such a statement, which was developed by the Council of Colleges of Arts and Sciences, is provided in appendix G.

At most institutions, a dean's appointment is for a set term, comprising a series of annual appointments. Deans serve at the pleasure of the provost or academic vice president, and so in many situations, with ninety days' notice of nonrenewal, their appointments can be terminated. Often this can occur without giving reasons, but the more humane approach is to base such action on the results of careful reviews of performance that are part of normal institutional practice.

A few institutions have no process for reviewing the performance of administrators. There may be advantages to such an arrangement, but it is difficult to imagine how a dean could make adjustments and accommodations with the goal of improvement if no feedback on performance is provided. The absence of periodic evaluations also magnifies the notion that the appointment is at the pleasure of the supervisor and that performance may or may not have much to do with decisions about renewal or term extensions.

STRATEGIC PLANNING

Most colleges and universities engage in strategic planning, and a new dean may come on board at some stage of the process. It will be important for the dean to discover how long the plan has been in place, as well as the extent to which its specific recommendations need to be respected. The fortunate dean takes up his or her position when efforts are about to get under way to develop a new strategic plan.

Undertaking such processes for the first time, most individuals imagine that the primary product will be a thoughtfully developed plan that will guide institutional decisions into the future. People imagine that such a plan will spell out where new monies should be spent or where cuts should be made as the institution reshapes itself for the future. Typically, this is only partly true at best.

Most experts agree that the primary value derived from developing a strategic plan is not the plan itself but rather the process of developing the plan that provides the greatest benefit. Certain aspects of strategic plans will often begin to look silly and irrelevant soon after they have been prepared, because they seldom anticipate the future very effectively. The process of planning, however, causes the university to engage in the collective activity of stock-taking and thinking about its future. In the absence of strategic planning, an institution runs the risk of having its evolution shaped by hundreds of departmental decisions, often made in disciplinary-myopic ways, with little reference to broader institutional possibilities.

The plans themselves are not worthless. When they are first constructed they can serve as a useful guide, and they serve to elevate department understanding of specific strengths and opportunities that might be exploited. As the years pass, however, both internal and external conditions will render the plan steadily less relevant. It is important, therefore, to use the plan as a general guide, not as a detailed prescription that must be blindly followed. Actions closely driven by a plan that is five years old will often be ill advised and inappropriate.

Some institutions develop annual updates to their strategic plans. Such revisions are probably worth the effort if the time spent on them is limited and if the plan is used in a detailed way (rather than as a general guide). At some point, sooner than one might imagine, it is best to start over with a new strategic planning process. It is easy to imagine that one can make simple midcourse corrections to the plan, but the pace of change and unanticipated events alter an institution's landscape in a surprisingly short time.

The dean's role in strategic planning will be to create a process by which the college's many areas and interests work together to assess where the college is and where it ought to be going, within the context of the university's mission and direction. A well-handled process will ensure ownership of, and buy-in to, the eventual plan. Suggested reading for those interested in learning more about strategic planning is the classic book by Keller (1983) and the more recent work by Nedwek (1997).

LEARNING ABOUT ONE'S NEW UNIVERSITY AND STATE

If one is assuming a deanship in a new location, one should spend time learning as much as possible about the history and culture of the place. Find a good book on the history of the state and its folklore. Find another one about the university and perhaps another on the city in which it resides. Keep track of significant items; they will be useful in talks the dean will be expected to give, and they will help him or her understand things that might otherwise seem inexplicable. Develop a list of the names of individuals who have been especially significant in founding and developing the university, along with notes on the roles they played. Again, this information will turn out to be useful. Furthermore, people will be pleased that you have taken the time to learn about these things.

Gather and study institutional data. This will reveal two things. The first is the university's sophistication (or lack thereof) in studying itself.

The second is the relative state of each of the units that make up the institution. Ask for data not just for your college and its units but also for other colleges and their units. If these are provided quickly and without difficulty, it means one is moving to an institution where data are available to all (a healthy state). If these data are not provided, it may mean one of several things. It might mean that a few people at the top guard such data. It could also mean that the institution's data are scattered in various files, making it almost impossible to aggregate or put together to form useful and comprehensive analyses. Under these latter conditions everyone is less well informed than they should be, and it will be more difficult to (a) make good decisions, (b) understand decisions that are made, or (c) justify, with data, the rationale for making decisions.

Often, there will be copies of formal reviews that have been conducted. Accreditation self-studies and reports can be especially useful. Strategic plans and SWOT (strengths, weaknesses, opportunities, and threats) analyses can also be rich sources of information about an institution. It is becoming common for such information to be available on an institution's website, so the serious candidate can locate, download, and print vast amounts of information that can prove useful. The existence of information on a website may also reveal something about the broader policy environment of the institution. Reports from some institutions stand alone; those from other institutions are embedded in broader system documents or the reports of state agencies and boards.

Obtain copies of whatever printed material is available about your new college and the institution. What impression does the material make on you? What things are omitted or confusing? Is there a coherent institutional "look" to the printed material? Is your college featured appropriately in the material? The answers to these questions will help you to determine if there are issues pertaining to the depiction of your unit that will need immediate attention. The materials will also give you a sense of how the university tries to present itself. Again, look at the institution's website as a useful source of information on the institution's marketing strategies.

LEARNING ABOUT THE BUDGET

The new dean should plan on devoting significant time to learning about the budget. In a typical institution a college will have more than one budget, and each one will function somewhat differently from the others. In state colleges and universities the printed, authorized budget is usually the primary budgetary document. It will contain a list of all ongoing positions by title and/or grade classification, by percent time (full-time equivalent), by salary, and by name of incumbent. Typically, it also contains operations monies as a line item, sometimes as a lump sum and sometimes broken into major expenditure types, such as travel, maintenance, service charges, supplies, and so on. There is usually a separate line for capital expenditures. Unless told otherwise, one should expect to live within the budget and to lose any monies not expended by the end of the fiscal year.

While university budgets have many common elements, there are also many differences from institution to institution. In some state colleges and universities, any unspent or unencumbered monies revert to the state at the close of the fiscal year. In other states a fixed amount or a fixed percentage of unspent monies can be carried forward. If a carry-forward provision is available, it is important to know what is possible and what amount will be available in the coming year.

Another tool useful for gaining a grasp of the financial operation is an expenditure analysis. Sometimes these are available, and sometimes they must be specifically requested. Such an analysis will help a person new to his or her position understand how money has been spent. Reviews of this nature will provide insight into the financial culture and habits of the college, and may also reveal undesirable activities (such as monies given out to friends or disciplinary colleagues, for patronage, or for questionable purposes) that will need to be discontinued or addressed.

Some institutions use cost-centered budgeting. An academic unit's "cost" of operation is determined by adding a proportional amount of university-wide administrative expenditures to the regular budget of the unit. This is considered to be the unit's full cost, which is compared to measures of its productivity. Some of the simple comparisons made are cost per student and cost per student credit hour (SCH) of instruction. More complex analyses focus on the generation of revenues by the unit. Included here would be revenues from tuition, gifts, grants, and auxiliary activities. A ratio is then created that expresses the relationship between the monies spent and monies attracted by a unit. When such budgeting practices are used, incentive systems are often put in place to cause units to become more productive. A new dean should be alert to one of the common complaints from those operating under these systems—that they often ignore where a unit starts, rewarding change in the desirable direction while ignoring (or failing to reward) units that are already efficient and have little room to improve.

There will almost certainly be other budgets, but they tend to be used to fill in or allow expenditures that would not be possible from the state budget. For example, most colleges have a foundation or local account from which they can pay certain entertainment expenses associated with fund-raising. Such expenses typically cannot be paid from a state account. The monies in these accounts normally carry forward into the new fiscal year, so one does not have to worry about spending the account dry each year. Other accounts are sometimes available for research (into which indirect cost recovery is deposited), for summer sessions (into which any profit generated is deposited), and for special revenue-generating entities (such as a preschool or child study lab), often referred to as "auxiliary" or "enterprise" accounts. Of these, the research account is usually the most important, since it is often large and is the one out of which faculty start-up equipment packages are funded.

SETTING UP ONE'S OFFICE STAFF

Moving to a new leadership position features a period of disruption. The length and depth of this disruption can be minimized by devoting some attention to the working arrangements of the new office. One should review the makeup of the office staff and determine the flexibility that exists for changing personnel. A good way to start is to begin communicating with the staff to hear their views about the functionality of the office and to learn about their expectations. One should also develop clarity on his or her preferred routines with a key assistant. How are telephone calls, appointments, unscheduled visits, e-mail messages, postal deliveries and mail sorting, fax messages, and voice mail to be handled? Ideally, decisions will have been made so that the office is ready and the staff has a general idea of how it is to operate on the dean's first day in office.

VARIATIONS IN THE NATURE OF THE POSITION

The sections above are based on the assumption that the dean has considerable authority, but the nature of the position of dean varies greatly among institutions. At the less desirable end of the continuum one finds deans who do not hold academic appointments, have no control over large aspects of the college budget (such as indirect cost recovery, travel, temporary salary, or vacancy savings from vacant positions), and enjoy little discretion in shaping bylaws or enforcing promotion and tenure standards. In such settings the dean will have little chance to make a difference. Some individuals are happy in such a role, as it is less demanding. The important issue, therefore, is to understand the limits of authority and to make sure one can operate under whatever constraints they pose.

SOME THINGS TO AVOID

Individuals appointed as dean sometimes act as if the mere fact that they have been selected means that they have been elevated to new levels of knowledge and insight. Unfortunately, almost the opposite is true. Becoming a dean for the first time means that the individual selected is moving to a position for which he or she has no formal preparation and little, perhaps no, experience. The newly appointed dean almost certainly knows less about what it takes to be an effective dean—in fact, knows less about what the job entails—than one would know for any jobs previously held. So rule number one on the list of things not to do is simple: One should not make the mistake of thinking one is prepared for the new role. Instead, one should set about getting prepared so as to be as effective as possible from the first day.

Another common mistake is to begin doing the job (actually begin to handle day-to-day matters of the college) before formally occupying the position. These matters should be left to whoever is in charge until one's appointment begins. People will be well-meaning in deferring to the dean designate, but it is best to resist the temptation to be drawn into this level of involvement. The newly appointed dean should use the time between when the offer is accepted and the appointment officially begins to develop deep knowledge about the college and the university in which it resides. It should be a period of study, reflection, and preparation. This can often be accomplished by having the employment package feature "consulting" time, with travel expenses and appropriate compensation provided for the designee to spend time on campus before the appointment officially begins.

It is also important to avoid making hasty judgments. One learns very soon in these positions that the first version of anything seldom tells the entire story. The first version is valuable only in that it represents one's first exposure to the issue. Sometimes that version will be quite good, sometimes quite bad, but most often mixed in its accuracy and usefulness. With time and experience one learns which sources can be trusted, but this is usually not the case for the newly appointed dean. Try to gather many perspectives and opinions. It is only through this process that one will develop a more complete understanding of the issues and have the background one needs to make sound decisions or effectively adjudicate differences.

These, then, are some of the dos and don'ts for the period between when one is named as dean and when one takes over in an official capacity. It will be a stressful time, with the need to bring things to a close in the place one is leaving, to relocate, and to get everything in order in the new setting. It will be critical, however, to find time to build one's preparedness for being a dean (and to continue that professional growth once on the job). The activities suggested above will go a long way toward achieving that goal. (For a broader range of perspectives on the nature of the deanship, suggested readings include the edited works of Allen [1999] and Bright and Richards [2001]. In each of these books a number of different deans from a range of institutions comment on topics important to deanship.)

CHAPTER 4

First Steps on Becoming Dean

There are many things to be done once the appointment officially begins. Many individuals settle into these positions and just let the flow of issues that come to their attention define their activities as dean. As a general rule, this is a mistake; many of the issues that come to the dean should be directed to others. A new dean may want to see everything for a short time and decide what sorts of things are to be automatically referred to others. If, however, the dean attempts as a matter of permanent routine to handle every item, he or she will be buried in minutiae and never accomplish anything of significance.

This chapter offers suggestions on a range of things the new dean can do to help protect his or her time, help others understand how the college will operate, and set a tone that will be productive for all members of the college. The chapter is divided into four distinct sections, each devoted to a different aspect of the deanship. These are aspects of process (not substance): (1) engagement and communication, (2) elements of style, (3) setting an agenda, and (4) the life of the college. Choices made in these four areas lay the foundation for the deanship. It is difficult to overestimate the importance of the impressions that are created and tone that is set in the first weeks and months on the job.

ENGAGEMENT AND COMMUNICATION

Members of the college will want to get to know the dean, and he or she will certainly want to become acquainted with them. This can be done directly through face-to-face gatherings or through written communication. Face-to-face meetings are usually preferable, at least initially, but are time consuming and inefficient. Written communication allows the dean to reach everyone and ensures that a message is not filtered, but this method is generally not a good way to get acquainted, since it allows no personal interaction.

The new dean should devote significant time to getting acquainted. Visits to each unit will help the new dean see where the people that make up the college go about their work. The dean should gather information and study each department before making the visit. He or she should also expect to make a few remarks and perhaps take some questions. It is useful to find a system that facilitates the learning of names. You will meet a huge number of faculty members, staff, student leaders, alumni, and others. If the dean knows whom he or she will meet ahead of time and then reviews the list after each meeting, learning names will be easier. It is also helpful to associate individuals with place or certain activities. These lists should be reviewed frequently until the names are easily recalled.

Special campus groups may seek out the new dean, but an effort should be made by the dean to initiate meetings with them. Perhaps there are Nobel laureates, or members of the National Academy, or individuals holding named or endowed professorships. There will almost certainly be women's and minority associations. There will be student groups. There will be community groups that are interested in your college. It is nice to reach out to such groups rather than wait for them to take the initiative and get an audience with the new dean. Meet the leaders of each group and discover the issues that are important to them. Each group will have an agenda. In most cases they will reveal that agenda and ask the dean to comment. Again, being prepared through pre-meeting study or briefings by staff is highly recommended. A hidden benefit of such meetings is the chance to interact with individuals who cross disciplinary lines. Inevitably, the perspectives will differ from those presented in disciplinary settings.

Change in any organization introduces uncertainty among its members. The absence of information in such circumstances exacerbates stress, because people know little about the new dean and so have no basis on which to reject any suggestion that is made about his or her manner, style, or intentions. It will be impossible to get to know everyone at once, and it can take months in a large college to visit all of one's units; therefore, a broader communication plan is essential.

Written documents will likely be read if they are sent infrequently and are reasonable in length. If they are many pages long and are sent often, few people will read them. It is a good idea to reserve written communication to all members of the college for special occasions when the importance is high and accuracy in wording is important. Such a communication that I once sent appears below as a sample. On most other occasions, information can be provided to the unit heads, who in turn can pass it along to the members of their units.

Dear CLAS Faculty:

As we enter a new academic year, I thought it might be useful to share with you my observations about the state of the College, and to comment on several items I know are of importance to you.

The past year clearly brought its share of concerns; the debates over workload, teaching "versus" research and creativity, and faculty compensation were distracting to everyone. Nevertheless, much good was accomplished because—to borrow a phrase from Lincoln—"the better angels of our nature" prevailed. Instead of being demoralized by things outside our control, CLAS faculty members showed resourcefulness, dedication, and grit, and through their efforts brought credit to themselves and their programs by improving things under their control.

During the past year CLAS faculty secured new external resources to improve academic programs, to help public schools better prepare students, and to support talented students at both pre- and post-secondary levels. Our departments continue to receive growing national recognition and are increasingly the choice of more of the best and brightest undergraduate and graduate students. A faculty of reduced size handled more students, and then volunteered in impressive numbers to offer first-year seminars (in addition to their normal assignments). CLAS faculty visited high schools, hosted campus "sneaker tour" groups, and served as ambassadors for good in numerous other activities. It is both humbling and gratifying to represent a college with such talented and considerate faculty.

During the spring and summer a number of College faculty members wrote to me about salary conditions in their units. After many years of Legislative inattention, virtually every faculty member is now significantly underpaid, and our inability to adjust salaries has resulted in many inequities. The President and Provost have assured the deans that they will do everything in their power to secure significant salary adjustment monies this year. It has been a long wait and good intentions do not pay bills; however, I expect we will continue to excel in areas where we have control while we wait patiently for overdue recognition and compensation to reach us.

Thank you for all you do on behalf of ASU and best wishes for a productive and rewarding year.

ELEMENTS OF STYLE

People will want to know about the new dean's manner. Is he or she approachable? Is there an open door policy for meetings? Is the new dean going to centralize or delegate decision making? Will the dean welcome e-mail communication and respond to it? It will be helpful to all concerned for the dean to reveal his or her preferences and inclinations as soon as possible.

Each individual has ways of operating that are uniform and predictable. They reflect both the general way that one thinks about things and how one goes about making decisions. This is a matter of one's underlying practical or operational philosophy. If one has thought about this and knows the rules by which one lives, it is useful to let others know so that they can better understand one's behavior and expectations.

Rules to Live By

No two individuals will have the same "rules to live by." I reveal mine here not because I believe they should be copied but to help the reader understand the nature of such rules and what following them would mean.

Rule one for me is to maximize good—whenever a decision must be made or differences must be adjudicated, attempt to find the course of action that accomplishes the most good. This may sound simple, but it is not. What is good for individual A might be not so good for individual B. What is good for one department may negatively impact another department. What might seem best for the individual may not be what is best for the group. In the end, a decision must be made, and the results will be better if one has weighed the good and the bad of each option and then makes the choice that offers the most good that the situation allows.

An example of this is annual adjustment of salaries. To the extent that there is flexibility that can be exploited, it is a good practice to follow the normal decision rules that have been set up to guide the process and see what kind of results it produces. In a normal case, a raise amount is determined for each individual; one could stop here, apply the raises to the salary bases, and consider the work complete. The problem, however, is that providing adjustments to salaries without then looking at the resulting figures as a whole is usually a mistake. It is typical to see many irrational conditions or discrepancies between what people are earning and what they should be earning, in comparison with their colleagues. Such conditions are often called internal inequities. Chairs might be instructed, therefore, to examine salaries and make modifications to the raise structure so as to move the salaries of the unit toward a more rational state.

The goal often has to be limited to moving things in the right direction rather than fully correcting them; there is almost never enough funding for raises to make all corrections that might be indicated. The point is that in making salary adjustments, one should try to make decisions that maximize the good that the opportunity offers. If the inter-individual adjustments reflect performance differences for the period of review and the raises have led to greater fairness in the resultant salaries, people will consider it good. People always appreciate attempts to maximize good.

A second rule I have followed is to operate on the basis of principles. It is simple to say that one plans to be guided by certain broad rules of conduct, but it is another thing actually to discipline oneself to be even-handed on a consistent basis. This is reminiscent of Benjamin Franklin's autobiography, where he describes his efforts to achieve moral perfection. He identifies thirteen virtues and devotes one week to mastering each virtue—thirteen weeks to moral perfection. Week after week he fails. The final week deals with Franklin's pride and the virtue of humility. At the end of the week Franklin concludes, "If I could conceive that I had completely overcome it, I should probably be proud of my humility."

My point in recalling this story is that one needs help in trying to be fair. Principles can be very useful in this regard. Here is what using principles means. When someone comes to the dean with a request, it is important not to think of the request as unrelated to everything else. Rather, one should try to think of the family of issues to which the request is related. There will always be other things that have and will come up that are similar to the request of the moment.

The dean should ask him- or herself this question: If I say "yes" to this request, will I be willing to say "yes" in every other like case made by every other similarly situated individual who might come in with the same request? If I say "no" in this case, will I say "no" in all other similar cases? Furthermore, if I accommodate this individual, will I make the opportunity available to those who were not aggressive enough to ask but that might like (and perhaps even better deserve) a similar accommodation? In establishing a principle, one is saying that one is going to be guided by the correctness of the action, not by the individual who is making the request. In being guided by principles, one's decisions will be blind to who might be perceived as "friends" or as "enemies." The dean should never treat anyone as an enemy; it is best to refuse to have enemies. Over the long term those who may see the dean as their enemy normally will be softened by the dean's unwillingness to respond in kind.

A personal example of this principle was an occasion when a humanities faculty member won a prestigious fellowship in a national competition but the fellowship would not cover the full salary of living costs for time to be spent abroad. The professor requested a supplement to make up the balance of the salary, as well as a temporary adjustment to compensate for the higher standard of living in the area where the fellowship would be served. In saying "yes" to such a request, a dean must be prepared to make a general announcement that thereafter anyone coming in with a similar request will be supported in the same way.

Sometimes the use of principles keeps a dean from doing something he or she might like to do but would later regret because of the bad precedent it would set. An example of just such an event occurred when a faculty member who had been on the search committee that recommended the dean be hired, and who had since been helpful to the dean, requested that his position be reduced to half-time and that all of that effort be devoted to research. If one thought only about the personal dimension of this request and failed to consider the broader implications, one might approve it. Had this request been granted, however, there would have been dozens of additional requests for the same arrangement; it would have been both inappropriate and unacceptable to approve them. The request was denied, because it could not have been done for all other equally worthy individuals.

The alternative to operating on the basis of principles is to handle things in an ad hoc way, seeing each case as unique and trying to decide as the requests come in which ones to approve and which ones to deny. Not only will this lead to unevenness in one's decision making, but it will required the dean to spend hours listening to different versions of the same request. With the existence of a principle to guide how such things are handled, members of the dean's staff can act themselves without taking any more of the dean's time.

A final dimension of this principle has to do with one's general temperament. Much of a dean's time is spent in problem solving. How one reacts to such problems sets the tone and defines the starting point for making progress toward their resolution. Often an individual's reaction is related to who has caused the problem. Consistent with the principle of acting consistently, it is a good idea to react to any issue with disappointment rather than with anger. Angry responses seldom facilitate movement toward a solution; instead, they usually introduce new obstacles to be overcome. Disappointment sets a very different tone; it suggests that one cares about the people involved and that one expected better. It is not a confrontational response that makes people defensive. I strongly recommend responding with disappointment and holding one's temper in check.

My third rule is to be optimistic and have fun. But isn't being dean serious business? The dean's office should be a formal, staid place. If one appears to be enjoying what he or she is doing, perhaps he or she is not taking the position seriously. Phooey!

It is critical that the leader of any organization be optimistic and set a tone in which people are put at ease and can have fun. It is almost impossible for an organization to be more optimistic than its leader. If the leader walks around lamenting "Woe is us," there is almost no chance for the larger group to have much hope about the immediate future. The leader must be credible in his or her optimism, but being upbeat and effective in helping others to imagine the possibilities is critical to a leader's success. If a dean cannot help the organization envision a bright future, it is unlikely that its members will be motivated to work in a way that brings about a better tomorrow.

How does one create a climate of optimism when budgets are tight, governing boards are agitating about workload, salaries have fallen behind those of peers, and so on? Here is a personal example. At a time when things looked bleak, I tried to get people to focus on the things that were under our control rather than dwell on things that were not. I told a story from when I had been traveling by train across China during the mid-1980s. My party had fallen into conversation with an elderly couple and had asked them how the Chinese viewed life in China. They answered that it depended on one's perspective. They said they were old and took the "vertical" view. They had lived through a world war that started in the 1930s, floods and famines, the communist takeover, the Cultural Revolution, and much more. For them, life in China now was wonderful, because it had never been better than it was at that moment. Young people in China had not lived through those difficult times and could only take the "horizontal" view. When they thought about life in China, they could only compare it with life as it appeared in the media to be lived in Japan, Taiwan, Hong Kong, Singapore, and the United States. In this comparison life in China seemed awful.

I asked people to think about our institution using either view. There had been times when budgets had been better and when support for higher education had not seemed so tenuous; however, in taking the vertical view, the university itself had never been as good as it was at this moment. It was getting better, and we were making progress on all the issues over which we had control. Further, looking at our situation using the horizontal perspective, we should also be thankful, because conditions at our institution were better in most ways than at other comparable places. There was much to be grateful for and much to celebrate. We had every reason to be upbeat about our situation and positive about our future.

Similarly, people spend a majority of their waking hours in the world of work. They are much more productive in their work and have better attendance if they enjoy the workplace. The demeanor of the dean should never be so serious that colleagues cannot joke with one another or lead a social existence that (in appropriate settings) ignores rank. A happy office is a productive office, in that time is not lost to conflict and emotional turmoil. An office that has fun retains its good people and is an easy place for members of the college to come for help, comfortably. In hierarchical settings, this is especially important with respect to those in support roles, such as administrative and professional support staff.

The dean who creates an optimistic organization in which people enjoy coming to work will have gone a long way toward being successful. This is an important dimension of "setting a healthy tone."

Practices One Intends to Follow

The preceding section dealt with the behavioral dimension of the deanship. This section addresses the functional dimension of leadership. Included here are the broad areas of decision making, delegation of authority, and the utilization of senior staff.

Decision Making

How will you handle decision making? Will you be like a dean I once served and hold a big pot of money in your office, making decisions on how to spend it in an endless flow of meetings with individuals bringing in ideas for how it should be spent? I hope not. If the size of your college is significant, you will want to delegate decisions on day-to-day things to your unit heads. You will want to delegate decisions on things that come up from time to time to your staff (assistant and associate deans). As dean, you will want to focus your attention on a set of annual decisions that collectively move the college toward its goals. This is best accomplished by addressing major decisions as comprehensive, collective, comparative exercises. I will take a moment later to describe this practice; the point here is to let people know who has authority for which decisions and how you, as dean, will go about making those that will not be delegated.

Each university will have its own peculiarities; however, if policies and procedures allow it, comprehensive, collective, comparative annual exercises can be very helpful in ensuring that the dean makes good decisions. Such exercises can be used for such things as decisions on permanent personnel, temporary personnel, capital, renovation, and computer infusion.

Using permanent personnel as an example, a typical exercise would work something like this. The dean would indicate to the heads of all units that he or she has some personnel monies (some new and some from position vacancies due to retirement and resignation) to allocate for the purpose of building the institution in ways that would help it achieve its mission. Referring to university and college priorities and indicating the criteria that would be used, the dean would ask each unit head to make a request, within certain boundary conditions (usually some percentage of the current base budget), noting any relevant considerations. The unit heads would be asked to develop a ranked list of items they sought. They could place on their lists items for other departments or interdisciplinary programs that would be helpful to secondary units, even if the appointment resided elsewhere.

In the case of faculty positions, it is usually a good idea to let people know what sorts of conditions will improve the chances of getting a new faculty line. I always considered the argument that "we need to make a new hire because old Harry retired" a very poor justification for a faculty position. Looking back at what had been was never particularly useful to me; looking ahead at what might be was far more compelling. Arguments to recruit that were most influential with me included: (a) a threat to the academic integrity of a program if some critical knowledge area were not covered, (b) a very high number of majors per tenure and tenure-track faculty members, (c) a very high instructional burden (student SCH or tenure-track faculty FTE) by existing faculty, or (d) a chance to make a key addition to a productive research group (within the unit or interdisciplinary group). I was always interested in knowing whether the unit thought the search area was one that would give us a better than normal chance of increasing our diversity. Finally, consideration was given to protecting positions that were vacant because unit decisions had been made to protect quality—that is, tenure denials and failure to fill positions because there were no attractive candidates in the pool.

Each unit would have two to three weeks to construct its request. In the permanent personnel example, each unit would assign its priority to faculty, professionals, staff, and graduate assistant positions (these were included because the positions in the budget were permanent, even though graduate students themselves moved in and out of the budgeted lines). At the deadline, the dean would have his or her budget officer create a spreadsheet featuring all of the requests.

The dean and selected members of the staff (whoever seemed appropriate) would review the requests using established criteria with a view to giving the college the biggest push toward its broader institutional goals. In some institutions this would be the end of the process. In others—especially where a similar process occurs at the university level, in the office of the academic vice president or provost—this set of recommended decisions is forwarded to the more central authority for review and approval.

Once a set of actions has been approved, either in the dean's office or above, units are informed about the results. They then know which positions they are authorized to advertise and which new personnel monies are committed to their budgets. (The new funds would not actually show up until the next year's printed budget, since the budgets are typically printed only once each year.) These decisions typically take place in the late summer, no later than early fall, in order to give units a good start on the recruiting season.

In the absence of such exercises, how are decisions made? One typical way, already mentioned, is to commit monies in a series of ad hoc decisions. There are several major problems with this practice. The first is that each given decision is made without knowledge of other possible investment opportunities. The second is that the sum of the decisions seldom has any coherence. What is done amounts to a number of things that may or may not make sense collectively in terms moving the institution toward certain goals.

The comprehensive, collective, comparative form of decision making works equally well for other sorts of considerations. Whether it be renovation priorities, purchases of major items of equipment, or other large expenditures that have to be dealt with no more than once annually, seeing all the requests at once, seeing all items of a given sort in unit priority order, and comparing the requests using known criteria provide a very sound basis for making decisions.

If this method is to work properly, the dean has to discipline him- or herself not to make out-of-cycle decisions on requests that should be part of his or her comprehensive decision making. Unit heads will almost certainly come in with such requests throughout the year; they must be told that these decisions are made in an annual exercise and to hold their requests until that time. This is useful also because if one allows unit heads to come in a serial way, they will do so on a regular basis, and each time the request will be their "highest priority." Forcing the requests to come in all together makes it possible to determine the true priorities.

The method described in this section is a good way to handle the general case. On occasion a special opportunity may come along. Special opportunities seldom fit neatly into one's planned annual decision making. A later section of this book will discuss cases where it may be advisable to deviate from standard practice (see chapter 11, the "Management Trends" section).

Delegation of Authority

Each institution is different, but the trustees of the institution always vest decision-making authority in the university president. The president, in turn, delegates some of that authority to the provost (if there is one) and vice presidents. In the case of academic affairs, some authority is further delegated to the deans, who retain some of it and delegate some to the unit heads. Although it is frequently imagined that decision-making authority is delegated to faculty, this is almost never the case. (Some decisions may seem to be the faculty's because administrators have historically and routinely made decisions that were consistent with faculty recommendations. The topic of shared governance will be covered below in more detail.)

In considering recommendations, the faculty voice is loudest where the collective faculty has the most information and the greatest expertise: the curriculum, admission requirements, and internal unit policies. The faculty voice is usually least influential in budget matters, and it falls somewhere between these extremes when matters of budget and academic quality are mixed, such as in faculty recruitment.

A good practice, as noted above, is to delegate all decisions on day-to-day matters to the unit heads. They will be best placed to make such decisions; in any case, the work of the college will "grind to a halt" if the dean tries to make all of the day-to-day decisions for the college. Included here are most student matters, travel authorization, the purchase of supplies and services, and so forth. In delegating authority and responsibility for some things, unit heads need to be reminded that the dean expects their decisions to be fair and sound, and that annual evaluations will be based in part on their quality. (A later part of this chapter deals with improving the quality of decision making in one's subordinates.)

Correcting Mistakes

Mistakes are inevitable. Chairs will make mistakes; others will be made by directors, assistant and associate deans, and by support staff. Even the dean will make mistakes! A well-worn joke tells of the new dean who finds letters in three sealed envelopes prepared by the outgoing dean. The instructions say to open one letter each time there is difficulty. Time passes, and a crisis comes up. The dean opens the first letter, which advises: "Blame your predecessor." The dean blames his or her predecessor, and the crisis passes. Soon another problem comes up, severe enough to cause the dean to open the second letter. The letter suggests: "Blame the budget." The dean blames the budget, and the problem is resolved. In time the dean faces yet another serious challenge. The advice contained in the third letter is not comforting: "Prepare three letters for your successor."

Blaming others for problems is not the way to resolve them. In the end the dean is responsible for everything that goes wrong; it occurred either at his or her hand or by his or her authority. Improving the talent of other members of the administrative team is a strong theme of this book because in the end the dean is held responsible for whatever happens. Effective chairs, directors, assistant and associate deans, and members of the support staff will make good decisions most of the time. When a mistake is discovered, every effort should be made to accept blame, address the error, and take steps to correct it immediately. If the error is one that leaves the university at risk of negative publicity or litigation, key officials in the offices of public affairs and the general counsel should be alerted, as well as those in the reporting line above. Apologies should be issued and corrective costs borne as necessary. A quick, effective response is the best insurance against escalation of the problem.

After the mistake has been remedied, devote time to understanding why the system failed and how future breakdowns can be avoided. *Problems that stem from an error in judgment often make excellent case studies.* Such cases need to be disguised, but they can serve as very effective vehicles for discussion at administrative retreats. Exposing other members of the administrative team to such examples in settings where appropriate actions can be reviewed is a good way to have the entire organization learn from the mistake.

Senior Staff and the Use of Meetings

So far we have dealt with the behavioral and functional elements of administrative style. This subsection addresses some of the more important structural elements. Included here will be discussions of the dean's staff and the use of meetings.

Senior Staff Organization

Unless the college is extremely small, the dean will have one or more senior staff. In the case of huge state universities, such staffs can become quite large. It is important for the new dean to consider how his or her staff is going to be organized and then let unit heads know which members of the staff have authority for which things. Widespread knowledge of how the dean plans to operate will save everyone a great deal of time and will help the college function smoothly.

The first consideration for the dean is the quality and character of the staff. It is essential to have individuals who are competent, who are trusted, and who see themselves as facilitators, not gatekeepers. Almost any method of organizing a staff will work with good people, but almost no organizational arrangement will offset the complications created by individuals who lack these basic attributes.

How do colleges typically organize senior staffs? If a college is small, the dean will normally have an associate dean, who handles student (and perhaps academic) affairs, and a budget officer. If the college is quite large, a decision must be made whether to organize the associate deanships along substantive or functional lines. In the substantive arrangement, in a comprehensive college of arts and sciences, there might be associate deans for the arts and humanities, for the social and behavioral sciences, and for the natural sciences and mathematics. In the functional arrangement, associate deanships might be created for budget and personnel, student and academic affairs, and research and facilities. If there is no graduate college, there is sometimes an associate dean for graduate affairs. There is nothing especially compelling about these methods of arrangement, except they are commonly followed. There are many variants. In large colleges there are also assistant deans, who frequently support the work of one of the associate deans or have portfolios with narrow scopes. For example, many large institutions have an assistant dean to help with student affairs. Other institutions have an assistant dean of development or outreach. Some have an assistant dean who works almost exclusively on class schedules and temporary staffing. In other settings, especially at large universities, the budget officer is an assistant dean.

The point is this: Give some thought to how you want the work of the office to be handled. If the office is large, a choice will have to be made between a substantive and a functional arrangement. In the substantive model, each associate dean essentially manages all the functions of a segment of the college. In the functional model, each associate dean manages selected functions for all segments of the college. Once the decision has been made and the positions have been filled, it will be important to let unit heads know where aspects of authority have been placed. The unit heads can then contact the appropriate assistant or associate dean for each sort of business that must be addressed.

Initially, people want to see the dean personally, even if the matter is one that the dean wants an assistant or associate to handle. This can be discouraged by refusing to act on requests that come up at such meetings, referring the individual to the appropriate subordinate. Unit heads will seek out the designated individual only if they know the dean will not act on their requests and they know the subordinate has the authority to do so. If the dean is inconsistent in this regard, unit heads will be confused about what to do, much time will be wasted, the assistant and associate deans will not be as effective as the dean would like for them to be, and the college will suffer as a result. It is critical, therefore, for the dean to operate in way that is consistent with the delegation of authority and responsibility to the staff.

Administrative Meetings

There are two types of regular meetings that are held in most colleges. The largest of these bring together all of the chairs/unit heads, directors, assistant and associate deans, and other important members of the college's leadership group. (Such groups have many names, but a common one, used on many campuses, is Administrative Council.) These meetings should be held on a regular basis—monthly meetings are common—with additional meetings called as needed. There will always be information that needs to be disseminated, but meetings that are limited to the dissemination of information fail to take advantage of an important reason for meeting.

If a dean wants such meetings to be worth the time devoted to them, each session should feature a group discussion of at least one important issue. Such a discussion will be engaging for the participants, will be valuable for the dean, and will allow the members of the leadership team to hear the various points of view and the arguments behind them. There is almost no better way to tap into the collective intelligence of the group than to have it regularly engage in discussions of important issues. These discussions are not meant to lead to motions or formal actions. Rather, they serve to develop richer perspectives on important questions and issues, and they help the dean develop a better-informed sense of what might be possible.

The second type of regular meeting involves only the dean's senior staff. If the college is large, with significant staff, the question of how to keep everyone informed must be considered. There is much to be said for a tidy, focused, twice-a-month meeting of the dean's staff. Since work is compartmentalized and delegated, the primary purpose for such meetings is to give each member of the staff a general sense of what is happening in other parts of the college. Time is precious, so it is important not to meet more often or for longer than necessary. It is a good idea to put a strict time limit on the updates provided by members of the staff; otherwise, each report will be longer than the one that preceded it. When this occurs the meeting drags on until people have to leave to go to other appointments; the last presenters will be heard by only a few, and the primary reason for meeting will not have been satisfied. These meetings should not duplicate the information sharing that occurs in the larger group meetings, which include chairs and directors.

SETTING AN AGENDA

The new dean is usually confronted with conflicting agendas. The president and the provost (academic vice president) will almost certainly have things on which they want the new dean to work. The faculty will have its own set of concerns and issues. Each unit will be wondering how it fits into the new dean's plans. There will probably be strategic plans, external department evaluations, and anecdotal information about the state of the college with which one should become familiar. What is missing, of course, is an agenda set by the new dean.

Is there an easy way out of this? Can a person be dean and have no agenda beyond reacting to the things that come up? It is doubtful that someone who felt this way would be selected as dean, and it is unlikely that he or she would remain dean for long taking such an approach. Why? We live in a time of change. Change represents an opportunity and a threat. Times of change offer opportunities for institutions to improve their placement if they make good decisions, but they run the risk of losing ground to others if their decisions are unsound. To the extent one can be proactive, it is possible to shape the agenda, whereas being solely reactive will mean that your existence is shaped fully by whatever comes along.

What to Emphasize?

To be successful, the dean's agenda really needs to be the college's agenda. If people do not take ownership of the ideas, do not buy into the directions indicated in the plan, the dean has little chance of succeeding. It is best, therefore, if an agenda can be developed through an iterative process informed by an environmental scan, institutional data, and a realistic look at the college's strengths and weaknesses. This review should produce a list of things that would be good for the college and a sense of direction for the overall effort. To be successful, college priorities must obviously be consistent with the university's mission, direction, and goals. (A later section will deal with the operationalization of a plan; the purpose here is to remind the new dean that he or she is expected to *do* something, so it is wise to determine the rough contours of an agenda, an agenda that reveals the general directions in which the new dean intends to move the college.)

Leadership for Change

Higher education is often described as being "operationally passive."[1] This is surprising, because the liberal tradition on which colleges and universities are based features optimism about the future, a belief that understanding can come from a critical examination of that which confronts us, and a confidence in humankind's capacity to make things better through reasoned choice. One would expect colleges and universities to be better situated than many other organizations when it comes to change. Consistent with this liberal tradition is establishing an institutional state of mind that is optimistic about the future. The dean's orientation should be that change represents opportunity and that success is expected. The college, through its own initiative, will get better.

Deans are well placed to provide leadership for change. Deans have been described as "brokers of time and relationships, and as institutional interpreters and mediators."[2] Deans are brokers of time in that they help determine how the institution's human resources are deployed and used. Deans are brokers of relationships because they help set a tone and facilitate various forms of interaction that occur in colleges and universities. Success in various forms of human interaction (faculty member to student, faculty member to administration, faculty member to faculty member, student to student, administrator to administrator, student to staff, faculty member to staff, and so on) is fundamental to the work of higher education.

Deans are also institutional interpreters and mediators. Deans are situated at the crossroads of conflicting values and priorities. The faculty typically sees the dean as too aggressive, and the provost typically sees the dean as too passive when it comes to such concerns as workload, enhancing diversity, pushing undergraduate reform, elevating the place of teaching (at the expense, in the eyes of some, of research), assessing outcomes, encouraging faculty advisement, or pushing any other institutional initiative of importance, such as outreach. Residing at the crossroads, deans interpret and mediate the discourse that surrounds these issues.

Leadership implies that there is a direction. Leadership for change suggests that the organization seeks to employ changes that facilitate its movement in an agreed-upon direction. Planning for such change should be seen as a normal, continuous process. Planning leads to agenda building; it will provide direction for the dean's leadership.

Styles and Strategies for Leading Change

What aspects of administrative style facilitate change? First, it is important to be open, not guarded. It helps to be well informed personally and to ensure that those around you and reporting to you are equally well informed about their own programs and those of others in the college. It is important that there be a broad understanding of how priorities are set and how decisions are made. It is important to operate on the basis of overarching principles (those of the campus and the college) rather than on acquaintances and patronage. When all participants know the rationale behind how priorities are set, when decisions are made through processes that are understood and predictable, and when fairness is revealed in decision making guided by principles, a condition of trust is established. Progress toward change is facilitated when parties trust one another.

A second element of administrative style that facilitates change is effective communication. There is much talk today about faculty and departments not responding to institutional needs, but it is often the case that the faculty either has not received clear signals or has received mixed signals as to what the administration expects. The mix of responsibilities for a typical faculty member is changing as colleges and universities evolve. The dean must effectively communicate the evolving expectations of the faculty. (This topic will be treated in greater detail in a later chapter.) A college will be most effective if faculty responsibilities are effectively integrated with institutional needs. This can happen only if the dean is successful in communicating what is expected and then urges that outcome.

A third consideration is how one most effectively urges a specific outcome. Pushing faculty members to do things seldom brings a satisfactory result. Much greater success can be expected if one takes proactive steps to draw individuals and units toward the desired outcome. This can be accomplished in a variety of ways. One approach is to identify best practices and publicize and celebrate them so others will copy them. Another is to evaluate units annually on the extent to which they are responding to institutional needs, rewarding those who are most helpful to the institution. Finally, alter reward systems so that individuals who are doing institutionally useful things in exemplary ways are recognized when it comes to annual salary increases, promotion, and tenure. (These strategies are described in greater detail later in the book.)

A fourth approach that facilitates change is to build and extend stewardship for the university's well-being. This occurs through delegation of authority and responsibility to chairs (unit heads) and faculty. Delegation only makes sense, however, if those whose authority is thereby enhanced make good decisions. It is important for every dean to stimulate the professional development of chairs and directors who report to her/him, thereby enhancing the general talent level of the college's administrative team. This is accomplished through such activities as administrative retreats that focus on problem solving. One approach that works well is to organize panel discussions featuring the most effective chairs. They can serve as models for new or weaker chairs to emulate. Professional development can be accomplished through workshops for new chairs, through continuous mentoring on the part of the dean, and through activities that improve the performance of the unit heads' senior staff. An important mentoring opportunity occurs each year in the annual evaluation of unit heads. Just as the review of tests provides a chance to enhance student learning, so going over an administrative performance evaluation with a unit head provides a wonderful opportunity to help the individual grow into a more effective administrative team member. (These ideas are covered in greater detail later.)

Stewardship is effectively extended when those who have been given additional authority and responsibility make decisions that can be supported. If the dean has to support a bad decision or has to overturn a bad decision and thereby not support the subordinate, an undesirable outcome occurs. By improving the talent level of chairs, deans can ensure that better decisions are made more often, decisions that can be supported to the satisfaction of all, and to the greater goal of extending a sense of stewardship more completely throughout the organization.

A sense of stewardship within institutions is proportional to the extent of influence of the many individuals upon whom success depends. It is also strongly influenced by the ownership that the faculty and unit heads feel about the directions of the college. To engage faculty and chairs fully and to make them most effective as partners in leadership for change, it is important to inform and involve them appropriately. This is more likely to occur if the dean's administrative style is (a) open and builds trust,

(b) effective in communicating university priorities, (c) skilled at using tools that draw individuals and units toward desired outcomes, (d) successful in deepening the sense of stewardship felt for the institution.

Does this approach mean that there must always be a consensus or at least majority support for a change agenda? Such a condition is always welcome, but it should not be seen as essential. There are many settings where the status quo will be the most popular condition but where change is clearly indicated. A good example of this was the effort to diversify the faculty in higher education. Strong leaders pushed to achieve this goal, not because it enjoyed popular support but because it was the right thing to do. The important questions for any change agenda are: Is it the right thing to do? Do key people support it? If these questions can be answered in the affirmative, the dean needs to push the agenda for change.

LIFE OF THE COLLEGE

What exactly is the college? Organizationally, a college is normally a collection of departments that share a certain intellectual orientation and purpose. The bodies of knowledge in the units that make up a college are frequently quite varied, as are the sorts of contributions that are deemed important if faculty are to be successful in their respective disciplines. Occasionally all the faculty of a college will be in a single unit (nursing is often organized this way), but more often there could be anywhere from three to over forty departments and centers in a college. In most universities, the largest colleges are usually those that encompass the liberal arts and sciences; professional colleges are often smaller and more focused intellectually.

The dean is largely responsible for determining if there will be life in the college beyond the obvious administrative functions. The wise dean works with unit heads, members of the dean's staff, and faculty to ensure that there is much more to the life of the college than budgets, facilities, schedules, catalogs, personnel decisions, and other sorts of organizational matters. A healthy college has numerous events that celebrate the successes of students, faculty, staff, and alumni; help to welcome and orient newly hired individuals to the academic community; and project the university into the community in which it resides. It is also a good idea to have a range of clothing and utility items, adorned with the college logo, that indicate membership in the college. These items might include jackets, shirts, umbrellas, leather notebooks, and so on; they can be given to people who serve on college committees, to students who make the Dean's List, to donors and friends. A later section will cover this topic in some detail, but the newly appointed dean should take steps to review current practices and consult with others to make modifications as is necessary to invigorate the life of the college.

The new dean has a great deal to think about and much of what is important may not come intuitively. Some deans spend their time preparing in appropriate ways, which dramatically improves their chances of getting off to a good start. Others come in ill prepared and learn as they go. If they are quick learners and have good instincts, they may survive if people are patient. Others do not learn as they go; they come in ill prepared, exhibit inexperience in their manner and decisions, and seldom last very long.

The advice offered in this chapter, if followed, will help the new dean immeasurably. Give thought to the kind of dean you want to be, in manner and in how you plan to organize to execute the duties of the position. Put a staff in place that will allow you to function as you envision. Get to know the people who make up the college and the university. Work with appropriate others to craft the rough outline of an action agenda. Orient yourself to be a catalyst for change, to be a leader. Finally, think of the college as something more than an organizational necessity of the university. Come up with a set of events that will bring life to the college.

Aristotle said, "Well begun is half done." The importance of getting off to a good start cannot be overemphasized. By itself it will not ensure success, but it certainly improves one's chances.

NOTES

1. G. Keller, *Academic Strategy: The Management Revolution in American Higher Education* (Baltimore: Johns Hopkins University Press, 1983).

2. J. Rameley, "Challenges for Deans," *CCAS Newsletter* 16, no. 1 (1984): 1–3.

CHAPTER 5

Improving the Abilities of Unit Heads

The talent of the unit heads exerts a strong influence on one's effectiveness as dean. If unit heads cannot be trusted to make sound decisions, the dean cannot easily delegate authority and responsibility. If the dean makes all decisions, there will be little time for anything else, and morale will suffer. If unit heads have authority and responsibility but make bad decisions, the dean will spend all of his or her time reversing decisions, adjudicating differences, responding to grievances and lawsuits, and reacting to what is urgent, while leaving unattended what is important. Improving the talent of unit heads is so important that I have devoted an entire chapter to this topic.

The talent level of unit heads can be improved two ways: by replacement of weak leaders with ones who are stronger, and by improving the talent level of those currently in office. The ease with which individuals are replaced and the control a dean has over that process vary from institution to institution; therefore, taking steps to improve the ability level of those currently serving as chairs, heads, and directors is probably the more universal option. There are, however, colleges and universities where the dean has a strong say in who is appointed to these positions, so both approaches will be discussed.

ENHANCING THE TALENT LEVEL THROUGH SELECTION

At most colleges and universities, unit heads serve at the pleasure of the dean, normally on annual administrative contracts that are renewed for a certain term (a four- or five-year stint is typical). At some institutions, these initial terms can be extended; at others, when the term is fulfilled the individual rotates out, and someone new is appointed. There are advantages to each system. When terms can be extended, an especially effective individual can be retained in the position. The downside of longer terms is that the ethos for taking one's turn is weaker. When people rotate through these positions they can usually keep their academic careers on track, while people who occupy these positions for extended periods sometimes pay a price in their academic careers. The primary problem with a strict rotation is that many individuals who are ill suited to the job will have a turn at doing it. While this might help them appreciate how difficult a job it is, the overall effect on a college is to make the mean talent level lower than when people well suited for such jobs spend more time in them.

Regardless of the arrangement of the term, it is in the dean's and the institution's interest to have the best people selected to fill such positions. The challenge becomes getting such individuals to agree to be candidates and then getting them appointed. This may sound simple enough, but more often than not it is difficult to do on a regular basis.

Choosing between an Inside and an Outside Search

Some colleges and universities look internally for the vast majority of their leadership appointments. Others frequently look externally when they are searching for new chairs, directors, or department heads. Here are the arguments for each approach.

An external search may be the preferred action if a unit is troubled and there appear to be no reasonable internal leadership options. An external search is also indicated when a department is very young and immature. Finding someone from a well-run institution with the experience to mentor and guide such a department can pay excellent dividends. Still another valid reason for external searches is to increase the diversity of the leadership team. Less compelling arguments that are sometimes made for an external search for a chair/unit head include that (a) no one wants to do it, (b) an external hire means the unit gets an additional position, or (c) an external person will be able to leverage more funds for the department. These latter arguments usually do not justify the cost and risk incurred in conducting an external search.

Is there risk involved? Yes, more than the inexperienced dean might imagine. First, it should be noted that external searches result in appointments that work out well enough to justify the cost only about 50 percent of the time. This means that although half the time the appointee accomplishes at least what was hoped for, the rest of the time you have added at high cost a tenured, senior individual who ends up failing, sometimes badly.

There are numerous reasons why such appointments fail. One of the most common reasons for failure is that the individual recruited has come from an academic culture so different that everything he or she tries is unsuccessful in the new setting. Occasionally, the person selected comes not because he or she is drawn to the challenge offered by your position but because the candidate is running away from a bad situation in a current setting. People who look good on paper and in an interview sometimes turn out to have character flaws that handicap them in a leadership role.

Risk also comes from the chance that a search will produce a candidate who is attractive but with whom it is impossible for the dean to come to terms. (If they are very good and from institutions where they are appreciated, counteroffers are often made, causing the candidate to remain where he or she is.) When a long search produces no appointment, morale can suffer, and the reputation of a department can be harmed. External searches are sometimes appropriate, but there is significant risk in seeking leadership through this method, and so it should be used judiciously.

An internal search is usually the best option. The selection then comes from a set of individuals who know the institution and who are known to one another. If a department sees this as the expected course of events, it will take more care in developing faculty to ensure that there is a steady stream of individuals ready to take on assignments. Departments in such settings often engage in "succession planning," whereby individuals with leadership potential are encouraged to serve as associate chairs, undergraduate or graduate coordinators, and in other quasi-administrative roles. This practice often reveals (to both the individual and the unit) obvious candidates for future consideration. Another reason internal searches are good is that new positions can always be filled with an eye toward building academic strengths, rather than using them for administrative purposes (in which the academic specialty is secondary and may not represent a unit's need for critical expertise).

Conducting a Search for a Unit Head

Faculty members, having come from hundreds of other colleges and universities, often have misguided views about such searches. It is therefore important to inform the faculty at the start of the search how things work under this dean at this institution. It is truly the case that "an ounce of prevention is worth a pound of cure" when it comes to searches for unit heads. The letter that appears below is one that I used to initiate searches. It represents the conditions that prevailed at his institution. It is included here not to be copied for use elsewhere, because what is said would be different in each setting. Rather, it is provided to give the new dean a sense of the kinds of issues that should be addressed at the start of the process and not be left to chance.

MEMORANDUM

TO: Department Chair Search Advisory Committee

FROM: Dean

RE: Some Thoughts on Chair Selection

Next to hiring, retaining, and advancing faculty, decisions on the selection of department leadership are among the most important personnel actions made in colleges and universities. Leadership is almost always undervalued when it is effective, but costs in productivity and morale can be enormous under conditions of dysfunctional leadership.

The best departments take care to ensure that their faculty members appreciate the need for effective leadership. They take steps to ensure that their members are exposed to the many dimensions of departmental operation so as to become familiar with the diverse activities and problems facing the department. They involve faculty in establishing practices to deal with the problems and opportunities available in the university community.

When no one cares enough about the department to be willing to serve in an administrative capacity, administrators in the university's hierarchy may easily dismiss the department as an unpromising place in which to invest. Therefore, it is important (1) that the culture of the department instill an appreciation for effective leadership, (2) that faculty members are involved in a variety of departmental activities that help develop administrative talent, and (3) that the faculty in its collective activity works to ensure a steady stream of qualified individuals ready to assume leadership positions.

Conducting a Search for Chair. Poorly handled searches can be divisive and stressful. The prospects for successful appointments made under these conditions are frequently diminished. If certain courtesies are extended in the search, many problems can be avoided, and the chances of enjoying a productive search resulting in an effective appointment can be enhanced. Some of the important courtesies are described below.

Courtesies to the Department. When conducting a search, the committee should be sensitive to the culture of the department as it determines, within what policy allows, the elements that will characterize the search process. Every decision should be made with an eye toward building confidence in the process and ensuring that all parties feel appropriately consulted. It is essential that all departmental personnel are informed and participate actively in the search process.

Courtesies to the Candidates. Steps should be taken to ensure that no one is devalued by the process. The selection of a chair almost always comes down to a difficult choice among qualified people. The candidates possess different strengths and weaknesses, but this does not make qualified candidates unacceptable. It is important to remember that the individuals not selected will continue to be colleagues in the department and might even be the choice of a selection committee in some future search. For these reasons, it is important to ensure that no aspect of the search be degrading to candidates. An important step toward this goal is the maintenance of confidentiality.

Although votes may be taken in the process, it is important to remember that departments do not elect chairs. Nevertheless, votes can provide important information about faculty sentiment. The publication of such votes is discouraged, because they can be demeaning to less favored candidates. Furthermore, a vote has served its purpose once the committee knows the results. Since the goal of the vote is to inform the committee, not to elect, there is no reason to distribute the outcome further. It is also the case that the contents of letters of recommendation and the discussions and minutes of committee deliberations should be kept confidential. Committee members breaching confidentiality are not serving the best interest of the process and are guilty of a breach of professional ethics.

Courtesies to the Committee. As dean, I will work to ensure the integrity of the search committee as the official body that provides advice on the selection of a chair. Furthermore, the committee is free to rank the candidates as long as a fully developed statement of strengths and weaknesses is provided along with the ranking. The results of votes taken to inform the committee can also be forwarded as part of the recommendation. The goal in the search process is to enjoy a condition of agreement at the end of the search; however, if my view differs from that of the search committee, I will meet with the committee prior to taking action on an appointment. The goal of this meeting will be to explore reasons for the discrepancy in viewpoints and to see if a consensus can be reached.

Avoiding False Expectations Related to the Appointment of a New Chair. Many individuals, and on occasion whole departments, hold false expectations about the conditions surrounding the appointment of a chair of an academic unit and the extent to which decisions on the allocation of resources are tied to new appointments. Contrary to popular belief, there is not an administrative salary scale for chairs. The current practice across the university is to convert the academic (nine-month) salary to a fiscal (twelve-month) salary when an individual assumes a position as chair. (A downward reversion occurs from twelve months back to nine months at the end of the term.) As is routine in all cases of promotion, a modest adjustment to the base pay rate is made, if appropriate.

Decisions about the allocation of resources to departments are never part of the department chair appointment process. It is only natural for someone entering a position to seek to "win" something for the department, but if this is the way decisions were made the "new kid on the block" would receive all the resources, and the department could expect to make gains only in years coinciding with a change in leadership. I cannot imagine anyone wishing to live in such an environment. Allocations made in this way and without an assessment of other competing needs would almost certainly result in ill-advised and inappropriate decisions.

When an individual agrees to serve as chair, I promise that he or she will have full access to competition for available resources, but that we will make judgments about their allocation in comprehensive, comparative, collective exercises wherein all needs can be contrasted and the benefits and costs can be maximized. If an individual is not willing to function administratively under this arrangement, there is no place for that individual on the university's administrative team.

This is mentioned here because colleagues frequently ask chair candidates what they will seek on behalf of the department as a prerequisite to accepting the position as chair. Such discussions are counterproductive and should be avoided. (Questions about the candidate's view of departmental needs and the candidate's view of priorities in seeking new resources as occasions present themselves are appropriate.)

I believe that if departments will take seriously the advice offered herein, our searches will be more productive, transitions in leadership more harmonious, and the possibilities for continued effective leadership enhanced. A desire for these outcomes is what prompted the preparation of this memorandum, and I hope it will be read in the spirit intended.

In instructing search advisory committees, it is important to make sure they understand that part of their role is to encourage people to let themselves be considered; this is the most important step in ensuring that the pool is both strong and diverse. (If units are small, getting one good individual to stand as a candidate may be the best one can hope for.) It is important for the dean to instruct the committee about the importance of acting affirmatively at each stage of the process. It is also important to let the committee know that your goal as dean is to appoint the person it recommends and that only if you believe its recommendation is flawed will you not conclude the search by appointing the favored candidate. (I always felt comfortable saying this because committees almost never recommended incompetent people, and I believed I could help any individual become more effective.) Nevertheless, the importance of quality leadership and the importance of diversity in that leadership are things that must be regularly emphasized if one expects to have good results.

Interviewing Prospective Chairs

An opportunity not to be wasted is the interview of candidates for chair/unit head positions. This interview provides the dean with a chance to let candidates know how the search will play out. It also allows the dean to thank candidates for their willingness to be considered and to let them know that the goal is to support the faculty recommendation. One should let candidates know that such searches almost always result in a difficult choice between good people. Thus, should the search turn to the other candidate it will mean nothing more than that the fit with the other candidate just seemed better at this time. The dean should also remind candidates about the general ground rules for the search and the appointment, and should spend a moment letting the candidate know about his or her general philosophy. The candidate may have questions and should be given the chance to ask them. Finally, the dean will have questions for the candidate. The questions listed below will normally reveal a great deal about the candidate's readiness to assume such a position. They are presented here as a guide; each dean will want to have questions that provide the insights he or she seeks.

1. What are the department's strengths, and what prime opportunities for investment are presented by the department?
2. What are the department's weaknesses, and what primary obstacles to progress are faced by the department?

3. If you were to be named chair, what would be on your near-term action agenda?

4. Tell me about your administrative style. What do you see as the role of the chair, and how do you see yourself operating in that role?

The answers to these questions—what is said and what is not said—reveal a great deal about the candidate's perception of the department and his or her readiness to provide the leadership that will be required. A candidate's response to the first question often reveals an awareness (or lack thereof) of broad university priorities in which the unit might participate. Responses to the second question provide an indication of whether the candidate tends to see the department as in control of its destiny or largely at the mercy of others. Responses to the third question often reveal those least suited to leadership roles, as the candidate might impulsively talk about "evening scores" or putting certain others "in their place." It also provides insight about the candidate's commitment to institutional goals like diversity in hiring. (When a unit exhibited under-representation of protected classes, I expected the candidate—without prompting—to mention this as something he or she planned to address.) Answers to the final question reveal the level of the self-awareness people have about how they operate. It is always interesting to compare what is said with what is known about the individual.

Appointing Unit Heads

When the time comes to make the appointment, the dean should operate on the basis of principles that apply to all such appointments. This is important, because some individuals will be more aggressive than others. To be fair to all individuals who will be appointed, they all should be treated alike. This means that the timid will probably do better than they might have, and the bold will do worse than might have been the case. What is important is that each will have been treated fairly.

What should the principles be? Here are the ones that I used for eleven years. (It is not suggested that these fit every institution, but there is a best set for each university.)

1. An equity and market review is conducted, and the base (nine-month) salary is adjusted upward, if such an adjustment is indicated.

2. The adjusted nine-month salary is converted to a twelve-month salary.

3. A new computer, printer, and software are provided for administrative use.

4. Other items deemed important to the administrative aspect of the appointment are provided as indicated.

5. No commitments are made for the department.

The more aggressive individuals will push for more, but the dean is on firm ground when he or she can say that what is being done is what is done for everyone. Most people appreciate knowing that it is the dean's practice to treat everyone fairly.

Occasionally there may be an individual who insists on special treatment. On the one occasion where this happened to me, the individual was told that what was sought was beyond what the college was willing to provide. He was thanked for his interest in the position, and his colleagues were informed that the search was continuing. The individual's colleagues were furious with him for standing as a candidate, knowing what was expected, and then holding out for more. The search was extended and produced an outstanding individual to serve as chair.

It is important to emphasize that there are many approaches to compensating unit heads. (An overview of chair appointment and compensation practices is provided on the American Council on Education website, acenet.edu/resources/chairs/.) Some places provide an administrative stipend that ends when the individual returns to the faculty. Other places provide two months of summer salary. In institutions with mandated teaching loads, some relief from the normal instructional load is often part of the compensation arrangement. The institution will provide the broad framework for what is possible; it is up to the dean to ensure that the offers are consistent with that framework.

HELPING NEW CHAIRS GET STARTED

When faculty members become chairs they often have a poorly developed sense of what the chair does, are not certain how the unit fits into and operates within the college, probably have had no training in academic leadership, and frequently lack a well-developed sense of broad institutional goals. Furthermore, with a turnover in the chair a great deal of institutional memory of departmental matters is lost. The wise dean takes steps to help the new chairs get started.

The things that a dean can do for new chairs fall into three categories: orientation sessions, retreats, and general mentoring. The subsections below provide suggestions for each of these approaches to improving the performance of new chairs.

Orientation Sessions

Each year, shortly before the new chairs take office, or at the latest shortly afterward, the dean should organize a half-day orientation session. (This should occur even if there is only one new chair.) The purpose of this session is to bring to the new chairs' attention as many things about the operation of a unit in the college as is possible. It is good to review the duties and responsibilities of the chair. If the chair is the product of an external search, he or she should be coached on the importance of an engagement and communication plan to connect with the unit's internal and external stakeholders. Most chairs take office at the start of the fiscal year, on July 1, so the communication should occur during the remainder of the summer and accelerate as faculty members return for the start of the fall semester.

The chair should be introduced to each member of the dean's staff and be informed about the aspects of college business that are handled by them. The major annual activities in which the chair must participate should be reviewed. These include major budget exercises, scheduling requirements and deadlines, important ceremonial and celebratory activities at which the chair's attendance is expected, personnel review schedules, and requests for renovation and new construction. This list will vary from institution to institution. Important college and university policies should be reviewed for such things as purchasing, fund-raising, sponsored projects, and special events.

Chairs should also be alerted to all the help resources to which he or she might turn when faced with difficult problems. These resources include the staff of the dean's office, the employee assistance program, the university's legal services, the office of equal opportunity and affirmative action, the ombudsperson group, and other chairs (with more experience). Finally, time should be spent to ensure that each chair understands the university's mission and goals, as well as how the department is expected to contribute to the university's needs. Having a session like this for new chairs is extremely important in getting them off to a good start.

Administrative Retreats

One of the best ways to help new chairs get started and to help all chairs become stronger is to provide them with an annual administrative retreat. These retreats should be daylong, involving three meals (with partners invited to the dinner), and should take everyone to a comfortable off-campus location.

A number of good things come from such a retreat. The unit heads begin to think of themselves as members of an administrative team. New chairs can see how experienced chairs conceptualize and deal with problems. The best practices of individual units can be reviewed so others will copy them. New friendships are created. Everyone (deans and chairs) can develop a deeper understanding of complex problems and issues. There is no better way for the new chair to be introduced to what it means to be a unit head than to participate in such retreats.

What makes up the program for a typical retreat? A complete set of the substantive elements is contained in appendix A, but the basic segments typically look something like the outline below.

Continental Breakfast

Welcome and orientation

Review of college and unit data (with discussion)

Roundtable discussion of some common administrative concern

Review and discussion of case studies (usually personnel related)

Lunch

Panel discussion by university officials who can be helpful to chairs

The chairs' clinic (three seasoned chairs respond to typical problems)

Panel discussion of some common administrative concern

A conversation with the provost (about university directions), with Q & A

Dinner, with participants and guests/partners

This generic overview may appear not very engaging, but an examination of the sample program elements will reveal sessions that are useful to chairs. In the typical session, three seasoned chairs, who are especially good at the issue being dealt with, are asked to make opening remarks on the topic; then everyone participates in a discussion, led by the panelists. Here are several examples.

In a session on making good decisions, three chairs started by telling the others how they go about making decisions for their units.

The first chair reported the following practices:

1. Fully communicate/discuss possibilities and learn the perspectives of others (good ideas will emerge, and decisions will be better accepted).

2. Know and follow applicable policy and bylaw provisions (these will provide guidance and reveal constraints).

3. Be knowledgeable about your unit (study all available data and collect your own).

4. Talk with others: chairs, deans, general counsel, affirmative action, employee assistance.

5. Gauge institutional and cultural pressures (they are always shifting), read the *Chronicle of Higher Education,* talk with colleagues elsewhere.

6. Understand idiosyncrasies of colleagues (different people need to be treated differently).

7. Do not allow yourself to get pressured into an immediate response.

The second chair reported the following practices:

1. Develop a process for reaching decisions—do not approach each decision as a new event.

2. Remember that opportunities frequently involve risks.

3. Establish a set of practices that you routinely follow (and that others can count on).

4. Find ways to stimulate new ideas.

5. Involve the department in sifting through ideas (think together about goals and fit, costs and benefits, virtues and flaws).

6. Actively lead in steering ideas (involve others, allow time, protect against railroading or sabotage, remember that anxieties and fear take time to overcome, consider that initial instincts may be wrong).

7. Show the idea in the big ring (represent honestly, recognize that at some point you may lose control, be attentive to context).

8. Remember that success does not occur with approval but over time with effective implementation.

The third chair reported the following practices:

1. Remember that the chair's principal job is faculty development, including leadership/stewardship development.

2. Save half of your time to deal with the unexpected.

3. Do not contrive work—efforts on every matter should never exceed the potential benefits.

4. Optimize productivity and rationality in ways that are consistent with an academic culture that is "democratic," is low in direction but high in supportive expectations, and enjoys gamesmanship.

5. Be prepared—this starts with being well informed.

6. Establish practices that allow the unit to act quickly but thoughtfully with deliberation and involvement appropriate to the issue.

7. Refer to guiding documents (mission statements, program review advice) and assess your situation regularly.

8. Operate from known rules/principles.

In the discussion that followed these introductory statements, retreat participants tried to come up with some common elements to sound decision making. The items that appear below represent the final list of things that, if present, will help to ensure that good decisions are reached.

1. The need to be informed
2. The need to communicate
3. The importance of policies and process
4. The need to orchestrate
5. The need to operate on the basis of principles
6. The need to articulate with the bigger picture

This session turned out to be very helpful for all of the chairs. The participants spent time thinking about the importance of making good decisions, and they learned about the practices followed by some of the best chairs in the college.

Two other examples of sessions are provided in abstract form below. Appendix A contains many examples of retreat program elements.

In a session meant to have chairs think about their role in orchestrating things, three chairs (with well developed senses of humor) were asked to engage in a role-playing exercise. The situation they found themselves in was this: The dean has just called and wants the department to look at the trailing member of an academic pair. The lead member of the pair is being recruited by another department in the college, but the appointment's success hinges on the ability to find a position for the trailing partner. The partner's expertise is in the field of the department being called but is not one of the priority hiring areas for that unit. Adding another male faculty member will make the department's diversity profile look worse than it already is. The person would probably not make a short list in a national search at his rank in his specialty. Nevertheless, the individual has a reasonable record and finding a job for him is a deal breaker in the primary search.

Each panelist was asked to present this to those at the retreat as if they were members of his or her department. The first panelist was asked to present it in the most negative way possible; the second panelist was asked to present it in the most positive way possible; the third panelist was asked to present in a totally neutral way, neither encouraging nor discouraging support for the dean's proposal. (The presenters did a marvelous job, and the entire group had lots of laughs.)

After the presentations the group entered a discussion about the appropriate role for the chair in such circumstances. The conclusion was that none of these roles is appropriate. A chair loses credibility when he or she pushes excessively for the outcome the dean seeks. A chair is not being a good university citizen if he or she presents this issue in a way that will kill its chances for a fair review. Even the strictly neutral presentation is not the best, because the chair is expected to act as a member of the broader university team and to encourage the department in a reasonable way at least to look at the candidate and decide if the faculty believes that the individual could be a valuable addition to its ranks. An appointment would never be made over the objections of the faculty, but the chair should encourage his or her colleagues to provide at least a fair review and interview. Again, the discussion of this case caused all chairs to think about their leadership roles. Thus sensitized, the chairs would probably have given a real case featuring similar circumstances a fairer hearing than they have before the retreat.

Another retreat session that paid many dividends was one that was suggested by a series of focus-group meetings with new faculty. The dean and associate dean hosted a series of lunches for about 80 faculty members who were in the first two years of their appointments with the college. These meetings had revealed vast unevenness in the extent to which new faculty were helped and supported in their new setting. The session featured three chairs who were perceived as doing the best jobs of helping new faculty and nurturing them during their crucial early years as independent academics. Each of the three chairs on the panel told about the things he or she did to help new faculty. Many of the other chairs were astonished and quietly embarrassed by the discrepancy between what these thoughtful chairs were doing and what they had been doing themselves, which was essentially nothing. The remaining part of the session featured questions and answers with the panelists and a general discussion of what had been discovered in the focus groups. The long-term result of this session was that each new faculty member received much more help in his or her relocation and other aspects of the job that we had learned were giving young people trouble.

Another type of retreat that can be useful is a seminar on professional development, offered for chairs by professional organizations. Many professional associations and academic disciplines have such meetings for chairs. The American Council on Education has a Department Chair Leadership Program that features workshops for chairs from all disciplines.

It also has a well-developed department chair online resource center (www.acenet.edu/resources/chairs). The Council for Colleges of Arts and Sciences (CCAS) has annual seminars for chairs heading departments in the arts and humanities, the social and behavioral sciences, and in the natural sciences and mathematics.

Many other national organizations offer seminars on professional development for chairs. Included here (as examples) are such organizations as the American Association of Higher Education, the Modern Language Association, the American Conference of Academic Deans, and the Assembly to Advance Collegiate Schools of Business. Chair seminars are also offered by the professional associations of specific academic disciplines. While seminars offered by these groups are generic in nature and deal with topics in a less campus-specific way than one can do internally, they are useful, and the wise dean happily pays the travel and registration costs for chairs who seek this form of professional development.

Active Mentoring by the Dean

The third important issue in helping new chairs become more effective is active mentoring by the dean. The dean should not be shy about his or her belief that part of the dean's job is the professional development of the chairs. Active mentoring means taking advantage of every "teachable" moment that comes along.

New chairs are often uncertain as to how to go about certain tasks. A good example is in acting affirmatively. A new chair may contact the dean seeking permission to proceed with a search by interviewing the top two candidates. In discussing the pool of candidates the dean (or his or her associate) discovers that the third candidate, a protected-class member, is seen on paper as slightly less qualified than the top two candidates but is strong and clearly one who meets all of the published criteria. This presents the dean with a wonderful opportunity to remind the chair of the institution's commitment to diversity and the need for chairs to provide leadership in acting affirmatively in such situations. This conversation should occur quietly and privately, so as not to embarrass the chair. Emboldened and encouraged by the dean, most chairs rise to the occasion and revise their recommendation so that three candidates are interviewed. Such action often leads to the appointment of the protected-class member.

Similar opportunities come along on a regular basis. In each case the dean should provide mentoring to the chair, along with strong encouragement to do the right thing. If the chair seems hesitant, it may be useful to refer the chair to another chair who you know has dealt with similar problems in a constructive and appropriate way. With such reinforcement the reluctant chair will usually exercise the positive leadership that is needed.

HELPING CHAIRS UNDERSTAND THEIR JOBS

The chair is often described as the "first among equals." This phrase contains an inherent contradiction; perhaps that is why the position of chair is often described as the most difficult in the university. In the typical setting, faculty members fear a powerful chair in general, especially one who might not side with their interests. Unit bylaws are often written in such a way as to constrain the authority of the chair. Bylaws, however, can never take precedence over higher authority, so in truth, no authority delegated to chairs can be circumscribed by unit bylaws. Still, deans should encourage chairs to remember that they can be effective only as long as they have the support of their colleagues and the dean. They should be appropriately consultative and support the faculty as fully as is possible. It is a privilege to serve in an administrative capacity. The power to be effective comes at least as much from the support of those who are being led as from authority that has been delegated from above. In the end, however, all departmental decisions are seen by the university as that of the supervising administrator, and he or she is responsible for whatever results from such decisions, whether or not they were consistent with faculty advice. The dean should help the chair understand the delicate balance inherent in the management of an academic department.

Another point to be impressed on new chairs by the dean has to do with what defines effectiveness. Many faculty moving into these roles wish to be evaluated on the basis of their academic performance, with no reference to their administrative effectiveness; therefore, a good idea is to have an instrument that features the basic elements of effective administration. (See appendix B for a sample evaluation form.) Chairs should know that they will be evaluated using this instrument. They can also be asked to provide a self-assessment of their performance with reference to the items in the instrument. Typically, this information is combined with faculty evaluations of the chair's performance and a retrospective look at what the chair has actually accomplished (or failed to accomplish).

There are numerous evaluation instruments available for use in the assessing administrative performance. Some of the more sophisticated ones assess such things as the chair's familiarity with areas and levels of importance of each item for the chair's overall performance. A rather complete review of this topic is provided in *Evaluating and Developing Administrative Performance* (Seldin 1988).

Many chairs imagine that their success will be driven almost entirely by the new things they can "win" for the department. This kind of thinking needs to be discouraged. It is good to remind chairs that they control vast budgeted resources; it is the stewardship of these resources that will be most important to the chair's success. If he or she uses what is already available in an efficient and effective manner, what the unit accomplishes will be maximized. To the extent that the chair fails to use these resources fully and effectively, he or she will be a failure. It is always difficult for chairs to attack unit wastefulness, largely because much inefficiency reflects what faculty members prefer to do rather than what the institution needs to have done. The letter below is an example of something the dean can do to remind chairs of the importance of using their budgeted personnel resources to maximize instructional effectiveness.

MEMORANDUM

TO: Administrative Council (Chairs and Directors)

FROM: Dean

RE: Maximizing Instructional Power with Budgeted Resources

You know from your own experience and from my presentations to the Administrative Council that we are in a difficult period budgetarily. As we make our budgetary and academic course scheduling plans for next year it is especially important, therefore, to ensure that we have taken every necessary and appropriate step to maximize what is accomplished with the funds recurring in our annual budgets.

I sense from my discussions with many of you that our current scheduling practices result in inefficiencies that cannot be justified. These problems must be confronted and overcome if we are to achieve appropriate levels of responsiveness and accountability.

Although department bylaws in some units may lead some individuals to believe otherwise, department chairs have the authority and responsibility to administer the budget, assign faculty loads, and plan and coordinate academic program offerings. It is certainly appropriate to consult with faculty in the process of building a schedule, but there is no inherent right to teach on certain days or times, nor is there a requirement to limit an individual to a certain number of classes or class preparations. The tests of reasonableness and fairness to the faculty and accountability to the institution should govern these processes.

University policy recognizes a number of activities that legitimately serve as partial equivalents of class instruction. These included laboratory development and supervision, the direction of student research and independent study, various administrative assignments, and approved curatorial activities or research. University service such as committee assignments are a normal component of university work above and beyond regular teaching loads. Faculty are expected to maintain office hours and engage in academic advising as part of their regular contribution to their faculty assignment.

On the basis of this broad array of considerations and concerns I am issuing the following guidelines to be applied in the process of developing academic class schedules and assigning faculty loads in the College. The implementation of these guidelines will (a) eliminate some of the arbitrariness that exists in teaching-load assignments across units of the College, (b) improve the instructional productivity, and (c) create opportunities to undertake new program enhancement initiatives. These are inherently worthy outcomes. Aspects of these guidelines that can be implemented for spring semester should be applied immediately. The remaining items should guide the preparation of class schedules and the assignment of teaching loads.

1. Chairs hold the authority and responsibility for managing department resources, establishing academic class schedules and making teaching assignments. Past practices or bylaw specifications must *not* be allowed to interfere with this condition.

2. Schedules must be built that are responsive to the need for instruction as expressed by (a) student demand, (b) concern over timely access to courses required in the major, and (c) general program considerations such as accreditation and course sequencing. Faculty teaching preferences must be subordinate to these broader institutional needs.

3. Fixed teaching loads (such as a 2:2 schedule) for all faculty are unacceptable. Research (the long-term record of scholarship) and service contributions vary significantly across faculty, which means effort in the area of teaching must vary for equity in workloads to be achieved.

4. Historically undersubscribed specialty courses should be offered less frequently, overly diverse graduate offerings should be trimmed, and indiscriminate load reductions for normal service should be eliminated, all for the purpose of freeing faculty effort to be applied in areas of greater need (particularly for the addition of lower division classes and general education offerings).

5. Chairs should develop schedules that allow more undergraduate students to be enrolled in introductory courses taught by our best teachers.

6. Our best teachers should be encouraged to teach larger sections and given an appropriate share of the department's support (TAs, secretarial, etc.) to manage the workload. Incentives in the form of preferred days and times, attractive class preparation conditions, and variable semester-to-semester loads should be utilized to encourage this outcome.

7. To the extent possible classroom scheduling should maximize the goodness of fit between the facility and the class. Classes should be scheduled in classrooms that: (a) are equipped with the necessary facilities (maps, audio-visual, etc.); (b) accommodate the teacher's instructional style; and (c) are not overly large or small considering the anticipated demand.

8. Chairs should consider how faculty members' teaching assignments might be adjusted to maximize the impact of faculty development activities. (For example, a faculty member who has just completed a workshop on enhancing critical thinking or developing writing skills might be offered the opportunity to teach a course especially conducive to employing what has been learned.)

9. As many of our new programs are interdisciplinary in nature, certain economies would be realized and intellectually stimulating graduate coursework would result from the creation of new graduate courses team-taught by faculty in different academic units. In this way interdisciplinary degree programs would feature something more than a selection of disciplinary courses (drawn from some set of existing academic units) and provide for fractions of instructional effort to be combined in a useful manner.

10. If a class is canceled due to low enrollment, the faculty member should be assigned to cover another class. This might be one that has either been added in response to enrollment demand or that would otherwise have been handled with salary savings. If this is not possible because of a lack of competence to teach such classes, then, as a last resort, the faculty member should be assigned to an additional class the following semester (thereby making up the deficit).

11. Ours is university with a large enrollment of nontraditional students, many of whom would prefer evening classes. Faculty

should be encouraged to teach classes in the evenings to accommodate the needs of these students. If volunteers are not available, faculty members should be assigned to teach evening classes
on a rotational basis.

12. In making assignments featuring variability in the distribution
of effort across teaching, research and service, chairs are encouraged to make decisions on the basis of a broad set of general
guidelines tailored to the department's needs, rather than adopt-
ing overly trivialized systems that constrain more than enhance
the process.

13. Assignments to probationary faculty must reflect recognition of
(a) a presumption that efforts in the area of research will lead,
or further contribute to a record of scholarly productivity, and
(b) the need to achieve a condition of equity among members
of this set.

14. All members of the faculty should teach. Instruction is at the
heart of the institution's mission and teaching must remain unequivocally a central function of the faculty. Buyout arrangements must be limited, cost effective for the unit, guided by fixed
rules applied to all unit members seeking such arrangements, and
approved by the College in advance.

15. Faculty annual performance evaluation and salary adjustment
procedures must be made more sensitive to variations among faculty in their contributions to teaching. Those individuals who
are exemplary in the quality of their contributions to the unit's
instructional activities must be recognized in a significant way.

One might expect that chairs hated receiving this memo. This was not
the case. A draft of it was shared with the chairs, and they provided input on the final version. A careful reading of the document will reveal
that it reinforces the chairs' authority, provides guidance without intro-
ducing fixed goals or unbending constraints or formulas, and urges something that is difficult to argue with—the full and effective use of the unit's
budgeted resources (the base budget on which a unit operates). The note
proved to be very helpful to chairs in addressing long-standing problems,
because it gave them the leverage to act.

It is often surprising to see how little faculty members actually know
about what being a unit head actually means. In addition to the suggestions above, many deans purchase books on chairing the academic department for each new unit head. One such book that is widely used to
provide chairs with a generic overview of the job is that by Tucker (1984).
Providing this book (or another of the dean's choice) is a nice way to help

new chairs and to remind them that their new job is quite different from that of a faculty member.

If a dean employs the many ideas conveyed in this chapter, he or she will improve the talent level of the unit heads. They will be more effective as leaders, more attentive to institutional needs, and more likely to make sound decisions. Proactive measures directed toward the professional development of one's administrative team will pay dividends in productivity and morale. A long and successful deanship depends on the talent and stewardship of all those in leadership roles. Deans leave this area unattended at their own peril.

CHAPTER 6

The Dean and the Faculty

Colleges and universities exist in the realm of ideas. It is at colleges and universities that ideas are created, tested, applied, revised, re-formulated, and passed on to the next generation. Colleges and universities are idea centered; this is what has always drawn serious students to engage in study at places of higher learning. Some institutions claim to be "student centered." This perspective recognizes the central role of undergraduate education in justifying the subvention of university costs. The public's inclination to support higher education would be drastically reduced if the education of students were not a major aspect of institutional missions.

In colleges and universities, the faculty drives the pursuit of ideas. The faculty defines the character of university academic life. It is the faculty members who create, discover, and apply disciplined reason to sort through the universe of ideas and select those that make up society's current knowledge base. This quest for knowledge creates the unique environment of university learning—a setting where the process and the products of discovery exist together in time and place. For the intellectually engaged student, time spent in shared discovery with faculty can shape directions, careers, and lives.

Deans have the incredible good fortune of being able to facilitate the work of faculty. One of the great benefits of serving as dean is that one can enjoy vicariously the work of so many wonderfully talented individuals. In a college of any size, hardly a day will pass without some notable achievement by a member of the faculty. It is important, therefore, for the dean to take time to follow the progress of the faculty and to share with enthusiasm the accomplishments that stem from its efforts. The role of the dean is to make decisions that have the effect of maximizing the good that can be accomplished by faculty, good that is consistent with the university's mission and needs.

Colleges and universities do not exist to provide faculty with a place to work. Colleges and universities exist to serve a societal purpose. They exist to provide places of unfettered inquiry. They exist as places where knowledge is passed on to the next generation. Faculty members are employed to do the fundamental work of the university. As important and central as the faculty role is to university life, one must remember that faculty positions serve an institutional purpose.

Critics of colleges and universities agitate a great deal about faculty. These detractors complain about what faculty teach, how they teach, and how few classes they teach. They find little value in the notion of unfettered inquiry, especially when it is applied to things that seem to be of no practical value, merely that of wanting to know or wishing to create. The public's distorted view of colleges and universities causes deans to spend time defending the nature of faculty life.

Unfortunately, colleges and universities are often not as conscientious as they should be about those faculty members who are least productive. Furthermore, the institution of tenure often makes it difficult to deal effectively with those faculty members who are performing unsatisfactorily. The deans must bring leadership to the college's efforts to ensure that the use of the faculty resource, the assignment of faculty responsibilities, is consistent with university needs.

The excerpt that follows represents the author's attempt to reconcile the two seemingly conflicting roles that must be played by the dean: the role of faculty champion and the role of institutional conscience regarding the use of faculty time. Each dean needs to find a way to play these roles effectively. In sharing the piece below, there is no intention to suggest that this approach should be copied or transplanted intact elsewhere. It is offered to give the reader a sense of how one might go about creating a coherent way of thinking about faculty life.

The Integration of Faculty Responsibilities and Institutional Needs

As legislatures and governing boards look for ways to provide access to higher education at a reasonable cost, attention frequently turns to the teaching loads of university faculty. The popular view is that faculty members are underutilized in teaching and preoccupied with their research. A redirection of faculty effort, away from research and toward teaching, is a common prescription for providing more classes without increasing costs.

It is widely observed that colleges and universities, especially research universities, generally resist efforts to alter the mix of faculty responsibilities, noting (without much explanation) that such a step would be detrimental to the reputation of the institution and the quality of its programs. The debate has been noteworthy in that it reveals a lack of information about faculty life on the part of those outside the university, and a failure of colleges and universities to provide a straightforward description or defense of faculty life in its current form.

How do faculty members spend their time? Is the distribution of effort appropriate in terms of kind, amount, and quality? What is the best use of faculty time from the perspective of those seeking intellectual growth and credentials, the students; or from the perspective of our sponsors, the taxpayers; or from our customers, a democratic society in need of an educated citizenry and those who employ our graduates?

The Public View of Faculty Work

In the popular view, a faculty member's time is spent in the supposed mutually exclusive areas of teaching, research, and service. It is imagined that these areas compete for time, so effort devoted to one area detracts from the others. These "distinct" activities are seen as unbalanced toward research (Figure 6.1).

In actuality, attention to what faculty members do serves to divert attention away from what is important: the learning, discovery, and practical utilization of knowledge that occurs in colleges and universities. A better way to think about colleges and universities is to focus not on what faculty members do, but on what is accomplished through their efforts. Some of the farmer's most visible work is the time spent on the tractor, but what is important is the yield of the

Figure 6.1 Left: This diagram is meant to suggest the imagined distinct nature of teaching, research, and service, and the size of the circles is meant to imply the relative effort given to each activity. Right: This pie chart visually depicts the public view of the distribution of faculty effort.

harvested crop. Time spent lecturing to students is a highly visible form of teaching, but in the instructional realm it is learning, not teaching, that is most important. Furthermore, learning guided by faculty occurs in many settings away from the classroom.

The University View of Academic Life

The important aspects of university life cannot be simply compartmentalized, except artificially. Each aspect interacts with and enriches the others, much to the benefit of students. It is the powerful lessons that come from participating in the process of discovery and the extent to which discovery is integrated with learning and service that distinguishes the research universities from other forms of education. Figure 6.2 illustrates this concept, depicting university academic life on the basis of its primary products.

This more elaborate illustration of university life (Figure 6.2) allows a number of important concepts to be more easily understood, once a brief explanation is provided. Notice that "teaching, research, and service," which are faculty activities, have been replaced by "knowledge transmission, generation, and application." These are the products of faculty, student, and staff efforts. The overlap of the ellipses (Figure 6.2) provides a means of visually depicting the richness added to the learning environment when the student (the recipient in knowledge transmission) is an active participant in the generation and application of knowledge.

In Figure 6.3, the darkly shaded area reflects learning that occurs as a result of direct instruction in formal classes and activities that support classroom learning. Such instruction is cost effective, especially with high-enrollment sections. Its primary drawback is that students tend to be passive recipients of lecture material. This is,

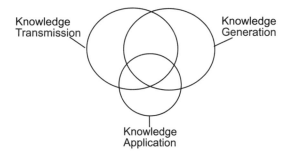

Figure 6.2   This diagram is meant to depict the "ideal" arrangement of university activities, revealing rich integration among the transmission, generation, and application of knowledge.

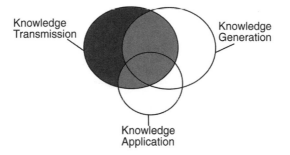

Figure 6.3   The shaded areas represent knowledge transmission. The darkly shaded area reflects learning that occurs as a result of formal teaching and advisement. The lightly shaded areas reflect learning that occurs through participation in non-classroom activities related to knowledge generation and/or knowledge applications.

however, a primary form of instruction, the main teaching activity for which the faculty is given formal teaching credit, and, in the minds of many university critics, the only faculty activity of importance. Other activities that involve the transmission of knowledge (many times without generating formal credit) are career and professional advising, office-hours meetings with students, holding informal study sessions, and responding by e-mail to student questions. To fully support knowledge transmission, time must also be devoted to class preparation, testing and grading, planning class laboratories, reading term papers, and developing new courses. The lightly shaded areas of Figure 6.3 represent less formal learning opportunities for students, all of which occur outside of structured classes.

Faculty research results in the generation of new knowledge. The shaded areas of Figure 6.4 represent the products of faculty, student, and staff efforts devoted to research and creative activities. Activities in the darkly shaded area reflect what is largely solitary time and includes library research and reading to stay current in one's field; time for critical thinking, contemplation and reflection; planning projects, preparing grant applications and manuscripts; data analysis and interpretation; and informally reviewing and critiquing the works of others. The lightly shaded areas represent activities in which knowledge generation is integrated with knowledge transmission or knowledge application; it represents hidden instruction of the most valuable kind.

The practical utilization of knowledge takes many forms. The shaded areas of Figure 6.5 reflect knowledge application that results

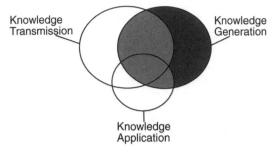

Figure 6.4 The shaded areas represent knowledge generation. The darkly shaded area reflects occasions when there is no concurrent knowledge transmission and/or application component.

from faculty, student, and staff efforts. These activities include the good that is accomplished through leadership of and participation in national organizations in one's field; reviewing and editing works (of others) being considered for publication; membership on panels, boards and commissions related to one's professional expertise; providing clinics and workshops; public talks; and writing letters of evaluation and recommendation (darkly shaded area). The good that is accomplished through activities is critical to the advancement of knowledge because it serves to organize, support, discipline, and ensure quality control over the dissemination of new ideas. The lightly shaded areas represent activities that integrate knowledge application with knowledge transmission or knowledge generation.

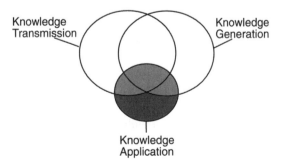

Figure 6.5 The shaded area represents knowledge application. The lightly shaded areas reflect occasions when there is concurrent knowledge transmission and/ or generation.

Contrary to the popular view, research and service activities of faculty do not detract from student learning. To the contrary, they enhance it. The shaded areas of Figure 6.6 are meant to suggest the enriched student learning experiences that result from activities that inherently integrate knowledge transmission with knowledge generation or application. The area labeled "A" reflects activities that are most well developed at research universities. It represents time of "shared discovery" by students and faculty. Students consider these activities to be among their most meaningful and exciting educational experiences. Such "informal learning" activities are common. When students talk about their undergraduate experiences, they frequently mention their involvement in intellectual activities outside the formal classroom—their participation in research projects or discipline-related volunteer work, almost always in collaboration with or under the guidance of faculty.

An example from our campus helps illustrate the point. A faculty member with interests in biology and society devotes part of her energies to examining the connection between knowledge provided by science and public policy that ought to be informed by that knowledge. Such work is considered to be research and perhaps service, but not teaching. Yet, undergraduate students involved in this project spend time in Washington interacting with policy makers, Congressional science advisors, Congressional staff, and members of the Congress. The public policy learning opportunity that this faculty member provides for her students is a far more enriching educational experience than could typically be provided in a classroom lecture.

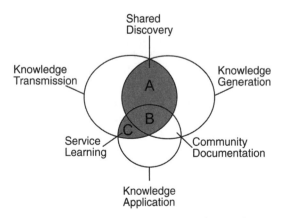

Figure 6.6 The shaded areas represent the enrichment of learning that occurs when knowledge transmission is integrated with knowledge generation and/or application.

Research-enhanced learning activities are engaging, hands-on, and problem-solving. This is where students participate in the creation of original ideas and the discovery of new insights and truths. Such activities occur in laboratories, seminars, field settings, and in various other forms of collaborative effort. An ancient proverb reminds us that "The mind is a fire to be lighted, not a vessel to be filled," and it is in times of shared discovery that life-changing intellectual transformations usually take place. These are frequently the most important moments in an undergraduate's academic life. Unfortunately, these opportunities are reduced when the quantity of teaching is emphasized at the expense of concern for the variety and quality of the learning experiences provided.

There are times when both research and service activities of faculty enrich the learning environment. Frequently, faculty members draw upon new ideas, constructs, technologies, or methodologies developed through their research as they help address problems in the community. A good example (again from our campus) is the use of instruments and remote sensing methodologies (developed under NASA grants) which are being employed to provide information which saves nearby municipalities millions of dollars in inspection costs. Students are involved in this activity and their learning is enriched because immediate, practical use is made of the knowledge they are acquiring.

Areas labeled "A" and "B" in Figure 6.6 represent learning opportunities that distinguish a research university from other forms of education. The activities that fall under these areas demonstrate the importance and significance of a culture where discovery and learning are drawn together in time and place, a culture where the process and products of inquiry reside together as natural partners. The attention given to knowledge generation results in vastly greater opportunities for shared discovery. It is a shame that these activities are largely unrecognized by the public. They represent some of the most meaningful learning experiences offered in higher education.

The shaded area labeled "C" in Figure 6.6 reflects those activities featuring the integration of knowledge transmission and application. Included here are internships, service learning, and field-work tied to classroom instruction. A current example of an undergraduate activity in this area (again from our campus) is service learning. Students taking classes in geography have the opportunity to participate in community outreach through internships that take them to inner city schools, where they help children learn about the relationships among people, places, and environments. In such settings the benefits flow both ways. Each party is simultaneously the enricher and the enriched.

Faculty responsibilities follow the general pattern described above. There is, however, significant variation among faculty members in the relative effort devoted to each area and in the specific activities that constitute their work. As university officials assign responsibilities they try to optimize the fit between faculty strengths and interests, on the one hand, and the institution's needs, on the other. Performance evaluation reflects the quality of the faculty member's work, with direct reference to the responsibilities to which he or she was assigned.

Workload practices that focus exclusively (or even excessively) on teaching formally scheduled lecture classes and ignore the full complement of faculty life lead to an impoverished learning environment. Such approaches result in an increase in the time spent on the least engaging forms of instruction and often come at the expense of those most valued, of those featuring active learning, of those the students find most meaningful.

Does every student at every research university participate in shared discovery? Probably not. Some students are interested in earning a degree, but with minimal effort. For those students who fail to draw on the full value of a campus experience rich with research opportunities, the credit hours earned may be comparable and the degree identical to that of a student who engages all the campus resources, but the educational experience is decidedly poorer. Both students may have degrees; only one has a full education.

Differentiation and Integration of Responsibilities

University officials are not interested in blindly protecting teaching loads. They are interested in assigning faculty to responsibilities that create a desirable balance between efficiency and effectiveness, between activities that support formal instruction and those that are essential to "informal learning." Absent an appropriate emphasis on the generation of knowledge, one no longer enjoys a primary benefit of attending a research university. Flexibility in assigning faculty responsibilities and the existence of a climate that encourages the integration of teaching, research, and service are fundamental to the soundness of the research university and provide the best use of faculty resources.

The integration of various activities is not unique to university faculty members; it is common in the professions. The typical surgeon spends a small portion of the day in surgery, but the time spent in such activities as patient care, continuing medical education and service to a hospital board or the AMA is important to his or her professional development and practice. Attorneys spend important time in court, but their success in litigation is strongly influenced by their other professional activities. Some of these activities are direct and formal, such as reviewing case law. Others, such as maintaining one's personal cultural literacy are more indirect, but empower the attorney to connect legal precedents and common experience, something critical with juries. Simply put, a surgeon's work extends beyond the operating room, the lawyer's beyond the courtroom, and the professor's beyond the classroom. It is the integration of a rich set of activities that leads to full effectiveness in each profession, and full benefits for the patient, client, or student.

Faculty as a Fixed Asset

It has been popular to criticize colleges and universities for their lack of agility, especially as corporate America has reduced the size of its continuing workforce, invested in the continuing education of its workforce, outsourced numerous support services, and turned to the employment of part-time workers to ensure a more adaptable enterprise. In contrast, university faculties have been seen as a large, fixed asset, resistant to change and out of step with the times.

If there is value in changing this condition—many people believe there is—the two primary options for converting the faculty to a variable asset are either (A) to create conditions where it is easy to change the faculty (eliminate tenure and hire a transient workforce) or (B) create conditions were faculty can change, but through practices that do not undermine academic freedom and tenure. Each option converts the faculty to a more variable asset, but only the latter option ensures continuity, unfettered inquiry, and the development of a sense of stewardship, all fundamental to a healthy university. Under option A (eliminating tenure and employing an itinerant teaching workforce), an institution might achieve greater economy in providing instruction, but at a cost to quality. Transient employees are highly unlikely to engage in significant knowledge generation or knowledge application. The development of significant research programs and the capacity to render knowledge-based forms of service require time and stability. The shaded areas of Figure 6.6 signify the aspects of university life related to student learning that would be lost if tenure were abolished and colleges and universities become reliant on a transient workforce. Under such conditions, knowledge generation and application would be severely diminished or lost, thereby weakening knowledge transmission by limiting its forms. Activities that provide some of the most important "learning moments" would be eliminated. Under option B (getting faculty to change), the key is to recognize that there is no single template for faculty life and there is no single mix of responsibilities that is best for either the faculty member or the university. Institutional practices must reflect these facts.

The Assignment of Faculty Responsibilities:
Faculty as a Variable Asset

The faculty asset is flexible when responsibilities can be assigned in a variety of ways. Concern should be directed at the appropriateness of the kind, amount, and quality of faculty responsibilities. "Kind" as used here means faculty contributions to knowledge transmission, generation, and application. "Amount" has to do with the sum of these contributions equating to a full academic assignment. "Quality" indicates the value of the work when referenced to discipline standards. The academic topics, content and methods used by faculty are aspects of academic freedom and not subject to administrative assignment or oversight.

The integrated model of faculty responsibilities provides an excellent way to visualize the differences that must exist among faculty if departments are to make full and effective use of their personnel resources in support of institutional needs. Recognizing that different faculty members will have talents and interests that are unique, a workload system must allow its participants to understand and agree upon the responsibility mix prior to the academic year and then refer back to it as the products of the year's work are evaluated.

Some examples (again based on real cases) of the variation in faculty responsibilities that will occur appear in Figure 6.7a. At the upper left one sees the responsibility mix for a faculty member who has a large research program in the sciences, and involves undergraduate and graduate students in virtually all of his nonteaching activities. The faculty member is an award-winning teacher, but teaches only one class a semester. There is significant overlap between energies directed toward knowledge transmission and knowledge generation, because much of this work occurs in nonclassroom settings in which students are actively involved. This faculty member is generous with time given as an ambassador for the university and for science, spending part of many days and evenings in the public schools. Students participate in these outreach activities, thereby experiencing important service learning opportunities. In a sense, this particular mix of responsibilities epitomizes the life of a faculty member at a research university, where the activities of knowledge transmission, generation, and application are highly integrated, thereby providing a uniquely enriched learning environment for students.

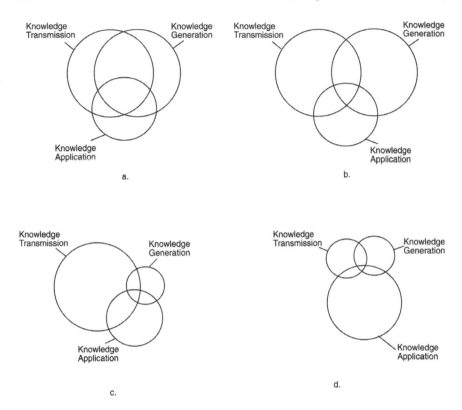

Figure 6.7   Sample profiles of faculty responsibility.

Another example (Figure 6.7b) is of a faculty member who works in the creative realm. This individual provides formal classroom instruction in two classes per term and is a distinguished poet. A significant amount of this individual's nonscheduled time is spent with students functioning together as equals, exploring ideas, contemplating possibilities, structuring arguments, or finding the most meaningful way to convey an image, grasp a concept, or create a mood with the written word. These are periods of "shared discovery," and are seldom fully captured in the university's credit hour accounting and billing mechanisms. In order to give his students experience performing before audiences and to simultaneously enrich the community, this professor regularly takes classes to nursing homes, where students give readings of their creative work and help place-bound members of the elderly population improve their skills of creative expression. This also serves as a wonderful example of service learning for students. Finally, this faculty member is called upon frequently to provide public readings, thereby bringing the products of his creative energy to other communities. Students frequently accompany this professor in these public settings, thereby further expanding their education and developing their awareness of the special public enrichment role played in society by those with talent for creative expression.

Over a career, a number of tenured faculty members will experience reduced interest and competitiveness in the generation of knowledge. In times past, these individuals were seldom asked to do additional teaching or service; rather, they were relegated to second-class status with no prospects for advancement and minimal raises to show for their efforts. These individuals often became disaffected and embittered, taking their frustrations out on students and colleagues. The remaining two examples in Figure 6.7 reflect the workload assignments and responsibilities that might occur with an individual who (for whatever reason) has become less productive in research, but who is effective in the classroom (Figure 6.7c) or is interested in devoting more time to service responsibilities (Figure 6.7d). A far more desirable way to utilize less balanced portfolios is to develop a work assignment that features a responsibility mix weighted toward the area(s) of current ability and interest, consistent with institutional needs. Figure 6.7c is the profile that might exist for a faculty member with a heavier than normal teaching load and a level of activity devoted to knowledge generation that is small and seldom leads to published products or external funding support.

In a shared governance setting, a small number of faculty members are called upon annually to provide extraordinary service contributions to the institution. Figure 6.7d represents the temporary work and responsibility profile for the President of the Academic Senate. This profile suggests the nature of this short-term assignment: reduced teaching, reduced time for the creation of new knowledge, and a significant intrusion on the time that would normally be available to spend with students. Nevertheless, such assignments are necessary in a healthy university, and the evaluation of the products of such an assignment should reflect the responsibilities to which the individual was committed.

Differential Profiles: Among Faculty and Disciplines

Just as a university functions best when each of its members has a full load but a responsibility profile tailored to his or her abilities and interests, so it is with departments, colleges, and campuses. A school of social work will have a very different profile than that of a theater department or a department of physics. The level of integration and mix of knowledge transmission, knowledge generation, and knowledge application will be influenced by differences in the academic and professional cultures of the various disciplines, and by the varying demands placed on units as a result of the institution's setting and mission.

Evaluation of the Collective Contributions of Faculty

When one asks what a department has accomplished, the response may be impressive to peers, but often reflects only moderate attention to institutional needs. This is because such a large fraction of faculty time is discretionary and devoted to activities of the faculty member's choice. While flexibility in a faculty member's life is essential to his or her academic freedom and productivity, it is important to remember that faculty positions are created to meet university needs. Members of the faculty and the university are best served when the faculty resource, which (when expressed as a proportion of the budget) is the dominant campus resource, is employed in ways that maximize attentiveness to institutional needs.

A way of calling attention to institutional needs and differentially rewarding units that are responsive is through the use of annual department evaluation. An example of such an evaluation instrument appears in Table 6.1. Departments are evaluated in three broad areas: (1) the extent to which they provide a quality learning environment, (2) the extent to which they are maintaining or enhancing their academic quality and reputation, (3) the extent to which they are responsive to institutional needs (that are not captured in items 1 or 2). The use of an annual evaluation provides a useful way of reminding departments of all the ways that faculty members can support the university, and is especially effective at informing everyone that many of the things that are important to the institution are given little attention nationally by the academic disciplines and their professional organizations.

It should be noted that the items featured in this evaluation instrument were not created by oversight boards or administrators. Rather, the items represent the things already being done in one or more units in the college. The form features a compilation of the best practices gathered from information contained in annual department reports.

The use of an annual unit evaluation helps a department chair negotiate faculty work assignments and responsibilities in such a way as to maximize what is accomplished collectively by the faculty of a unit. By assigning responsibilities prior to the start of the year, one can ensure that all the institution's needs are attended to and that each faculty member (through some mix and level of integration of knowledge transmission, generation, and application) has a full complement of activities that support the university's mission. Under such an arrangement, departments that are most valuable to the

Table 6.1
Annual Evaluation Department Contributions to Institution Building

Key Codes	Relevance	Status	Grade
	Relevance	Status	Grade
	PR, of primary	EX, exemplary	A excellent
	relevance	AVG, typical; average	B good
	SR, of secondary	MIN, absent or	C Fair
	relevance	minimal	D Unsatisfactory
	NR, not relevant		E Failing

Department: _____   Year: _____

	Relevance	Status	Grade
I. Creating a Quality Learning Environment			
A. Special Classes Being Offered			
1. writing intensive			
2. time flexible (jumbo, stretch)			
3. honors			
4. new student seminars			
5. enhancements (labs; reading; recitation; discussion sections; field trips)			
6. broadened perspective (integrative; capstone; inter-, cross-, and multi-disciplinary courses			
7. enrollment limited			
8. faculty taught			
9. undergraduate research experience			
10. innovative instruction (collaborative learning; critical inquiry; learning cycle; technological enhancement)			
B. Special Facilities/Support			
1. mediated learning labs/classrooms			
2. tutors/advisors (hours extended)			
3. modern equipment/adequate stations			
4. colloquia, symposia series			
5. audio/visual support			
6. class scheduled in appropriate facilities			

Table 6.1   (*continued*)

	Relevance	Status	Grade
C. Special Efforts at Enrichment/Recognition	▓	▓	
1. honors societies, majors clubs			▓
2. organized study groups			▓
3. student awards			▓
4. development of "involvement profiles" (job résumé)			▓
5. junior fellows program			▓
6. conference paper presentation support			▓
D. Attracting Student Talent	▓	▓	
1. scholarship support			▓
2. recruitment activities			▓
3. campus visits			▓
4. student preparation for awards competition			▓
5. co-enrollment of majors in the honors program			▓
E. Department Climate (attentiveness/sensitivity to students)	▓	▓	
1. faculty/student diversity			▓
2. protected classes mentoring/networks			▓
3. undergraduate printed guidebook			▓
4. senior reception			▓
5. program of study workshops			▓
6. student interviews (entry, junior year, exit)			▓
7. brown bag lunch discussion groups			▓
8. social events for all			▓
F. Efforts at Continuous Improvement	▓	▓	
1. TA training/evaluation/mentoring			▓
2. graduate training attentive to future requirements of the professorate			▓
3. faculty development			▓
4. unit development (retreats)			▓
II. Building/Sustaining Nationally Prominent Programs	▓	▓	
A. Encourage and Support Faculty Research/Creative Activity	▓	▓	
1. external funding			▓
2. publication			▓
3. invited presentations			▓
4. editing/reviewing			▓
5. clusters of strength			▓
6. collaborate with faculty in other disciplines			▓

Table 6.1 (*continued*)

	Relevance	Status	Grade
7. career development grants			▓
8. support of interdisciplinary activities			▓
9. collaboration with industrial partners/national labs			▓
10. access to special facilities (e.g., NASA's Space Telescope), collections, archives, etc.			▓
B. Provide Leadership for the Discipline	▓	▓	
1. hold office in the national professional organization			▓
2. service as program director, section head in federal agencies			▓
3. serve on panels, boards, accreditation bodies			▓
4. host/organize conferences and workshops			▓
5. house national/international journals			▓
C. Build Graduate Student Quality	▓	▓	
1. graduate student recruitment visits			▓
2. GRE scores of enrolled students			▓
3. Ph.D., M.F.A. placement			▓
4. graduate school admission of undergraduate majors			▓
5. appropriateness of teaching assistant workload			▓
6. competitiveness of stipends			▓
III. Serving the Broader Institution	▓	▓	
A. Full and Effective Use of Resources	▓	▓	
1. space and facilities appropriately utilized			▓
2. faculty time and effort directed and distributed appropriately			▓
3. staff utilization optimized to work to be accomplished			▓
4. resourcefulness in handling instructional replacement (due to the unavailability of faculty because of leaves, unfilled positions, understaffing, etc.)			▓
B. Responsiveness to Institutional Needs	▓	▓	
1. offer courses responsive to demand			▓
2. SCH generation (protection of the funding base)			▓
3. providing coursework to support general studies			▓
4. summer bridge offerings			▓
5. use of faculty in undergraduate, lower division courses			▓
6. supporting interdisciplinary instruction			▓
7. providing quality advising			▓
8. support universitywide student recruitment/career days			▓

Table 6.1   (*continued*)

	Relevance	Status	Grade
C. Unit Culture			
1. depth of concern for, loyalty to the university			
2. service on committees at all levels			
3. good communication between chair and faculty			
4. appropriate levels of consultation/shared governance			
5. effective internal problem solving mechanisms			
D. Active Outreach			
1. service on state boards/councils			
2. sponsorship of external events			
3. workshops for public school teachers			
4. campus events for high school students (science fair)			
5. hosting community college personnel, high school counselors			
6. participation in faculty ambassadors program			
7. operation of clinics, labs, museums, galleries			
8. programs for disadvantaged			
9. participation in state and local organizations			
10. hosting campus tours			
11. participation in alumni events			
12. school demonstrations			
13. radio, television programming			
14. telefund follow up			
15. friends groups			
16. newsletters			

institution can be rewarded, and the many kinds of faculty work that make a department valuable to an institution can be recognized.

The ideas contained herein are not just conceptual. They have been utilized in the author's institution since 1994 and have been woven into the reward structure of the College. Under this arrangement the responsibility mix for faculty features greater variety than was the case in the past, when the relative effort devoted to "teaching, research, and service" was essentially the same for all faculty. Significant merit, given on the basis of quality of contributions in the assigned areas, has reached a much larger number of faculty than was the case when more traditional practices were used. The differential allocation of merit to units based on their collective achievements has resulted in changes in unit salary bases ranging from 15% to 26% (due to differential rates and compounding) over a four-year period. Those departments receiving the highest cumulative increases have been those that responded most effectively to the institution's needs, as determined by the annual evaluation.

With many acceptable profiles of faculty life (rather than one) it is possible for a much wider distribution of merit than traditionally has been the case. By using an integrated model of faculty responsibilities, and employing an annual department evaluation, there can be many valued roles for individuals working collectively toward common goals. Such an approach reduces attention paid to hierarchies of things a faculty member might do, and magnifies attentiveness to the quality of the work provided by the faculty member in handling assigned responsibilities. As recently noted by a colleague, "it is important to recognize good whatever its form and wherever it occurs." Both the character and productivity of our colleges and universities benefit when this is the case.

The excerpt above is an attempt to help conceptualize faculty work so that critics of higher education have a better sense of what university life is like and how it is different from other forms of education. At the same time, it is important to think in constructive ways about how the faculty resource can be used most effectively. The basic principles featured here are that: (1) faculty positions exist to serve an institutional need; (2) each faculty position should have a mix of responsibilities that adds up to a full load; (3) there is no single template for faculty life— rather, there are hundreds of mixes of responsibility that are acceptable; (4) an individual faculty member should expect that his or her portfolio of responsibilities will change from time to time, reflecting his or her abilities and interests and the department's needs; (5) faculty members should expect to be evaluated on the basis of the mix of responsibilities they have been asked to carry; and (6) the performance of entire departments should be annually evaluated, with some portion of merit allocated on the basis of collective performance in support of university needs.

FACULTY ISSUES AT VARIOUS CAREER POINTS

Since the work of the faculty is such a central part of college life, the dean will spend a good deal of time on faculty issues. These issues change with individual faculty over time; since deans will be responsible for faculty at all stages of their careers, deans will be attending to issues that cover the career span of faculty on a regular basis. The subsections that follow address some of the important faculty issues that appear regularly in the office of the dean.

Normal Faculty Recruitment

When budgets are favorable, colleges engage in recruiting. It is perhaps more accurate to say that unless budget conditions are highly unfavorable, colleges annually engage in some recruiting. At most institutions, the dean sets the ground rules for faculty recruitment. The process of recruitment is superficially similar for all colleges and universities, but when examined in detail, recruitment practices are seen to vary significantly from place to place.

Typically, someone first determines that money exists in the amount necessary to pay the salary and benefits for a position and to pay for the equipment, renovation (if needed), and other forms of support necessary to get the position started (the "startup"). A university officer, through some process, then authorizes recruitment. Such an authorization typically identifies the specialty sought, the academic rank, the appointment home, and a salary range. It is important to take care in determining the nature of a position to be filled, because at most institutions (perhaps all), one can fill only what is advertised. University hiring policies normally prohibit advertising a position at one level (say, assistant professor) and then filling it at a higher level (such as associate professor) with someone who possesses qualifications that (a) are stronger than those of others in the pool and (b) may well warrant appointment at the higher rank. Had the position been advertised at the higher level, the pool would have been different and, in all likelihood, far stronger.

After authorization to recruit has been granted, an advertisement is normally created. The job description and the advertisement as well as the advertising plan typically must be approved by the campus office of equal opportunity. Once approved, the advertisement is placed in appropriate outlets.

When the deadline for applications has passed, a committee reviews the credentials of the candidates who have applied, comparing candidates with the criteria appearing in the position description. A short list of candidates is then established, and additional information is gathered on the candidates on it. Committees are instructed to make every effort to act affirmatively in advancing the cases of qualified protected-class members at this and every subsequent stage of the process.

A proposed interview list is then established and sent to the equal opportunity office for review and approval. Once approval to interview is secured, candidates are invited to the campus and interviewed. An offer is extended to the most qualified candidate. Candidates are typically given two weeks to respond to the offer. If there are other attractive candidates, every attempt is made to keep them interested until the position is filled.

In recent years there have been a growing number of breaches of recruitment ethics. For this reason the American Association of University Professors (AAUP) and the Council for Colleges of Arts and Sciences (CCAS) have developed a statement on recruitment ethics. Most American colleges and universities have endorsed this statement. It can be found in its entirety in appendix C.

Crafting Offers of Faculty Appointments

There are two institutional approaches to making offers of appointment to prospective faculty. One approach is to set well-defined parameters for an offer at the start of the process. Limits are established on the salary, startup costs, and relocation costs (if provided). The offer is then made to acceptable candidates in ranked order until someone accepts it. The foregoing is often the practice in places with unions or with rigid salary scales.

The second and more common approach is to have only the rough contours of an offer in mind but to craft an offer that strikes a balance between (a) what one thinks it will take to get the candidate's acceptance and (b) the kinds of salary distortions (compression/inversion, defined below) that can be tolerated by the department that will serve as the tenure home. This may sound like an odd compromise, but at most institutions the salaries of resident faculty do not keep up with what is being offered in the marketplace for top new faculty. In this latter approach, other aspects of the offer beyond salary also reflect this compromise. If an institution wishes to land its first choice, it often has to stretch and do things that are not being done for existing faculty.

One might think of institutional approaches as reflecting any of perhaps three levels of aggressiveness. The lowest level is to be firm in what the position features in terms of salary and startup. The middle level is to try to balance what the candidate is requesting and what the institution can bear, both in terms of salary and resentment. The highest level of aggressiveness in recruitment is to match or surpass every element of the best competing offers. As an institution moves through these levels of competitiveness, it increases its chances of landing the top choice. It also increases its chances of creating inequities that generate resentment, hurt morale, and may undermine the acceptance of the new faculty member. Deans typically work with chairs to decide on the final contours of an offer and then work with the chair over time to undo any inequities that have been created. (It should be noted that private institutions can keep confidential most details about faculty offers. Public institutions are subject to open-records legal provisions and often have to make salary information available to everyone.)

What does an offer to a new assistant professor typically feature? Salaries vary greatly by discipline, by the type of institution, and by the cost of living of the area in which the university is located. The attractiveness of an offer is not always easy for a candidate to sort out. As states reduce health benefits or access to managed care, for example, prospective faculty may also weigh the costs of health insurance for themselves and their families. Increasingly, new faculty are savvy about broader considerations and will compare such things as retirement contributions, health care costs, and the cost of living and housing as they examine competing offers. A dean should know how the circumstances of his or her institution compare with those of others so as to be able to respond fully and accurately to candidate inquiries.

Each year the *Chronicle of Higher Education* publishes salary data. Oklahoma State University also publishes an annual report featuring national salary data by discipline, rank, type of institution, and region of the country. For colleges of arts and sciences, the CCAS publishes the results of an annual salary survey. This latter survey is especially helpful because it contains information not only about salaries but about all components of offers that have been accepted by faculty who have moved to new positions the previous year. Some disciplines also collect salary data annually. Information about what is happening in the marketplace is extremely valuable to the dean and his or her chairs. It is therefore useful to have an annual subscription to these publications (and others like them) as appropriate for the disciplines featured in one's college.

Open-Ended Recruitment

While most recruitment is of the conventional sort, colleges and universities have tried many unconventional things to improve their success. One such approach is to do an "open rank" search. The field is specified, but people of all ranks are encouraged to apply. The position is then filled with the individual who provides the best value.

A variation on this approach is the "open field" search. Recruitment of this type has been used most frequently to attract applications from members of protected classes. Only well-staffed colleges and universities can consider this approach, but if one has the luxury of looking for faculty talent without regard to the field of expertise, very strong appointments can often be made that simultaneously strengthen the university and increase its diversity.

Senior Hires and Targeted Searches

The vast majority of academic hires—at least those without some administrative component—are at the junior level (in a typical year over 80 percent). There is always some interest in searches at the more senior levels, especially when institutions are attempting to build clusters of strength in certain areas or when they believe a senior scholar is needed to provide intellectual leadership for an academic area that consists mostly of junior faculty. Recruitment of senior faculty is complicated and risky. It is complicated because colleges and universities do not like to lose top faculty and take great pains to retain them. The very best faculty members are usually so well set up in their home institutions that it takes a formidable offer to pry them away. Such offers typically involve endowed appointments and other "perks."

Senior searches are risky because no potential candidate wants to become the person not chosen. Theses searches are risky also because they are highly visible. If a university makes an offer to a senior faculty member and he or she declines (perhaps due to a counteroffer), there can be embarrassment for the institution that extended the offer. There are many other aspects of concern with senior hires. Sometimes these scholars will accept offers but merely take leaves of absence from their home institutions rather than resign outright. (Often the hiring institution has no knowledge of this arrangement.) This is considered to be unethical by many institutions, but at least as many will extend this privilege to senior faculty members whom they hope not to lose.

When a faculty member accepts an offer, the hiring institution goes to some lengths to relocate and set up him or her in the new setting. If the faculty member returns to his or her previous institution after only a year, the recruiting institution has been very shabbily treated. To avoid such circumstances, some colleges and universities insist on seeing a copy of the letter of resignation, as a condition of the offer. Other risks include the unwitting hiring of a senior faculty member who turns out to be a fading star looking for a comfortable place to "wind down." A final risk is that of the individual accepting your offer not because he or she is especially drawn to your institution but because he or she wants to get out of the current setting, either for personal or professional reasons.

It has become more common in recent years to conduct searches for senior scholars using "target of opportunity" strategies. Under this scenario, a position does not exist unless and until the specific individual sought is interested in relocating to your institution. This process reduces or eliminates many of the risks inherent in senior recruitment. At most institutions, the office that oversees equal opportunity and affirmative action must grant a waiver to make an appointment without conducting an advertised search. Such waivers will usually be granted if the institutional benefit is significant and if the individual being recruited is truly distinguished.

Searches of this sort might better be described as courtships. In the typical case the individual being sought is invited to campus to give a talk. The individual receives an honorarium and is hosted to several days of low-key intellectual and social events, introduced to key members of the administration, and exposed to all of the faculty and facilities in which he or she might have an interest. At some point the individual is asked whether or not he or she might have any interest in relocating and becoming part of one's faculty. If there is interest, more visits follow, maybe involving a spouse or partner and more detailed discussions. If the courtship is successful, an appointment is eventually made.

A variation on the target-of-opportunity approach is to hire an entire group of individuals in a targeted area. Such searches might feature four or five individuals from different institutions, attracted by the opportunity to be together in a strong research group. Alternatively, the individuals might already be part of a group but have become disenchanted with their current location. These are complicated searches, because success depends on all members of the group being of like mind in their willingness to relocate, but if successful, such an approach can be transformative. During the author's tenure as dean, a few such overtures were made; several were successful, and one was not. In one of the successful cases, all members of a prestigious institute, complete with its intellectual property, assets, and board of directors, were recruited. In another successful case, key people from a variety of places were recruited to become part of a large team of scientists that, working together, subsequently won for the university a privileged position to secure funding from one of the major funding agencies. In the unsuccessful case, an attempt was made to move an entire institute in the sciences. In the end the home institution made a generous counteroffer to keep the institute.

Another aspect of senior recruitment, one that differs from traditional practice, has to do with broad institutional initiatives, which are becoming more common. In times past, recruitment decisions were typically weighted heavily toward department interests, which frequently were largely unresponsive to broader institutional goals. In the past few years many states have begun to see their colleges and universities as potential economic engines in the "new," or "knowledge based," economy. In many states, significant monies have been appropriated for the purpose of strengthening university research in areas possessing special promise for discoveries that, once commercialized, will lead to the creation of new wealth-producing companies in the state. The recruitment that comes from such initiatives is usually interdisciplinary and driven by specific lines of research that seem most promising, given the institution's existing strengths and the existing strengths of industries located nearby that might offer opportunities for collaboration. Such recruitment can be distorting, resulting in units with more faculty than they can reasonably use in some areas, while other areas are left with too few to cover the workload.

Dual-Career Academic Couples

It is becoming common in conducting faculty searches to discover at some point that the individual in whom you have interest has a spouse or partner who is also an academic in need of an appointment. Typically, finding a suitable position for the trailing member of the academic couple becomes a deal-breaking condition. In such cases some institutions just move on to the next candidate. Other institutions go to various lengths to see if an appointment can be arranged for the spouse/partner of the preferred candidate of the primary search.

For colleges and universities that will consider the appointment of the trailing member of an academic couple, the range of accommodation is enormous. At one extreme, some very large universities with many positions to fill actually place an advertisement in the *Chronicle of Higher Education* listing all the vacancies they plan to fill that year. This is called a "cluster ad." An explicit invitation to apply is then extended to dual-career academic couples who have specializations matching any two of the vacancies. Universities taking this approach see the opportunity for both members of such couples to be simultaneously considered in different searches as a way to attract two strong candidates who otherwise might not be recruited.

At the other extreme are colleges and universities that will at least make an effort at accommodation. The university will accept the resume of the trailing member of the academic pair and provide it to appropriate academic units within the university, in nearby community colleges, and in other colleges and universities in the area. This has the best chance of producing results if the hiring institution is in a large urban area with many other educational venues. In truth, however, this strategy seldom results in a satisfactory arrangement.

One of the most frustrating conditions for those conducting searches is when no mention about a trailing partner is made until the very end of a search, when an offer is extended. Some candidates will reveal up front in their letter of application that there is a trailing partner. Candidates are not certain what to do, because they fear that revealing this condition will keep them from being interviewed. They hope the interview will create such a favorable impression that the hiring institution will be receptive to the news. Some colleges and universities make a practice of asking candidates this question during the interview: "Is there anything else about your personal or professional circumstances that you would like us to know as we go forward with the search?" It would be inappropriate to ask directly about this personal matter, but the open-ended question gives the candidate a chance to make this requirement known. For colleges and universities inclined toward making some accommodation, if possible, disclosure at this point in the process usually works well. It is especially helpful if the candidate can be given a copy of the institution's written policy. The candidate is relieved to have the issue on the table and almost always quickly produces a resume for the trailing partner.

It should be noted that the view expressed above is not universally held. Some individuals believe strongly that until an offer is made, the candidate should not reveal that the deal will not be consummated if a position for a trailing partner cannot be found. Those who hold this view will argue that such a revelation made earlier often causes a college or university to drop a candidate from consideration.

If a university is going to make any attempt at accommodation, it is important to have a set of guidelines to standardize the process. This is important because any perceived inequities in making such accommodation will quickly be raised by those who believe they have been slighted. For this reason it is considered good practice to develop a written policy and then share it with departments and with candidates during the search process. A copy of such a policy is in appendix D.

The Special Circumstances of New Faculty

The recruitment of new faculty members represents a considerable investment of time and expense. It is therefore in the institution's interest to make the transition from graduate school, or from a "post doc" appointment, to a tenure-track faculty appointment as smooth as possible. Some colleges and universities have elaborate orientation and welcoming programs; others have nothing. A growing number of colleges and universities take new faculty on a road trip to learn about the state. Since recruitment of faculty is an investment for the long term, special efforts should be made to welcome newcomers, create positive first impressions, and help them adapt to the new setting. If a university does nothing in the way of orientation, the dean might do something for faculty new to the college.

Deans should check annually with new faculty to find out both what facilitated their moves and what complicated them. Then steps should be taken to repeat what was helpful and extend similar support to others. Likewise, attention should be given to how problems encountered by new faculty can be eliminated.

Positive and negative factors will be different for every institution, and perhaps for every unit within an institution. The list below provides a taste of what one might expect to hear from new faculty. The items in the list are from a single campus with forty-four new faculty reporting.

Things they especially liked or found useful:

1. Welcoming social events
2. Faculty orientation
3. Opportunities to meet new faculty from other units

Things they disliked or that caused them difficulty:

1. An overly long and complicated presentation on benefits
2. Too much printed material—information overload
3. Delay in activating health coverage
4. Lack of parking options when trying to move into campus office
5. Lack of permanent parking options
6. Delays in getting computer and e-mail set up
7. Lack of information about housing options
8. Lag time in getting reimbursements
9. Office or laboratory not ready for occupancy

Things they would have found to be helpful:

1. A specific contact person to answer questions
2. A list of things "to do" right away
3. A new faculty website with information on relocation, orientation, important dates, intramural grant programs, contact information for other faculty, etc.
4. Information about how the university handles student problems such as:

    Aggressiveness (students as "customers" to satisfy)

    Pressure to "dumb down" classes

    Large range of student abilities

    Passive, poorly motivated students

    Large classes (most had no experience)
5. Information about academic issues such as:

    Policy on "withdrawals" from classes

    Grading expectations

    Handling religious observances

    Class attendance

    Academic dishonesty

    Process for introducing new courses
6. Information about organizations and programs

    College faculty organizations and committees

    How the honors program fits with other units

    Opportunities to participate in interdisciplinary programs
7. Information on academic support services available to faculty

    Media services

    Technical support for mediated instruction

    Computer setup support

    Access to online journals and library holdings

    Electronic interlibrary loan
8. Information about tenure standards

Unique observations expressed by minorities and women:

1. Male students were viewed as more aggressive by women faculty members.

2. Both women and minorities would have liked more interaction with other women and minorities, even if they were in other units.

3. Both women and minorities felt a special mentoring burden for students who were also protected class members.

4. Women and minorities were often asked to engage in more service than were their majority male counterparts.

As one can see from reviewing this list, there are many things that members of a university's continuing workforce take for granted that may cause problems for junior faculty. It is important for the dean to find out what the world in his or her college looks like to new faculty. Once the specifics are known, an action plan can be put into place to help future hires find a smoother road.

Annual Performance Reviews

All colleges and universities engage in reviews of faculty performance, and most perform annual reviews. These reviews serve the twofold purpose of (a) providing feedback to the faculty members about their performance, and (b) serving as the basis for salary adjustments. These reviews typically start with the submission by faculty of materials to update their academic record. This information helps reviewers understand the nature of the faculty member's workload and the quality and volume of the academic work completed during the review period (usually the previous twelve to thirty-six months). Faculty personnel or compensation committees typically start the review and pass their recommendations to the chair of the department, who either makes the final decision or makes recommendations to the dean.

Deans of large colleges will find themselves reviewing cases far outside their range of academic expertise. Several good reference works that will help deans better understand academic performance in fields other than their own are those by Diamond and Adam (1995) and by Middaugh (2000). The former work focuses on the individual work of faculty, while the latter considers both individual and collective (unit) performance.

Most institutions have some mechanism by which a review can be appealed. Typically, such a review is limited to a "formal inadequacy" or a "procedural irregularity." A formal inadequacy occurs when individuals conducting the review failed to follow established policies in reaching their decisions and recommendations. In a procedural irregularity, established policies were followed in terms of the process but equivalent accomplishments were judged not in fact to be equivalent. Again, it is important to have written guidelines on what can be appealed and to whom such appeals are directed. An example of such a policy appears in appendix E.

Salary Concerns of Faculty

Unless a university has a rigid salary schedule tied exclusively to rank and years in rank, it is almost inevitable that faculty members will approach the dean with perceived inequities. In responding to such inquiries, the dean should keep several things in mind:

First, academic life is dynamic, and changes in the value of each individual are continuous, while salaries are adjusted at discrete intervals. This means that it is nearly impossible to get salaries in a perfect order and keep them there. The correct order will be changing as milestones are reached and significant changes occur in the cumulative records of those who make up the faculty.

Second, while a college almost always can afford to adjust the salary of a single faculty member, to be fair any adjustments should address all similar cases of inequity, not just the individual bold enough to plead his or her case.

Third, in systems that feature adjustments to salaries—that is, where the attention is on the size of the adjustment rather on the resultant salary—significant irrationality can develop between what individuals are worth and what they are paid.

Finally, new hires and counteroffers to keep faculty on board can be very distorting, creating salary compression and inversion, and market inequities for continuing faculty. "Compression" occurs when the spread of salaries is inconsistent with the spread of value of the faculty members. "Inversion" occurs when certain faculty members earn more than colleagues who have been equally productive over a longer period of time and are, therefore, further along professionally. Market inequities occur when an individual is paid less than what is normal for similarly situated individuals at peer institutions.

Given these conditions, it is foolhardy to imagine that there is only one salary problem and that fixing it will not open the door to dozens (perhaps hundreds, in a large college) of similar claims. For this reason, the dean must deal with all members of a class of individuals or deal with no one. If one has the money to address all cases, a comprehensive study can be undertaken to look at issues of compression, inversion, and market equity. Most colleges and universities never have enough money to completely correct all such problems; therefore, they might decide to solve

40 percent of the problem for each case, hoping to make further corrections on another occasion.

Another strategy, one that is sometimes taken in institutions with sufficient flexibility, is to determine the "marketability" and "market worth" of each faculty member. Marketability has to do with the likely mobility of the individual—that is, his or her attractiveness to other institutions. A highly marketable individual is one who may have standing offers to go elsewhere or is constantly being encouraged by other colleges and universities to join their ranks. Market worth is the salary that similarly situated individuals command at peer institutions. "Similarly situated" means that the individuals being compared have similar career profiles (year the doctorate was completed, rank, years in rank, and quality of cumulative record). In this case an institution that cannot address all salary problems might elect to correct 80 percent of the problem for the most marketable faculty (which it is most likely to lose and whose loss would be most devastating). It might correct 60 percent of the problem for the next tier of marketability, 40 percent for the next tier, and 20 percent for the lowest tier of marketability. The lowest tier would likely represent those individuals who could not get other university positions, at least at current rank, at an equivalent institution. In most colleges and universities, acceptable performance is required for any salary adjustment.

These adjustment strategies are possible only at institutions that are flexible. Where union contracts or highly structured scales are in place, there is little opportunity to look rationally at salaries, and so deans are left without the use of one of the most valuable tools one might have for encouraging and rewarding academic productivity. Deans in such settings can console themselves that they do not have to deal with the difficult issues that surround making salaries rational.

Probationary Reviews of Untenured Faculty

Consistent with AAUP guidelines, the typical probationary period for new faculty at most colleges and universities is six years. This means that a tenure decision is rendered near the end of the sixth year of appointment; the faculty member serves the seventh year either with tenure or as a terminal year (i.e., if tenure is denied). At most institutions, there are from one to three reviews during the probationary period. Their purpose is to provide a candid assessment of the candidate's progress (or lack thereof) toward tenure. While chairs like to be encouraging in such reviews, it is critical that they note any warning signs. Failure to provide accurate feedback is unfair to the candidate and leaves the university vulnerable to litigation if at the end of the review period tenure is denied. Inevitably in such cases, the litigant will cite favorable reviews as an indication that everything seemed to be "on track."

At some institutions, candidates who are struggling are placed on conditional contracts. When this occurs, specific shortcomings and explicit conditions for recovery are noted. If in a subsequent review the conditions have not been met, the candidate is terminated early. If the conditions have been met, then the individual is considered to be making satisfactory progress, although this is no guarantee that the final decision in the sixth year will be favorable.

Promotion and Tenure

The academic career ladder is very compressed. It features only two basic states, untenured and tenured. It features only three ranks: assistant, associate, and full professor (or just "professor"). The typical faculty member faces a tenure decision (or promotion to associate professor and tenure decisions together, if the two are coupled in an "up or out" arrangement) in his or her sixth year. Five to eight years later, productive individuals normally move to the rank of professor, where they remain for the remainder of their careers.

Tenure decisions are extremely important, because they represent a lifetime investment in an individual; they must, however, be made after watching only five years of performance (the review begins at the start of the sixth year). The standard for tenure and promotion to associate professor is demonstrated achievement and promise for continuing success in a career featuring excellence in teaching, research, and service, or in productive scholarship as defined by the institution in which the tenured appointment is to be granted. Typically, the standard for full professor is demonstrated success in teaching and mentoring, a national scholarly reputation, and significant national leadership in one's discipline.

Deans of large and comprehensive colleges face a special challenge when they move outside their own disciplines and make decisions about the futures of individuals from other fields. There are three things new deans can do to improve their ability to review and comment on records outside of their area of expertise. One is to talk to deans who have come out of the fields of candidates under review. Another is to review samples of recent successful cases from given disciplines. The third is to secure external commentary from experts in the field. External letters are often a formal part of the review. When this is the case the dean should rely on the letters supplied.

The specific requirements for meeting these standards vary greatly from discipline to discipline. This makes the evaluation of cases difficult for faculty committees and for academic administrators. For this reason it can be very helpful to require each unit to prepare generic profiles of what a typical successful case will look like for each discipline or specialty. These profiles should be created at a time when there are no active cases under consideration, or the profile might be written with a specific case in mind. Faculty committees creating such statements will take care not to make the requirements unduly difficult, because that might lead to a negative decision on someone who has the department's support. Likewise, the committees will take care not to set the standard too low, because they will not want it to produce a favorable decision on someone they do not support. These profiles, once created, should be shared with faculty (especially new faculty), so that they understand the benchmarks in greater detail, along with information that is appropriate for their disciplines or specialties. The profiles are especially helpful to faculty committees and the dean, because they can contrast actual cases with the generic profile, thereby developing with a better sense of how a given case under consideration compares with a known standard. In colleges and universities that use this practice, it is common for the unit head to use part of his or her letter of recommendation to compare the record with the generic profile. This analysis is also very helpful to understanding the case in the context of the discipline.

When generic profiles are used, one should be developed for each specialty where the nature of the expected record will be different. For example, a department of English might have one profile for its literature faculty, another for its composition faculty, another for its faculty in English education, and yet another for its creative writers. Another department might well be able to operate with a single profile, since its expectations are virtually identical for all of its specializations.

A final concern is the need to protect faculty who are devoting significant time to centers, institutes, and interdisciplinary programs. Such individuals, because they often direct their efforts outside the mainstream of the discipline, are systematically undervalued by those whose work is more clearly centered in the discipline. For this reason, it is useful to have such work independently evaluated by an appropriate faculty group representative of the nondepartmental entity and to include that evaluation in the promotion or tenure file, for the purpose of informing those in the formal review stream, starting with the department. Such an evaluation is often called a "supplemental review." An example of supplemental review guidelines is included in appendix F.

The standard for tenure at most larger institutions continues to be dominated by the research record. Many colleges and universities have noticed that they have in their ranks individuals who have only modest research credentials but are doing what they are asked to do in an exemplary way and are very valuable to the institution. Such individuals often languish unappreciated at the rank of tenured associate professor. Included in this category of faculty members are individuals with special assignments, such as directing the freshman composition or mathematics programs. Other such individuals might be housed in an academic discipline (say, physics) but are committed to science education. These faculty members are doing work that is important to the university but that often does not seem to colleagues in their disciplines to be worthy of promotion.

Some colleges and universities have taken steps to promote such individuals to the rank of professor. When the promotion occurs, one view is that "the university is lowering the bar"; the contrasting view is that the university is not diminished by such action but rather is enhanced, because a good citizen who has excelled in ways that are important to the university's mission has been rewarded. This is not lowering the bar; it is merely creating another appropriate way for a person to get over the bar for promotion. As dean I never regretted supporting such a promotion. Interestingly, in his reminiscences about his time as chancellor of the University of California at Berkeley, Kerr (2001) observes that he probably erred in giving too little credit for activities that contributed to institutional good.

Post-Tenure Review

In the past decade the practice of establishing some form of post-tenure review has gained popularity. At most institutions oversight boards concerned about the expense of higher education and the appropriateness of faculty assignments have driven this review. The primary issue is often faculty teaching loads; the common complaint is that "faculty members are only spending six or fewer hours a week in the classroom." The review is also driven by anecdotal information about abuses of faculty time. (Faculty seen mowing their lawns during the Monday through Friday, 8:00 A.M.–5:00 P.M., workweek is a popularly repeated complaint.)

Where such systems have been successfully put in place, faculty members have worked in collaboration with administrators and members of the oversight board to create a system with which all parties can live. The

best such systems are performance based and typically feature elements
similar to those that appear below.

1. A definition of the lower threshold of satisfactory performance; such
   statements typically contain phrases such as:

   "The faculty member's workload reflects a reasonable set of institutionally important activities for someone who is fully employed."

   "The activities are performed at an acceptable level of quality."

   "Teaching and service activities are acceptable in amount and quality."

   "The individual is institutionally useful."

   "The individual conducts him- or herself in a professional manner."

2. A statement that gives definition to *un*satisfactory performance; such
   statements are prepared for each discipline. They contain phrases such
   as:

   "Fails repeatedly to . . ."

   "Shows no evidence of . . ."

   "Does not participate effectively in . . ."

   "Fails on a consistent basis to . . ."

3. Guidelines for various forms of intervention:

   Remediation (voluntary)

   Rehabilitation

   Revitalization and renewal

   Reassignment of responsibilities (for a better fit with abilities)

   Remediation (involuntary)

   Performance contracts

   Employee assistance (counseling)

   Dismissal for cause

Each university has its own process for carrying out post-tenure review.
Those institutions that have embarked on this process have discovered
that it is not as time-consuming as they had imagined, because it takes
very little trouble to identify the borderline cases. Once the cases to be
scrutinized have been identified, time is spent giving special study to the
problematic cases, while the rest of the faculty, having been judged as
comfortably satisfactory or better, is not bothered with further review. The
other surprise has been that colleges and universities are good at evaluating positive aspects of performance but relatively unskilled in objectively
assessing unsatisfactory performance (the absence of good things or the
presence of undesirable things).

Where employed, post-tenure review has been an effective tool for addressing long-standing problems, such as the faculty member with 40 percent time for research who annually produces nothing of consequence in the research and creative realm. In the past such individuals probably did not receive merit-based salary adjustments, but there was little other consequence. With post-tenure review, such a case would be judged as unsatisfactory and would be addressed. The goal is always to take steps that make the individual more effective and more valuable to the institution; everyone benefits from this outcome. If, despite all efforts, there is no improvement, an institution has no choice but to proceed with dismissal for cause. Dismissal has eventuated in very few cases nationally, and in those cases it was almost certainly justified.

Faculty Development

With or without post-tenure review, a dean should always be concerned about faculty development. Some colleges and universities have sabbatical leaves that serve this purpose, but many do not. At many institutions sabbatical leaves are almost never approved for anything other than pursuing research. This is unfortunate, because there are many wonderful uses for sabbatical leaves that can strengthen other dimensions of academic life. Occasionally a bias against people focused more on instruction than research occurs because of quirks in the system. At some colleges and universities a faculty member can take a sabbatical leave only if other faculty members are available to cover his or her classes. It is more difficult to cover the teaching responsibilities of someone who teaches a larger than usual number of general, high-enrollment classes. This condition might work against the approval of those with larger teaching portfolios. The dean should always be on the lookout for, and work to correct, such inequities.

When an institution has sabbatical leaves, that privilege is best protected by establishing clear policies on their use. Poor policies lead to uneven decisions, which lead to disgruntlement. It only takes a few complaints to move legislators to eliminate these important programs.

When a faculty member's performance is below par, there is always a reason (or reasons) to which one can point. Knowing the probable cause often helps to find ways to remedy the problem. Sometimes alcohol or drugs are implicated. Life events can often introduce emotional stress. Discoveries by others may render insignificant a line of research that one has pursued throughout one's career. Whatever the cause, the correct step is faculty development. In cases where performance is undermined by mental or emotional health problems or substance abuse, the dean should enlist the services of other campus officers and work together with them and the employee to develop a plan for recovery. Employee assistance programs (see below) can be especially useful in this regard.

Not all faculty development, however, is directed to problem cases. A good faculty development program provides opportunities for all interested faculty to improve themselves. Some such programs are best handled at the university level. Others can be provided by a college and should be, especially if they are unavailable from any other campus source. In large state systems (the University of California or the University of North Carolina), the system office often sponsors seminars or initiatives featuring specific faculty development opportunities.

The sections below provide a glimpse of faculty development activities that might be contemplated by a college, although in almost every case it is perfectly fine, perhaps even preferable, if the activity is university-wide in nature.

Employee Assistance Programs

Employee assistance programs are

> worksite-based activities designed to assist: (1) work organizations in addressing productivity issues, and (2) employee clients in identifying and resolving personal concerns, including, but not limited to, health (this may also involve physicians at a student health center), marital, family, financial, alcohol, drug, legal, emotional, stress, or other personal issues that may affect job performance.[1]

Such programs are typically directed and staffed by individuals with training in clinical psychology or family therapy. Readers interested in learning more about employee assistance programs are directed to Herlihy, Attridge, and Turner (2002), and Fogg (2003).

Involving a neutral third party, such as a professional from a campus employee assistance program with expertise in handling such cases, can be enormously helpful. For example, in many cases of substance abuse, a department's caring actions actually enable the habit. A professional will see a condition for what it is and will be able to offer advice on the best way of attacking the problem. Most deans have no training for such matters, but they do have the authority to create strong incentives for the affected faculty member to get help. Advice from the office of general counsel should also be sought, especially if leave without pay or other punitive steps are being considered. This will ensure that the path toward resolution is not only behaviorally appropriate but legal and within the scope of what institutional policy allows.

Targeted Professional Development

It is often the case that a faculty member is quite good in most dimensions of faculty life but struggles in one area. Here are some examples:

1. An individual who lacks training in the use of technology for on-campus or distance education.
2. An individual who is assigned to teach a writing intensive class in the major with no training or experience on exactly what is required.
3. An individual with no training or experience in using inquiry-based learning is located in a department that has decided to use this method of instruction.
4. A faculty member who has difficulty projecting his or her voice is assigned to a large classroom not equipped for amplification.
5. A faculty member with a heavy accent has difficulty with verbal communication.
6. An individual with little or no experience working with specific student populations, ethnic groups, women, adult learners, or graduate students is assigned to work with these groups.

In each case, specific steps can be taken to help the individual involved gain the competence needed to address the problem. This usually requires the commitment of time by the faculty member and the commitment of some resources by the college. It is money well spent, because faculty members usually welcome the opportunity to improve themselves and are pleased that the university is willing to invest in their further development.

Interdisciplinary Fellows

It is not uncommon to hear a university described as a place with many silos. Department isolation is common in many colleges and universities. This condition runs contrary to the powerful forces—especially in the sciences—for broad integrative work that requires participation from people in a number of disciplines. How does one combat departmental balkanization? One idea that is used at a number of colleges and universities (and across universities in larger systems) is to institute an interdisciplinary fellows program. Such a program provides faculty members the opportunity to spend a semester in another department, while providing monies to the home department to cover the lost instruction. These might be thought of as internal sabbaticals, although technically the "fellow" is not on leave. Rather, he or she is on reassignment, with specific objectives in mind. Programs such as this lead to significant new interdisciplinary connections that produce important benefits in the areas of instruction and research. An example of guidelines used for one such program appears below.

Interdisciplinary Fellows Program

The Interdisciplinary Fellows Program offers College faculty an opportunity to develop inter- and cross-disciplinary scholarship and instructional activities. The College will provide a maximum of $10,000 to the home unit of each Fellow to cover class sections. If the unit plans to replace the Fellow with a professorial-level visitor, the Chair (or Director) may request permission from the Dean to reallocate unit-internal funds to supplement the award. Such requests will be considered on a case-by-case basis.

Interdisciplinary Fellows will be selected through a competitive process. Competition is limited to tenured faculty of the College, and the fellowship period may be spent in any cooperating unit on the Main Campus. Fellows are required to report on their activity at the close of the fellowship period; they will be asked to participate in follow-up evaluation of the Interdisciplinary Fellows Program.

Guidelines:

1. The purpose of the Interdisciplinary Fellows Program is to provide an opportunity for College faculty to have time reassigned outside their home unit to explore connections between their research and teaching areas and other disciplines. (It is expected that during the period of reassignment, faculty will continue to work with their graduate students in the home unit.) In consultation with one or more sponsors and the department chair or program director in the potential host unit, an applicant to the Interdisciplinary Fellows Program proposes a systematic program of activities that will be undertaken during the reassignment period. These activities may include conducting research within the host unit, auditing courses or undertaking independent study with members of the host unit, or developing collaborative teaching opportunities. In the selection process, greatest priority will be given to projects focusing on both teaching (graduate or undergraduate) and research. The applicant must have the support of

the chair (director) of both the home unit and the host unit, and is strongly encouraged to be physically located in the host unit (or, if this is impossible due to severe space limitations in the host unit, to spend a significant proportion of each work week in the host unit).

2. There must be a well-supported relationship between the applicant's research and teaching specialization(s) and the proposed focus for the reassignment project. Applications will be judged according to the potential for innovative inter- or cross-disciplinary outcome(s). (Participation in the Interdisciplinary Fellows Program does not affect accumulation of time toward sabbatical eligibility.)

3. Applications will be due in the College by (date), for fellowships to be awarded the following semester. Announcement of the Interdisciplinary Fellows will be made by (date). This will allow time for necessary planning and adjustments to the course schedule.

4. Applications for the program will be reviewed by the Interdisciplinary Programs Committee. The committee will make recommendations to the Dean, who will grant up to 3 FTE spring semester awards.

5. Three broad criteria will guide the selection process. It will be the applicant's responsibility to address these in the application materials and to make the proposal intelligible to the non-specialist reader:

   a. There should be a clear rationale for the proposed period of exchange in the host unit, and a clear indication of the anticipated outcome(s).

   b. There should be a clear indication of the innovation and originality of the proposal.

   c. There should be a clear indication of the benefits of the proposal to teaching and learning (undergraduate or graduate).

6. All other things being equal, and depending on the number of projects proposed, priority will be given to proposals involving beginning collaborations (rather than to the support of projects already under way).

Application for Interdisciplinary Fellows Program

Materials and information specified below are required; further information may be provided at the discretion of the applicant. An original and five copies of the completed application, plus an original and five copies of an abbreviated (no more than five pages) up-to-date curriculum vitae, should be submitted to the Office of the Dean.

Required materials and information:

A. 1. Name of the applicant

2. Home department or program

3. Rank and years at present rank

4. Primary area(s) of specialization

5. Letter of support from Chair (or Director) of home unit

B. 1. Name of host unit

2. Faculty sponsor(s) in the host unit

3. Requested period of exchange

4. Location of office or laboratory space in host unit (if provided)

5. Letter of support from Chair (or Director) of host unit

C. Statement, of not more than three pages, describing the proposed project. Include a description of your present specialization(s) and the proposed new area that will be developed; how this project will broaden and strengthen your inter- or cross-disciplinary competence; and how the project will enrich your scholarship and instructional activities. See review criteria listed in program announcement.

Early Retirement

There will be occasions when despite the best intentions of all parties a nonperforming faculty member makes no progress or improvement. When this happens, one alternative that should be explored is early retirement. Some states have formal programs to encourage early retirement, although these tend to be available in some narrow window of opportunity rather than being generally available over time. Other states have enacted "phased" retirement programs, which allow faculty members the opportunity to reduce to 50 percent effort for a period of time (usually three years) and then retire.

Most colleges and universities have no formal program but do have the flexibility to enter into early retirement agreements. Such agreements normally feature some incentives for faculty members to retire before they might otherwise choose to step out of their tenured positions. The university provides whatever perquisites are featured in exchange for a signed letter of resignation, effective at some future agreed-upon date. The incentives can take many forms, depending on what the policies of a university will allow. Sometimes these incentives provide a supplemental contribution to a retirement account. Agreements may provide for guaranteed summer salary for the last year or two. Reduced teaching is sometimes featured in these agreements, as is the selection of courses to be taught. There are sometimes important health care implications for the individual, the institution, and the state when retirement comes before the age of sixty-two years. Health benefits factors should be clearly understood before parties enter into formal agreements.

The problem with early retirement agreements is that they cannot just be offered to problematic faculty members or to individuals who are facing possible dismissal through post-tenure review. If early retirement agreements are available, they have to be made available to all members of the faculty. For this reason, it is a good idea to have guidelines that indicate what will and will not be done in crafting such agreements. A sample of such guidelines appears below.

Retirement Guidelines

There is no requirement to enter into early retirement agreements; therefore, agreements will be made only when conditions that are acceptable to the faculty member, the department, and the university can be found. Assuming that the conditions outlined below are satisfied, the balance of benefits and costs that accrue to the institution serves as the primary criterion for determining the acceptability of an early retirement proposal.

Adjustments to the base salary are never part of an early retirement agreement.

Enhancements to income are sometimes featured in retirement agreements. These enhancements typically take the form of access to summer teaching, supplemented by summer research support. These forms of salary supplementation do not alter the base salary, but provide additional income in the final year or years of employment and, for those on the state system, provide a higher annual average income, which serves as the basis for calculating the retirement benefit.

Modest lump sum payments can be made to optional retirement plans such as TIAA/CREF or Valic, as part of retirement agreements, if the employee is a participant in an optional retirement plan.

Retirement agreements may feature assignments that exclude the teaching of formally organized classes for a semester or two, but they never provide release from all campus duties and responsibilities in a way that occurs during sabbatical leave. A sabbatical leave year (or semester) may be part of an early retirement agreement as long as it is sought and approved through the normal mechanism and the Board requirement of returning to the university for further service is met.

Agreements must result in retirement within no more than thirty-six months of the date they are approved by the university and accepted by the faculty member.

Hire-backs up to forty-nine FTE are permitted for faculty on the state retirement system.

The benefits available to tenured faculty upon retirement are described in the policy manual. Departments are free to agree to other conditions (such as the use of an office or access to secretarial/clerical help) for items over which the department has authority. With this single exception, retirement agreements do not contain a commitment of benefits beyond those provided by university policy.

Execution of a retirement agreement includes the requirement for the faculty member to sign a waiver in which he or she confirms that employment rights are being relinquished coterminous with the resignation, and that the decision to retire will not be revisited.

Retirement agreements deal with the individual with whom the agreement is struck. Such agreements do not include accommodations for others.

As one can see from these guidelines, the only way an agreement can be struck is if all parties agree on the conditions. There is no entitlement to an early retirement agreement. A faculty member who holds out for some perquisite has leverage only to the extent that the department wants her/him to retire. The risk in doing more for such an individual than one might do for someone whom the department would like to have continued is that unfairness creeps into the process. This is another example of why principles and guidelines are so important. They discipline or constrain the process in ways that ensure fairness.

DIVERSIFYING FACULTY RESPONSIBILITIES

Most faculty members are strongly drawn to their research and creative activities. The opportunity to spend a lifetime in such a pursuit is typically what initially drew them to academia. Many faculty members find teaching very rewarding. These individuals are generous in the time they give to students, both within and outside the classroom. A few faculty members, however, are drawn most strongly to service roles either in their professional organizations or in various institutional roles.

Modern colleges and universities seem always to be taking on new initiatives that require faculty time and attention. The culture of higher education, however, makes it difficult to marshal the efforts of the faculty toward new endeavors. It often falls to the dean to take steps to draw faculty toward new responsibilities that need to be covered. Examples of such activities are provided in the following:

Undergraduate Student Recruitment

At most institutions the faculty view of undergraduate recruitment is that it is handled by those reporting to the Vice President for Student Affairs. Faculty members teach whoever comes and often see their role (especially in lower division classes) as one of winnowing out those who do not belong. The general faculty view toward undergraduates is that there are too many of them and that a significant number lack motivation and/or possess academic deficiencies.

University rankings almost always include one or more measures of student quality. The variables chosen most typically feature such input measures as high school rank, high school grade-point averages, and standardized test scores; occasionally they include output measures, such as retention and graduation rates, honors won, or graduate or professional school placements secured. The competition for straight-out-of-high school, high-achieving, parent-financed, full-time, residential students is increasing, and colleges and universities are becoming more aggressive in recruitment. Such recruitment often involves members of the faculty who enjoy interacting with high school students and their parents.

When colleges and universities seem overrun with students and feel understaffed, it can be difficult to get faculty involved in the recruitment of undergraduates. The most successful approaches to this activity occur in settings where departments are evaluated, in part, on the quality of the students they are able to attract and where the university works to reshape the student body so that it features an increasing proportion of high-achieving students and a smaller proportion of marginal students.

Extending the Reach of Campus Academic Offerings

Colleges and universities typically direct their attention primarily to the campus mission, although narrow aspects of programming are often provided at off-campus sites; this is especially true in the case of land-grant institutions, through extension services or in classes taught through extended education programs. Many people believe that the on-campus living-learning arrangement is the best way to experience a university education; however, there is growing pressure to take education to place-bound students who cannot travel to a campus location. A survey of public opinions on higher education indicated that almost 60 percent of

Americans expect that in the near future, "students who want a college education will take most of their courses over the internet."[2] The possibilities offered by technology have increased efforts to extend degree programs to the growing population of adult learners for whom such alternatives represent the only hope of securing a diploma.

Again, it is often the dean who is called upon to find ways to encourage faculty to participate in activities that extend the campus. Sometimes such course offerings are considered part of the faculty member's regular load; at other times it is considered to be off-load and is compensated through a supplemental pay mechanism. Occasionally, especially when such programming is handled through a central office and the courses are taught on load, other forms of compensation are provided to the individual or his department. Compensation might include research and travel funds, equipment purchases, or additional operating funds.

At many institutions, lack of faculty interest in the extended mission leads to losses in academic quality and control. When faculty members have no wish to devote time to the development of programs tailored for and taught to specific cohorts, quality control can be lost as others step in to construct programs. When faculty members will not teach in such settings, instruction is left to less qualified adjunct faculty. Again, the quality and reputation of the institution is jeopardized. Deans should find ways to reward units that keep their faculty involved in activities to extend the campus. Many people see this as the future of higher education.

Research Experiences for Undergraduates

At all but the most elite institutions, the student academic mix covers a great range. Some students want to find the path of least resistance through and out of the university. At the other extreme, campuses attract students who fully engage the academic culture. Such individuals become deeply immersed in the full range of campus activities. Of course, one finds every sort of student between these extremes.

The challenge for campuses with heterogeneous student bodies is to keep the weaker students from "dumbing down" the courses and to provide significant out-of-class opportunities for student-faculty interaction. One currently popular way of responding to the latter challenge is to encourage faculty to bring bright and motivated undergraduate students into their world of discovery and creativity. Other popular activities include service-learning programs.

Writing, Speaking, Ethics, and Critical Thought across the Curriculum

It is comfortable to imagine that every student leaving every university with a degree possesses a well-developed set of habits and skills and an intellectual orientation that will allow him or her to live life more nobly. Unfortunately, this is not always the case.

Colleges and universities have taken many approaches to addressing this problem. One popular approach is to include in the requirement structure classes that feature academic content but are taught in such a way as to simultaneously strengthen a student's writing or speaking skills, ethical bearing, or ability to reason. Inevitably, such approaches fall to members of the faculty, who must learn how one effectively changes the course methods so as to ensure progress in developing these basic skills.

There are dozens of other examples that might be cited, but it should be clear that each new university initiative pulls the faculty in a new direction. Deans are often charged with ensuring that such new practices are adopted. In trying to move the faculty toward such new roles, several things are especially important. First, doing something new seldom means that the university is abandoning any of the existing items in the faculty portfolio. This needs to be emphasized; otherwise, many individuals will imagine that the emphasis on new things somehow devalues old things.

Second, it is important to develop the idea that there is no single way to be a faculty member; rather, there are hundreds of ways to serve effectively. No faculty member can do everything, so it is the faculty collectively that must cover all the required activities. The only way an institution can make good progress on developing faculty attentiveness to institutional needs (rather than to disciplinary-valued activities exclusively) is to ensure that no institutionally important faculty responsibility is stigmatized and that individuals are rewarded not by what institutionally important responsibilities they carry but how effective they are in carrying out the responsibilities they have been given.

Third, the dean must find incentives that draw faculty to the new areas of need. This is typically done with summer support to attend seminars, with funding for graduate student support, or with the release from other activities. It is through such steps that a university can slowly reshape itself by altering the responsibility mix of its faculty.

NURTURING THE "DIFFERENCE MAKERS"

Colleges and universities have all sorts of faculty. Some work hard, others are lazy. Some are productive, others accomplish far less. Some achieve prominence, others work in obscurity. Some are balanced and fully integrate their teaching, research, and service; others are more one-dimensional, attending to their preferred activities and ignoring almost everything else. Most faculty members are good citizens and credits to the university. Most earn more than what they are paid and lead productive lives. Then there are a few faculty members who are real difference makers in the institution.[3]

What are difference makers? Typically they are respected academics, but often they are not the most distinguished members of the faculty. They tend to be younger and intellectually broader than the typical faculty member. More often than not, they are engaged in work that integrates knowledge areas. They are individuals who are masters at moving from ideas to action. They are patient and persistent. They are flexible, accommodating, and adaptable. They test their ideas and readily revise them to make them stronger. These individuals are concerned with getting things done, not with who gets the credit. They are successful in the larger competitive arenas, able to attract significant grant funds (in disciplines where this is essential) from the major foundations and agencies. These individuals see change as opportunity. They think strategically, not selfishly. They engage students and involve them in their work. Most of these individuals are great with external audiences and tell the university's story with effectiveness. They think about the broader good and contribute significantly to the greater good. They lift others around them to higher levels of productivity. They might be thought of as catalysts for good.

The dean should watch carefully and identify the difference makers in the college. Once identified, he or she should take proactive steps to support such individuals so they are not tempted to look elsewhere for employment. Fortunately, these individuals often exhibit stronger loyalty to their university than is typical—but that does not mean that the risk of losing them to a strong effort from elsewhere is low. They typically do not look for jobs; special opportunities look for them. It is almost impossible to replace one's difference makers, and it is certainly impossible to replace them either with a single appointment or at anywhere near what a university typically spends to support them. A good way to recognize these individuals and facilitate their work at the same time is to place them in named, endowed positions, where the earnings on the endowment are available to support their programs and interests.

This will be a sound investment and will help secure the future of the college.

OTHER CONTINUING "FACULTY" POSITIONS

Some colleges and universities have another class of faculty—those on long-term contracts, renewable, but not in the tenure system. Such individuals typically have unique skills that are important to the field, but they fill positions that result in a record that is hard to tenure in the normal sense. Examples of such positions are people in theatre, such as designers (set design, lighting, etc.), or acting or voice instructors, and others for whom publication or independent creative activity are not really possible. Artists in residence might also be placed in this category. These appointment arrangements are therefore used for both short- and long-term contracts with individuals in the arts areas.

NON–TENURE TRACK FACULTY

At most colleges and universities, faculty members who do not have tenure-track appointments carry out a significant portion of the instruction and a more modest portion of the institution's research. In the instructional realm, these individuals are normally hired as graduate assistants, lecturers, instructors, and faculty associates. In research, they hold many titles, including postdoctoral fellow, academic professional, research professional, service professional, clinical professor, and research scientist. These individuals can make up a sizable proportion of a college workforce.

Graduate Assistants

Graduate assistants support instruction in many fields, but in departments with heavy lower-division instructional burdens it is not uncommon for them to be the instructors of record, carrying full responsibility for all aspects of their classes. This is especially true in English, mathematics, and language instruction. There are numerous issues regarding this practice. Many graduate students are ill prepared to take over formal instruction. The workload at some institutions exceeds twenty hours per week, which is detrimental to progress toward graduation. Graduate assistants are becoming more aggressive and demanding; they have unionized at a number of campuses, engaging in work stoppages over issues of workload, benefits, and the need to make a working wage. Many foreign-

born students with limited English speaking skills struggle to be understood by the undergraduate students in their classes and discussion sections. Finally, in making admission decisions, some departments pay more
attention to the number of classes to be covered than to the academic
preparedness of the students. In such settings the workload is often high,
and the time it takes to graduate can be deplorable.

In spite of these problems, colleges and universities will continue to hire
graduate assistants in large numbers. The use of graduate students has been
a historically economical way to provide instruction. Such teaching assignments also enrich the educational experience of the graduate students
by providing them with the opportunity to develop their teaching skills.
Nevertheless, a dean should be attentive to the rising cost of this form of
instruction and to the many issues that surround the use of graduate assistants for instruction. Abuses of any kind should be remedied at once.

A proactive activity on many campuses in called "Preparing Future
Faculty." This program was started with funding from the Pew Foundation and is intended to help graduate students learn about career opportunities in higher education. These programs, where they exist, expose
students to the wide range of career possibilities that are featured in all
types of institutions of higher learning. Students who have gone though
these programs are more fully familiarized with the professional aspects
of faculty life than would be the case for the typical student.

Lecturers, Instructors, Faculty Associates, and Adjunct Faculty

Colleges and universities use a variety of titles for the non–tenure track
instructional faculty, but they are often called lecturers, adjuncts, instructors, or faculty associates. If colleges and universities had their choice,
individuals in these categories would be employed only where there were
special needs to be filled. Constrained budgets, however, have caused
colleges and universities to rely ever more heavily on non–tenure track
faculty. Under the best circumstances (for the employee), these individuals
are hired on full-time contracts that provide full benefits and a three-year
notice of nonrenewal. They have offices and participate in appropriate
ways in departmental governance.

Under the worst circumstances, these individuals are hired by the
course at low rates (sometimes as low as five hundred dollars per credit
hour). They receive no benefits, have no assurance of how many
courses they will be contracted to teach from term to term, and may
not know if they will be hired at all. They have no offices but share
spaces with many others so that they can fulfill their office-hour

requirements. They do not participate in departmental governance and are largely unknown to the faculty.

These are the two extremes for non–tenure track faculty. Most institutions fall somewhere between these extremes. The American Association of University Professors (AAUP) has developed a statement of "Guidelines for Good Practice: Part-Time and Non-Tenure-Track Faculty." The statement is available on its website at www.aaup.org/Issues/part-time/Ptguide.htm. These guidelines can be helpful to the dean who is trying to create conditions that are seen as generally acceptable for this important part of the instructional workforce.

At some colleges and universities up to 40 percent of the undergraduate instruction is provided by these individuals. Often the younger members of these groups have training and credentials that are roughly equivalent to those of the tenure-track faculty. Over time, however, few such individuals remain competitive for regular faculty positions, because their heavy instructional loads leave them little time to pursue other forms of scholarship, especially activities that would lead to publication. Many new Ph.D. recipients take these positions if they are unable to secure appointment in a tenure-track capacity. If they are unable after a few years to move to the next level, they are likely never to be able to make such a move.

The AAUP position on such appointments is that if they are full-time and are held for seven years, a condition of de facto tenure exists. As a result, some colleges and universities will not hire such individuals for more than six consecutive years. Other institutions believe that their state laws and institutional policies clearly spell out the nature of such appointments in ways that protect them from being vulnerable to claims of de facto tenure. Court decisions on cases that are certain to be litigated will bring clarity to institutional liabilities in this area. What is certain is that letters of appointment must state clearly that these appointments are not on the tenure track and are time-limited in nature. The dean should review and approve the language that is used in all letters of offer to non–tenure track faculty.

Research and Clinical Faculty and Postdoctoral Fellows

Each faculty member is engaged in research and creative activities as an aspect of his or her appointment, but many colleges and universities have a special class of faculty that is normally supported by grants and contracts. These positions exist only when grant and contract monies are adequate to cover the salary and benefits. If the money runs out, the individual is left without a position. Nevertheless, many of the people who end up in these positions are very successful researchers, able to attract the external funding necessary to maintain their laboratories and fund the positions they hold. They receive contracts that coincide with the terms of their funding. When funding is renewed, their appointments are renewed.

In many ways these non–tenure track employees represent an invisible workforce within colleges and universities. They attract grant monies and contribute to the research productivity of the institution, but they have narrow roles and little job security. At a few places these individuals carry titles that sound like other members of the faculty ("assistant clinical professor" or "associate research professor," for example), but they do not earn tenure or serve as faculty in the full sense. Some participate in doctoral education or help in teaching on a volunteer basis, but these are exceptions. In the normal case they live one-dimensional lives. Many are happy to be able to use the university as a base, appreciate being able to have lab space for their work, and relieved not to be involved in teaching. Many, therefore, are content with these roles and enjoy long and productive careers.

Postdoctoral fellows normally take such appointments to strengthen their research credentials by working in new settings and demonstrating independence from their Ph.D. mentors. These appointments typically last from one to five years but can run on indefinitely. In the best scenario, an individual spends a few years in such a role and then moves on to a tenure-track appointment. A postdoctoral fellowship has become almost essential in some disciplines. Searches at the level of untenured assistant professor in the biological sciences, for example, typically draw a large number of highly qualified applicants from postdoctoral fellow positions. In such a pool it is very difficult for a new Ph.D. recipient to be competitive.

When one hears the word "faculty," one normally thinks of those serving in the traditional tenured role (or on the tenure track). In fact, people carrying out the faculty function serve under a wide range of appointment types and enjoy quite different privileges. Often, the tenure-track faculty are the only ones with a full voice on matters of curriculum, even though many, most, or all sections of some lower-division classes are taught by "faculty" that are neither tenured nor on the tenure track. The dean should take steps to ensure that the governance arrangements of his or her units are consistent with university policies and that, to the extent possible, all those with an investment in the activity have a say in its form and management.

NOTES

1. *Employee Assistant Program (EAP) and EAP Core Technology* (Arlington, Va.: Employee Assistance Professional Association, 2002).

2. J. Selingo, "What Americans Think about Higher Education," *The Chronicle of Higher Education* 49, no. 34 (2003): A12–A17.

3. See G. S. Krahenbuhl, "Are We Preparing Institutional Difference Makers?" *Quest* 55 (2003): 25–29.

CHAPTER

Student Affairs

There are many student matters to which the dean should be attuned. Student matters are so important and so time-consuming that it is typical to have one or more associate or assistant deans who work exclusively with students. The dean sets the tone for how students are treated, but the day-to-day interaction is usually delegated to other members of the staff.

STUDENTS AS "CUSTOMERS"

The business idiom is frequently applied to higher education. It is common to read of colleges and universities as competing in the "marketplace," and books have been written on the commercialization of higher education.[1] Institutions often describe themselves as "student centered" and "customer oriented." This perspective, popularized during the Total Quality Management (TQM) craze of the 1990s, was no more effective than many other approaches to improving conditions for student learning, but it caused unending headaches from students who imagined that it was up to the university to ensure that they were satisfied customers.

Colleges and universities are in fact *idea* centered. Educating the next generation of leaders is central to the mission of higher education, so institutions of higher learning must be attentive to student needs. Nevertheless, it is the pursuit of ideas that is central, and mature students come for this purpose. The problem with thinking of students as customers to be satisfied is that it ignores the inescapable fact that learning is internal and requires student engagement and effort. One does not become religious by attending church; one does not become physically fit by hanging out at a fitness club; and one does not become educated merely by attending classes. In each case the services provided might be outstanding, but if the individual does not engage, does not apply him- or herself, he or she derives no benefit. This would not be the fault of the organization; it would be the fault of the individual.

Colleges and universities have many customers, but the students are not among them. If forced to use the business model and idiom to describe the university, graduates could be thought of as one of its most important products. Other products are discoveries, services rendered externally (such as consulting), licensed and patented inventions available for new business ventures, and so on. When it comes to graduates, the customers are the employers who seek educated individuals for their workforces and the society in which the graduates become adult citizens. The education of students is a very important function of colleges and universities, but students are not customers to be satisfied; rather, they are the product that must satisfy in the world of work and society.

Some in higher education will disagree with these observations. They will argue that students and their parents see themselves as customers and come to their interaction with the university from that perspective. A student-as-customer orientation creates demands on deans and their colleges, and probably helps to ensure that an appropriate level of attentiveness is given to student needs.

ADMISSION STANDARDS

Most colleges and universities have admission standards that apply to all majors, although a few places admit students not into the university but directly into a specific college. In the latter case the published admission standards merely indicate one's eligibility to be considered; the actual record of admitted students will vary from college to college.

Standards are set with an eye toward many concerns, some which conflict and must be balanced. Most institutions would like their standards to be as high as possible, because the faculty prefers to work with bright and motivated students. Countering the urge to admit only the elite few is the reality that enrollment yields are lower with this group. Being overly selective, therefore, can hurt enrollment and undermine the generation of tuition revenue. Public colleges and universities are expected to provide access to students; if the university does not appear to be providing access to qualified students, funding ramifications may ensue. Colleges and universities also should be committed to providing access to opportunity to members of historically oppressed and under-represented groups. Until such time as university campuses look like America, efforts need to be made to encourage diversity in the student body and in the graduates of every institution.

STUDENT RECRUITMENT

At many, perhaps most, colleges and universities the recruitment of undergraduates is left to an office of admissions. If a college is content with the makeup of its undergraduates, it can comfortably leave this task to others. If, however, the college wishes to reshape the profile of the undergraduate class in a particular way, it will have to expend some additional effort.

How might a class be reshaped? Perhaps there is a wish to add more top students and reduce the number of students admitted with deficiencies. This may not increase costs; at the author's campus it was discovered that a million dollars per year was being spent on remedial classes for students admitted with deficiencies. The question was asked: How might the class be reshaped if we stopped admitting students with deficiencies and used the million dollars to create a thousand scholarships of a thousand dollars each, or five hundred scholarships of two thousand dollars each? The gamble here is that a thousand-dollar scholarship will change the enrollment decisions of the required number of students. If the additional high-achieving students are attracted (using scholarship support), then for no additional money the institution will have reshaped the class by replacing marginal and ill-prepared students with high achievers. With the entering classes thus reshaped, graduation rates might also be expected to improve.

There are many other ways a class might be reshaped. Steps to attract members of protected classes will help with issues of access and diversity. Almost every university needs to pay constant attention to this goal, because the demography of America is changing. It will be a challenge to shape the population of students attending America's colleges and universities to look like the population of America, but this should be our goal.

Some colleges and universities seek more residential students; some want more full-time students; yet others want more students in critical areas, such as teacher education. A college dean should examine the makeup of the undergraduate class and then, if deficiencies are revealed, become proactive in reshaping it.

How does a dean become proactive about enrollment management? The first rule is to become acquainted with the institution's enrollment management philosophy to ensure that each effort is consistent with the broader goals. An admissions officer or an enrollment management office is normally a good source of information. One simple request the dean can make is to be provided a list of all students who have been admitted (and have designated the college as their area of interest) but not enrolled, along with addresses and telephone numbers and information about their ethnicity, gender, academic record, and other items of importance. Once the reshaping goal has been identified, all students who if enrolled would move the college in the desired direction could be personally contacted by the department of the designated major. Often a simple personal call will make the difference in a student's decision or cause the student to carry through a general intention and enroll.

COURSE REQUIREMENTS

In a shared governance setting, the administrative voice is stronger in some areas while the faculty voice is stronger in others. On issues pertaining to curriculum, the collective wisdom of the faculty certainly exceeds that of the dean. For this reason, the faculty voice is more significant in establishing requirements for students. The dean, however, often has to provide leadership for the process of curriculum review. Whether it be general requirements or the requirements of majors, it is important to focus on what is to be accomplished. Absent such a focus, faculty discussions frequently degenerate into "turf wars," where every special interest wants its course on the requirements list. To avoid such a condition, it is usually helpful to proceed in a two-step process. The first step is to identify the knowledge and competencies to be instilled. Once these have been agreed upon, the second step in the process can identify classes that meet the stated objectives. Individuals and departments are free to suggest possibilities, but a faculty committee, with reference to agreed-upon criteria, determines which offerings will serve to satisfy the requirement.

RETENTION AND GRADUATION RATES

The success of colleges and universities is frequently judged by numbers of retained and graduating students. To the uninformed reader, such statistics often seem to imply more about the institution than about its students. That is, a school with a low graduation rate must not be taking very good care of it students. On closer examination one discovers that nothing could be further from the truth.

The undergraduate enrollments at some colleges and universities consist almost exclusively of straight-out-of-high-school, high-achieving, full-time, parent- or scholarship-supported, residential students. To no one's surprise, the graduation rates for such groups are high. Other institutions are required by their governing boards to take a more heterogeneous mix of students. Yet others have many students who must work. While working students may be classified as full-time, schedule conflicts often prohibit them from taking the coursework sequences that lead to graduation in four or even five years. Some colleges and universities have more commuting students, while others have more nontraditional students. Foreign students often accumulate massive numbers of hours before graduation so as to preserve their student visa status. The point is this: Retention and graduation rates reveal more about the student mix than about the university and the attention it pays to students. Stratified samples quickly reveal that high-achieving, residential, full-time, scholarship-supported students (with the possible exception of student athletes) graduate at high rates at all institutions. All other mixes of students graduate at lower rates at all institutions.

This is not to suggest that one should ignore either retention or graduation rates. There is always room for improvement. Colleges and universities typically provide all sorts of help for students having difficulty. The services include tutoring, special study sessions, counseling, study guides, and all kinds of formal methods of accommodation for individuals with known disabilities. A good first step is to survey the help resources and see if the faculty is aware of them. The major problem at most institutions is not failing to provide the services; rather, it is the failure of faculty members to direct students who need help to the services that are available. The following is an example of a letter sent by a dean to his or her faculty, urging them to refer students to these support services when it appeared they were in need of help. The second item is a reference card containing information on (a) some typical situations that might arise and call for intervention, and (b) all of the services that were available.

MEMORANDUM

TO: Instructional Staff

FROM: Dean

RE: Improving Student Success

In the not too distant past, faculty members strived to provide quality-learning experiences with high standards, thereby ensuring reasonable comprehension of the subject matter in those students who earned passing grades. Students either made the grade or they did not; the reasons why were not given much attention.

Colleges and universities ought to be sensitive to the needs of students and concerned about the reasons for cases of poor academic performance. Although responsibility for success in learning has and will always fall largely to the individual student, there are academically appropriate ways for us to help our students.

In addition to providing solid, well-taught courses, the best way to improve the success rate of our students is to be sure they have access and are referred at appropriate times to the many campus resources that exist for students. This will require faculty to be more assertive in exploring student difficulties than has traditionally been the case.

The attached reference card, entitled "An Instructor's Guide to Student Resources," was prepared to help instructors advise students who are having difficulties. The front page of the guide identifies situations that occur frequently and offers suggestions for exploration and action. The back of the card provides summary information, telephone numbers, and Web addresses for student resources in six areas: academic advising, affirmative action, behavioral and bureaucratic concerns, health, safety, and tutoring resources.

By distributing this guide, I hope to encourage faculty members and all others providing classroom instruction to work with troubled students, when and if appropriate, in order to guide them to professional help. The goal is to ensure that we are a caring institution, being appropriately helpful with students who are experiencing difficulties. Although not all students have the attributes necessary to earn a college degree, we need to ensure that those who can benefit from help resources are referred to the appropriate office in a timely fashion.

Thank you for helping students meet the academic standard for success. I hope you find this resource guide to be a useful tool.

AN INSTRUCTOR'S GUIDE TO STUDENT RESOURCES

Situations often arise in the classroom that suggest a student needs referral help beyond what the instructor can provide, but one may not know precisely what to do or where to direct students with difficulties. The following is a sample of typical student problems and available resources.

1. Some students have done poorly on the first exam or quiz.

   The instructor may meet with these students, take a look at their notes, ask them about reading the text, inquire as to study methods, ask about the outside work load. The instructor then may suggest study groups, doing note reviews, tutors, referrals to the Learning Resource Center, Writing Center, or Disability Resources for Students, as well as meet with the student during office hours.

2. Despite doing all the "right things," a student is still performing poorly.

   Gently inquire. If the student is looking for help and a disability is suspected, suggest that he or she contact the Disability Resources for Students.

3. An otherwise consistent student exhibits erratic academic performance or difficulty in concentrating.

   Ask if there is any way you can help. Referral to Counseling and Consultation or to Student Health may, in some instances, be helpful. Some students may also appreciate being reminded of the various campus ministries.

4. A student may request specific accommodation for test taking, e.g., extra time, an oral test, testing in isolation.

   Request that the student bring his or her materials from Disability Resources so that the appropriate accommodation can be made. If the student does not have materials from Disability Resources, refer him or her there. So that students be treated equally, they must have documentation from DRS before an accommodation can be made.

5. A student may express concern about his or her academic standing and overall progress toward a degree.

   Refer the student to an academic advisor.

6. A student is having difficulties in another class.

   Refer the student to the instructor, the department chair, or an ombudsperson.

7. A student confides an incident of harassment or problematic issues of diversity that arise in the classroom.

   If the situation involves faculty or staff, refer to the student to Affirmative Action. If the situation involves another student, refer the student to Student Life. If there is any question of safety, refer the student to DPS. The Intergroup Relations Center should also be contacted to provide consultation and services for those students, faculty, or staff.

8. A student seems to be emotionally or mentally troubled.

   If one seeks your help, refer him or her to any one of the following: Counseling and Consultation; Student Health; Disability Resources for Students; Clinical Psychology Center in the Department of Psychology (fees charged for services). If you wish advice on the situation, strategies may be discussed with professionals in any of these offices or with the Employee Assistance Program.

9. A student is so hostile that the instructor's safety or that of other students is threatened.

   Call DPS for immediate crises. Call Student Life for conduct problems. Call the Assistant Dean for Academic Programs at X-XXXX to discuss options for dealing with disruptive students.

One final note: If an instructor has any question about the personal well being of a student, he or she is encouraged to call Counseling and Consultation, Student Health/Mental Health, or the Employee Assistance Program. The professionals in those offices will be happy to discuss the types of things that are appropriate strategies in support of maintaining student health. Confidentiality is respected.

STUDENT HELP RESOURCES

(Although not shown here, a telephone number, an office location, and an e-mail address are provided for each service listed.)

Academic Advising

The college specifically serves students who have been academically disqualified and those who are transferring into the college. All other academic majors are advised in the department of their academic discipline. Majors seeking advisement are referred to their respective department or college.

Cross-College Advising Services (CAS) is the advising home for No Preference students, as well as select populations in other categories (e.g. freshman Pre-Business majors). CAS also coordinates various workshops.

Affirmative Action

Office of Equal Opportunity/Affirmative Action is responsible for employment monitoring, discrimination complaint resolution involving faculty or staff, workshops/training programs, and the Affirmative Action Plan.

Intergroup Relations Center (IRC) offers faculty and teaching assistants four services related to diversity: 1) consultation on diversity-related issues, curriculum, and intergroup conflict; 2) in-class diversity presentations; 3) out-of-class learner-centered experiences; and 4) student advocacy.

Behavioral & Bureaucratic Concerns

Academic Programs Office deals with course registration issues, academic advising, and is also a resource for scheduling and helping with disruptive students.

Student Life handles student conduct complaints and also is the referral point for students who must leave campus for emergencies.

Ombudspersons are faculty who facilitate problem solving for students in their college.

Health Resources

Counseling and Consultation (C&C) provides confidential psychological and career counseling services for all ASU students.

The *Employee Assistance Program* offers assessment, counseling, referrals and consultation for faculty and staff.

Student Health Services provides Out-Patient Health Care and Wellness Services for students.

General Medical Care: Call to schedule a medical appointment.

Mental Health Services: Call _____ to schedule an appointment with a mental health care provider.

Safety

Police Services: ASU Department of Public Safety has police jurisdiction over the campus. Emergencies: call 911.

Safety Escort Service is a free volunteer service that provides a one-
or two-person escort between campus locations to ASU affiliates and
campus visitors. Electric carts are generally provided when need dic-
tates. Hours of operation: 6:30 P.M.–midnight.

Tutoring Resources

Disability Resources for Students (DRS) facilitates equal access to educational and co-curricular programs, campus activities, career exploration, and employment opportunities for qualified ASU students
with disabilities.

Freshman Year Experience is a program that helps coordinate student-
support services for all freshman students. Tutoring, advising, and
computer resources are available in _____.

The Learning Resource Center (LRC) provides students with tutoring
in over 110 courses.

Math Tutor Center provides walk-in math tutoring. This service is
primarily for students in lower level classes.

Student Success Center is a multiple-service unit housing a test bank
and a resource library.

Writing Center provides one-on-one tutoring for any writing-inten-
sive subject. For more information about Writing Center programs
or satellite locations, call _____.

STUDENT FINANCIAL AID

Financial aid is normally handled by a university office, not independently by colleges. Nevertheless, a dean should be familiar with the nature of financial aid (scholarships, fellowships, loans, grants, stipends,
work-study wages, etc.) available to students and have an understanding
of the affordability of education at his or her institution. For example, the
affordability of a high-tuition, high-aid institution may be no different
from that of a low-tuition, low-aid institution. A high-tuition, low-aid
institution would be at a huge recruiting disadvantage and would have
to scramble to recruit parent-financed students from well-to-do house-
holds. A low-tuition, high-aid institution would be at a competitive advantage from a financial aid perspective and would have a greater chance
than most to shape its class in desired ways. Low-tuition, low-aid institutions tend to be attractive to all but the poorest students.

Financial support can be a hardship reducer for students from middle-
class families, but it is a barrier breaker for students from lower-class fami-

lies. It is often the case that low-tuition, low-financial-aid institutions struggle to attract and retain students from disadvantaged settings, because for them any cost is prohibitive and there is little or no scholarship money available. Such students often receive student loans, but far too many of them fail to graduate, thereby leaving with financial debt but no degree. If financial aid is a problem, part of the dean's fund-raising efforts should probably be directed toward building a scholarship endowment. (Fund-raising is covered in a later chapter.)

In some settings, department chairs have control of scholarships from earmarked endowments. In establishing any collegewide policy or allocating resources to be used for scholarship purposes, the dean should get an all-funds picture of the scholarship support available to chairs in the college. It is only then that the full impact of any student support decisions can be known.

STUDENT OUT-OF-CLASS EXPERIENCES

When one thinks of a university education, the focus is typically on the formal classwork that leads to a degree. A campus-based experience, however, should consist of a great deal more than the formal coursework. The activities that supplement classroom-based learning are a mix of more independent credit-bearing work and participation in the rich milieu of campus activities. These experiences can range from time spent in a faculty member's laboratory to attendance at theatrical performances or special lectures. They may involve special study groups or recreational activities. They may involve public service or service learning. In short, the range of activities that is available to enrich the campus-based experience is enormous.

The dean should visit with students about their campus experiences. He or she should find out if there are important things that are unavailable to students. It is useful to see what activities the students would like to see provided. Often, a small grant program can be initiated to introduce new opportunities. The most talented students typically seek a wide range of experiences to supplement their classroom learning. The dean should take steps to ensure that such opportunities are available.

An example of such a program is one that was developed by the author at the instigation of students, a Scholar Citizen Grant Program for undergraduates. The program provided funds to support students who wanted to apply what they were learning in ways that were useful in the broader society. Students who were supported by this program engaged in some wonderful activities. One spent time working with children with AIDS. Another helped minority diabetics learn how to manage their disease. One recipient developed a translation service to help non–English speakers through health care episodes and such simple processes as getting one's driver's license. Another recipient used her knowledge from a dual major in history and Chinese to write a book containing the oral histories of first-generation immigrants to the area. (The book was published while she was still an undergraduate.) The description and application form for this program are shown below.

Undergraduate Scholar-Citizen Small Grants Program

The College announces an undergraduate competitive small grants program to support projects based in scholarship and serving the community. This exciting new program seeks to go beyond existing research programs or public service projects by combining the strengths of the student as scholar and as citizen. Projects may represent a broad range of academic disciplines and service interests, and must be based in the student's academic and intellectual experience. Proposals may originate from any undergraduate student, currently in good standing at the sophomore level or higher, who will work in partnership with a faculty member and with students, graduate students, faculty, staff, and others as appropriate. Grants range from $250 to $2,500 and will last from one semester to a full year, with possibilities for renewal. Preference will be given to projects with long-range results.

Application Deadline: (date), for grants beginning during the winter break.

Submit: Application form including the proposal and resume.

Obligations: The successful applicant should complete the project, of course, must provide regular reports to the advisor, and will have the opportunity to present results at a conference for grantees.

Application:

I. Abstract. 250 words.

Briefly outline your project, goals, and methods. Explain how this project builds on your scholarship (meaning your coursework and any research and writing experience) and other relevant experience to date (what you know about the community you are proposing to serve). What community needs are you addressing?

II. Proposal. 750 words.

Describe your project in more detail. Explain your goals and specifically what you intend to do, with a proposed work plan and estimated timetable. Explain how the project is valuable for the community and show that you are not duplicating existing efforts. For example, a project to address substance abuse education in the dormitories should demonstrate that neither Student Health nor the Residence Hall Association nor any existing student club provides that service or could provide that service. Many things are possible and important. You might propose a weekend day-camp to promote literacy or an overnight at the zoo to advance environmental awareness, workshops for school teachers or students, service learning experiences, a conference with community outreach, or the development of exhibits, publications, or websites, for example. Projects may be completed in less than one semester or last more than a year, but should have longer-term scholarly or service implications. The program challenges students to draw on their studies to become engaged in the community, on the assumption that a central focus of a liberal arts education is to make scholars who are better citizens.

How does the project draw on your own scholarly work and what do you expect to learn from the project? What experiences and studies have you done that make you the appropriate person for this project? This could involve a study of the impact and results or you could write a paper documenting the process. You must work out the research component with a faculty advisor, who will serve as collaborator and supervisor for the project.

III. Expected Outcomes. 250 words.

Explain what you hope to achieve with this project. The review committee is interested in both "discoverables" and practical "deliverables." It is better to have realistic expectations, so that you can deliver what you propose, than to promise too much.

For longer-term projects, you will provide an interim evaluation of the project at least once per semester. Are things working or would other methods or personnel work better?

IV. Budget Justification.

Establish a realistic budget including specific estimates and explanation of each item. Revisions in the budget as the project progresses must be fully explained. You may request support for a variety of expenses, but not for salary or stipends for personnel.

Form

Name

Student ID#

Address, Phone, E-mail Address

Major, Number of Hours Completed, GPA

Faculty Advisor: The advisor must attach a letter of support for the student and the project, demonstrating that the project is realistic given the student's scholarly preparation and the project itself, and explicitly expressing a willingness to serve as a collaborator and mentor.

I. Abstract. 250 words. Briefly outline your project, goals, and methods.

II. Proposal. 750 words. Explain your project, goals, methods, and your qualifications in more detail.

   a. What is the project?
   b. What do you hope to learn and what do you hope to accomplish for the community?
   c. What is your timetable and your proposed work plan, including other personnel?
   d. What methods will you use (meaning what skills will you use, how will you do your work)?
   e. Why is the project valuable for the community?
   f. What experience have you had to prepare you for this project (meaning what coursework, work experience, and community activity)?

The University of Nebraska takes another approach to encouraging students to engage in a wide range of campus activities—an "Essential Experiences Certificate." To earn the certificate students are required during their undergraduate years to be involved in a minimum of six essential experiences in each of eight categories, for a total of forty-eight outside-of-class enrichment experiences (or twelve each year over four years). These categories are: arts appreciation, career planning, cultural understanding, health and wellness, intellectual development, personal development, social responsibility, and values and ethics. When a student participates in such an activity, he or she completes a one-page form with the basic information about the event or activity, answers two questions, and has the attendance verified by a university official. The two questions are: (a) "What did you do and what did you learn from this experience?" and (b) "How did this experience affect your education, goals, lifestyle or personal values?" The student affairs office evaluates the materials submitted and determines if the student has successfully completed the requirements for the certificate.

CELEBRATING STUDENT SUCCESSES

Each year students are recognized and rewarded in many ways. It is important to celebrate those successes and to bring them to the attention of the broader campus community. Two activities that proved to be very popular at the author's institution were an annual dinner for student award recipients and guests, and an annual awards convocation where all college, university, state, regional, national, and international award winners were recognized. Such events raise the campus and community consciousness to student achievements, but the successes of these students also bring honor to the college (and university) in which their work was completed.

Of course, the major success to be celebrated is graduation. In the past, especially at large institutions, commencement ceremonies recognized the students en masse, unable to afford the time to recognize them individually. For this reason, most large campuses have moved in one of two directions. One is to have multiple commencement ceremonies, each featuring some portion of the university. Each ceremony is kept to a manageable size, and each graduate can be individually recognized without making the ceremony overly long.

The other common approach is to have several days of celebratory events, starting with a university-wide commencement exercise of the traditional sort that recognizes all baccalaureate recipients as a group. This university event is followed by individual college convocation exercises. Each college is given a place and time to conduct its own event, where each graduate (baccalaureate or graduate level) is individually recognized. This has proven to be extremely popular with students, parents, and relatives, but it tends to detract from the significance of the university-wide event.

It is also common to have departmental receptions for students and their parents as part of the celebratory package. This gives parents a chance to meet the faculty and tour the facilities where their students have engaged in study. These events are typically more informal, featuring a reception with snacks, brunch, or a light lunch.

Many faculty members dislike participating in such events, but in the eyes of the public a university's graduates are its most important product. Celebratory events surrounding the successful completion of studies and the earning of degrees represent some of the best opportunities that colleges and universities have to build public support for their existence as publicly or privately supported entities. Deans should encourage faculty members to attend such events. Their presence at graduation reinforces their central role in student learning, draws them into the celebration of achievement, and adds to the pageantry of the event (because of their academic regalia).

MAINTAINING STANDARDS

Deans typically have the authority to waive requirements. Occasionally there is a good reason to do so, but many requests to have requirements waived have little merit, except in the eyes of the petitioner. It is a good idea to keep in mind that the university's accreditation is based on the earning of diplomas by successfully completing all, not just most of, the applicable requirements. University catalogs serve as a contract between the student and the university. The student agrees to complete the requirements as published, and the university agrees to award the appropriate degree in return. Students sometimes need to be reminded that the enforcement of requirements protects the value of the degree to be earned, as well as all the other degrees that are conferred by the institution. If requirements were routinely waived, the university's accreditation would be at risk, as would the worth of the degrees earned by any of the university's students.

Most colleges have a standards committee that is made up of faculty and students. This committee reviews petitions and appeals and makes recommendations to the dean or his or her designate (usually an associate or assistant dean). The focus of such committees is on protecting the academic integrity of the institution while making reasonable accommodation for special circumstances. Such committees are involved with requirements and competencies rather than "seat time." Such committees seek to ensure that fairness is extended to the student, both in terms of meeting the published requirements and of not being victimized by inappropriate faculty grading or evaluation practices.

STUDENTS AS INDIVIDUALS

The time has long passed when colleges and universities treat students as if "one size fits all." Each student engages the university in unique ways. By disposition and life experience each student brings certain attributes, abilities, and interests to, and draws different lessons and forms of enrichment from, his or her university experience. Some students thrive in settings featuring different people in each class; others to be comfortable need to be with some of the same students in as many classes as possible. Students vary in their level of ease in diverse settings. Small class settings with rich discussion are preferred by some students, large lecture sections by others. In short, each individual student has preferred methods of instruction and settings for learning.

Deans should take time to see how the university looks through students' eyes. Efforts should be made to publicize the learning approaches available to students and the learning approach featured in each of the college's courses. Other popular strategies, especially for freshmen, are (1) forming cohorts of students taking the same classes together, (2) creating packages of interdisciplinary courses that feature common themes—the environment, for example—and are taught by faculty members who work at connecting the content, and (3) offering various forms of "service learning," which connects classroom learning with community service of various sorts.

STUDENT PLACEMENT SERVICES

Deans often see their connection to students as largely academic. This can be a mistake, especially if the institution's placement services do not understand the college or are not inclined to promote a college's graduates. It is good to become acquainted with placement personnel. This will help the dean learn how graduating students from his or her college are being represented to employers and will help build a sense of shared responsibility for the placement of a college's graduates.

Placement personnel often seem to forget two important aspects of working life. One is that most positions that require a college education do not specify a major. (Certainly, many vocations and professions require specialized training, but these represent a small proportion of all jobs for college graduates.) The other factor is that a large number of college graduates end up working in areas not closely connected to their degree work and often change jobs many times during a lifetime of work. A dean should make certain that the placement office is steering graduates aggressively not only toward those positions for which they are clearly and directly qualified but also to those where their more generic skills and abilities may also predict success.

If the placement services director is skeptical about promoting students with good generic skills, it might be good to have her/him meet some graduates of your college who have been successful in the workplace outside of their undergraduate fields of study. A quick review of one's graduates will produce a long list of such individuals, who are usually more than happy to help the dean make this point with placement officials.

In the not too distant past, professors would tell students in lower-division classes, "Look to your left, then look to your right. Two of the three of you will not make it to graduation." Faculty took a certain pride in winnowing out underperformers. Colleges and universities are now judged by such measures as student persistence and rates of graduation. The admission and enrollment of a student carries with it at least an implicit commitment to look after the student's success. The thoughtful dean should stay abreast of new ideas and work to keep the goal of providing the best possible student experience at the heart of the academic agenda.

NOTE

1. D. C. Boc, *Universities in the Marketplace: The Commercialization of Higher Education* (Princeton, N.J.: Princeton University Press, 2003).

CHAPTER 8

Development and External Relations

Deans at private colleges and universities have always been involved in fund-raising. There was a time when state support allowed public institutions, in contrast, to operate comfortably with the monies that came from annual appropriations and collections (tuition being the major one). Today, however, the portion of the budget made up from appropriated monies is steadily declining almost everywhere. How does a university remain competitive under such conditions? The first step taken by most institutions has been to raise tuition. The second step is to look for other revenue streams. One of the most desirable sources of revenue is the university's endowment. Almost every American university has engaged in one or more capital campaigns over the past two decades with the primary purpose of building the endowment.

Most deans have no training in fund-raising. As noted in the section on getting ready to assume a deanship, there are many excellent seminars offered regularly by the Council for Advancement and Support of Education (CASE), at www.case.org/. This chapter is intended to review some of the basics of fund-raising, but enrollment at one of the CASE seminars is highly recommended, because fund-raising is now widely expected of deans, and fund-raising ability is a factor of growing importance in searches for deans. The growth of time devoted to fund-raising represents the most significant change in the role of the dean over the past twenty years.

Deans have always been active in alumni relations, although an alumni office, which may be part of or separate from the university, typically coordinates alumni activities. Large institutions sometimes have a university alumni group (sometimes called the "parent organization") and smaller, more focused alumni groups for each college. Most colleges and universities have active alumni chapters across the United States and around the world where significant numbers of their graduates are located. Shared "constituency-based" fund-raising highlights alumni importance and the role of the dean in both fund-raising (which extends beyond alumni) and alumni relations.

Alumni care about their university. This makes them some of the university's best friends and biggest critics. Part of the dean's job is to participate in campus events that involve the alumni, such as homecoming and award recognition ceremonies. Another activity that is almost universal is the publication of an alumni newsletter or magazine. The university will publish one or the other on a regular basis, but whatever the format, it will feature items from across the university. Many issues may come out without a single mention of one's college. For this reason it is becoming more common for individual colleges to publish and circulate their own materials. Such publications can focus entirely on the college and can contain such items as targeted gift solicitation, an honor roll of giving list, and news about current and former students and faculty.

WHAT IS FUND-RAISING?

Most individuals inexperienced in fund-raising imagine that it is asking people for money. The thought of spending one's time engaged in such activity can significantly reduce enthusiasm for the job. Fortunately, fund-raising almost never involves what most people imagine: making cold calls and asking for gifts. Thankfully for all parties, the process of raising funds is much more intelligent and comfortable. The following sections cover major aspects of the process.

Self-Assessment

The first step in fund-raising is to know what is going on in one's college. What are its strengths, its weaknesses, and areas of special opportunity? Where would the availability of additional monies make the biggest difference? Perhaps it is money for student scholarships or fellowships; perhaps it is endowed positions; perhaps it is money for a new building (often referred to as "bricks and mortar"). The assessment of needs should refer to the institution's strategic plan and identify the items that are essential for moving the institution to its next level of development. Potential donors and sponsors will have many questions about such matters, so be prepared.

Preparing a Case Statement

Once the period of self-study has been completed, a case statement can be prepared, laying out the college's needs and opportunities and making the case for how private monies will make a difference. At many institutions this statement is always in draft form and is never committed to a brochure. At other places case statements are formally printed as elegant promotional pieces. A college statement is almost always part of a larger institutional case statement and must be consistent with broader institutional goals and priorities.

The case statement is sometimes shared with donors, but its most important value is to the dean and members of his or her development team. One never knows where a conversation with a donor will go, so if they have thought through and written down the case for supplemental funds, the dean and staff will be better prepared.

Suspects and Prospects

As the story goes, Jesse James was asked why he robbed banks. He is said to have replied, "Because that is where the money is!" The preparation of a list of "suspects" represents an attempt to identify everyone who might have the means and the inclination to make a gift, grant, donation, or bequest, or to contribute something of value to the college. This list would include individuals, foundations, businesses, and governmental agencies. The idea at this stage is to think comprehensively about who might have an interest in the activities for which you intend to seek financial support.

A suspect becomes a "prospect" when, on further study, it appears that there is both capacity and an inclination to provide the type of support you are seeking. Sometimes this transition is simple and straightforward. Foundations almost always have publications that describe the kinds of things they support as well as the processes by which they receive and consider requests. In other cases, determining if a suspect is a prospect is more complicated.

A university has many constituencies, each connected to the university by certain activities or areas of interests. Many potential donors are members of multiple constituencies, because they have interests in many aspects of university life (perhaps athletics, the arts, and business). Some fund-raising consultants believe that the best approach to identifying donors is through a "constituency based" development model. Such an approach highlights the importance of screening lists of potential donors with members of the faculty, staff, alumni, and friends. Conflicts and the extent of existing relationships can then be fully assessed.

If the potential donor (or donor's area of interest) is unknown to you, an acquaintance must be made and a relationship developed. In the time spent becoming acquainted and cultivating a relationship, there will be many conversations about the college and the potential donor's interests. It is a good idea after each such meeting to commit to writing anything of potential significance that has come up in conversation. (At some institutions, travel reimbursements are not processed until such a report is entered in the record.) Such notes are often referred to as "contact reports." As these accumulate, some clear impressions about what does and does not interest the potential donor will emerge. When a match is found between a donor's interests and one of the college's needs, more focused discussions can occur.

Companies, foundations, and individuals with substantial financial capacity are interested in particular things. Those with histories of giving will expect the conversation to move toward potential areas of opportunity for the donor or grant provider. Experienced fund-raisers often say that the answers provided by a potential donor or the officer handling gifts and grants for a foundation or business will "write the proposal for you." One may learn that a prospect never gives money for "bricks and mortar" but is very interested in supporting students. Another might only be interested in providing support that takes something that is very good and makes it excellent. Yet other donors might want to start something that does not exist, such as a program in applied ethics. (In this case, the dean would have to consult with faculty to see if there is interest in moving into the new area identified by the donor.) Foundations often publish reports of all the projects that they supported the previous year. The dean and members of the staff use all of the information they can gather to begin to formulate a proposal.

A word of caution is in order here. Colleges and universities typically have ground rules for the cultivation and solicitation of donors. They seek to avoid the agitation created by multiple individuals from the university approaching the same prospect for different things. Donors want colleges and universities to know what their priorities are and hope that the person representing the highest priority in their interest area will see them. There is typically a clearance process to determine if a prospect that you wish to cultivate is available to you; the university may instead have cleared some other college to approach that individual for what is perceived as a higher-priority need.

Cultivation

As suspects are sorted and prospects emerge, significant time must be devoted to the cultivation process. It is through time spent with prospects that deeper relationships are developed and well-informed understandings of prospective donors are formed. Cultivation should be fun. It involves having the prospect as your guest at lunches and dinners, musical, theatrical and sporting events, and such special activities as open houses, dedications, special lectures, and celebratory events that are consistent with the prospective donor's interests.

In the conversations that occur throughout the cultivation process, it is not uncommon for the prospect to indicate an interest in supporting some activity. When this occurs, the dean has a perfect opportunity to suggest possibilities and gently steer the donor's general interests toward a specific need. Finding a match between a donor's general areas of interest and specific needs of the college is often the key to attracting a gift. When a match is found, it represents an opportunity for the donor to do something that will be meaningful for her/him. At this point all that must be worked out are the details.

Developing a Proposal

Once a general idea for a donation has been found, it is time to develop a written agreement that commits the donor to the gift and commits the college to using the gift in the way the donor intends. Such agreements can be reached easily if what the donor wishes to do essentially matches what the college seeks and there are no strings attached. When the donor's interests do not line up neatly with what the college seeks, or if there are other requirements, many months of discussions and negotiation may be required to reach agreement. Occasionally the differences cannot be reconciled. When this happens it is best to recognize that the opportunity the college feels comfortable offering does not and will never match what the donor wishes to do. It is time to move on to the other prospects.

The ideal gift is one that goes to the college's endowment and is unrestricted in its use. Such a gift gives the dean flexibility to apply the annual payout to the area of greatest need or opportunity. The corpus of the gift is protected, and the endowment provides in perpetuity a stream of funds with which the dean can do good or cause good things to occur.

Unrestricted gifts, however, are rare. More commonly, donors, foundations, and agencies insist on certain provisions. They often seek matching commitments. In this case, the grantor would expect each dollar given to a project to be matched by a dollar from the college. (Some states will automatically match gifts of a certain size that are made to its state colleges and universities. This can be a strong incentive to a donor, because it doubles the impact of his or her gift.) Another requirement sometimes stipulated is that if the college uses the gift to start a new activity, it must commit to continuing the program in perpetuity; this is often referred to as "institutionalizing" a program. Other requirements involve endowments carrying an individual's or company's name, stipulations that all service charges be waived, or that academic units be named after the donor. So that donors are treated fairly, a policy guide should be developed that lists naming opportunities (colleges, departments, centers, buildings, rooms, laboratories, etc.) and the giving level required for an entity to carry the donor's name.

Sometimes such stipulations are acceptable, and sometimes they are not. The many colleges, rooms, and buildings that carry donors' names attest to the fact that this is becoming common in higher education. There have been many cases, however, where such provisions were not acceptable, and in the end both parties walked away without reaching an agreement. This is a far better outcome than agreeing to something that is unwelcome and inappropriate.

Stewardship

Interaction with donors does not end when a gift is made. Rather, the relationship intensifies. The donor, having invested in some new thing, will have a deepened interest in it. As the recipient of the gift, the dean is responsible to ensure that stewardship practices are put in place to keep the donor informed about how the gift has been used and what good is being accomplished through its use. The dean should be aware of each source of private monies and be familiar with the restrictions on their use.

The dean should have processes in place to see that the monies are being spent correctly. For example, if a donor creates an endowment that provides scholarship support, arrangements should be made to let the donor know about the students being supported and to let the students know about the donor, so they can write letters to the donor telling about their lives and interests and expressing their thanks for the scholarship support. (Such feedback may be required by the endowment agreement.) Sometimes donors do not wish to receive such information. One should not assume this to be the case but should honor such a request if it is made.

Working within the broader university development context, deans should develop a system for acknowledging gifts and thanking the givers. For example, for gifts under five hundred dollars a generic typed letter that will satisfy tax requirements for the donor might be used. The department chair might send letters acknowledging gifts from $500 to $999. The dean and the chair might send letters (sometimes typed, sometimes handwritten) to acknowledge gifts from $1,000 to $9,999. The president, the dean, and the chair might all send letters for gifts of $10,000 and more. The amounts given here are entirely arbitrary. What is important is that there is a reliable process to ensure that each donor receives proper, timely acknowledgment and thanks for a gift.

It is important to recognize another aspect of stewardship as well. A donor who is displeased with how a gift has been recognized or used will make no more gifts in the future. If, however, the donor is pleased with what has happened, he or she may make even larger gifts in the future. Once relationships with donors have been built they deserve continuous nurturing by the dean. A word of caution is in order here. Deans come and go, but donors remain to be cultivated. *It is very important for a new dean to learn the identity of the college's external friends and sponsors and to ensure that the transition in leadership does not leave important donors unattended.*

DEVELOPMENT OFFICERS

If there are significant fund-raising expectations on a dean, he or she will normally have the support of one or more development officers. These individuals are fund-raising professionals who understand well all the information provided above. Sometimes these individuals report directly to the dean; in other cases they report to both the dean and to a central development office, or solely to a central office. In the latter arrangement a development officer may support activities in more than one college. For example, the individual may be a specialist in corporate giving, with responsibility for cultivation of and solicitation from certain companies for all colleges in the university. When development officers report to a dean, they tend to represent the interest of that college to all external prospects; however, all development officers should work in ways that serve the best interests of the broader institution.

Development officers are extremely helpful to a dean. They can help with cultivation and stewardship and can see that the many details are handled well. When the time comes to make a proposal or "make the ask" for a gift, however, it is unusual for the development officer to be charged with that task. The dean (or the university president in cases of a very large gift) should actually make the proposal. If the cultivation efforts have been effective, the response should be almost a foregone conclusion.

CAPITAL CAMPAIGNS

Capital campaigns are university-wide efforts to increase substantially the contributions of monies from various sources, public and private. Sometimes there is no particular emphasis; other campaigns are directed toward specific goals, such as building the university's endowment. Capital campaigns have phases. The first phase typically features a feasibility study, wherein the university's capacity to raise money is assessed. The next phase is a "quiet" phase, in which monies are raised toward the eventual goal but the campaign is not publicly announced. The third phase is the "public" phase, where the campaign and its goal are announced. The announcement of the public phase usually occurs at a preselected date, perhaps two years into a five-year campaign, or when about 40 percent of the funds have been raised. If the former method is used, the final goal is often based on a projection from the monies raised over the first two years, during the silent phase. The public phase ends with a celebratory phase, which closes the formal campaign.

The campaign described above might be thought of as traditional. Variations on comprehensive campaigns of the traditional sort are becoming more popular. Some institutions are having more focused, specialized fund-raising drives. Others are engaging in mini-campaigns and rolling campaigns. These variants are popular in more difficult economic times.

TELEPHONE FUND-RAISING

Another form of fund-raising that has become common is direct telephone calls to alumni. Colleges and universities often hire students to make such calls, which can go on year-round. There are professional firms that will organize and administer such activities; such firms are used for three reasons. First, they know the business of raising funds through telephone solicitation. Second, their use keeps the university from having to employ additional continuing personnel. Third, the companies claim to raise significantly more money that can be used for discretionary purposes than is raised through university-administered efforts.

Such claims, however, have not been well documented, and there are several drawbacks in using such firms. They typically keep a large percentage of the money that is raised (sometimes as much as 40 percent). Donors are reluctant to give if they know that such a large portion of their gift is spent on overhead. A second drawback is that such firms focus on squeezing the largest possible gifts or pledges out of donors. The scripts they prepare are very aggressive and do not serve the purpose of building long-term relationships between the institution and the donor. In the typical script the individual is pushed to make a first-time gift that is out of most people's comfort zone and perhaps beyond what the individual can afford. People occasionally say "yes" to such requests, but typically the caller follows the script down the scale to more modest and reasonable levels.

Another problem with the use of professionals is that the script often features the ruse that the university (or alumni association) wants to update its records on graduates. This helps to keep people on the line long enough to hear the question about a donation. Unfortunately, when updated information is provided it often does not get entered into the alumni records; when a call is placed the second year everything that the previous year's call was ostensibly to correct will still be there, in its original, inaccurate form. This is very off-putting to alumni.

Finally, some alumni will imagine that the call is really as personal as it is intended to sound. Professional callers cannot, however, have comprehensive information about the institution and so are unable to answer even the most basic questions.

Some colleges and universities also use telephone solicitation as a way of identifying potential candidates for major gifts. For example, if an individual responds to the first telephone contact by giving five thousand dollars or more, the potential for an even more substantial gift is indicated. The dean or his or her development officer should follow up to thank such individuals for their gift and to become better acquainted with their personal circumstances. Given thoughtful stewardship of the initial gift and effective cultivation, donors thus identified often make major gifts in subsequent years.

For the many reasons cited above, however, plain solicitation through direct calls is falling from favor as a fund-raising approach. Not only are the calls impersonal and aggressive, but they are part of an oversaturated and unwelcome (to most) marketing approach. Colleges and universities are not anxious to be seen as "just another telemarketer." Congressional controls may well put an end to this method of fund-raising in any case.

METHODS OF GIVING

Donors provide support in many ways. The gift most valued and least often received by colleges and universities is an unrestricted cash gift. The monies are available immediately for the institution's highest-priority use. However, as noted above, gifts almost always come with restrictions. Sometimes the restriction is on the form of the gift, and sometimes it is on the permissible uses. Some of the forms that gifts take are shown below.

1. Cash or checks
2. Matching commitments (over six hundred companies in the United States offer matching-gift programs for their employees)
3. Gifts in kind (this can be buildings, land, equipment, or other tangible assets of value to the institution)
4. Planned gifts (this can include bequests, insurance policies, annuities, wills, and legacy trusts)
5. Securities (appreciated stocks help donors avoid capital gains taxes and still receive a charitable income tax deduction).

In most cases the gift will not be unrestricted; the donor will specify its use. Usually the final gift agreement is not struck until the donor and the recipient agree on the use of the gift. No matter what form the gift takes, the university can direct the proceeds to many needs as long as they are consistent with the donor's wishes. Some of the more popular uses of gifts are these:

1. Creating endowments in which the corpus of the gift is protected and an annual payout from earnings (usually 4 to 5 percent) is made available for expenditure (for example, to support faculty, student scholarships or fellowships, program expenses, or many other needs)
2. Funding bricks and mortar (new buildings, new wings to buildings, renovated space, and so on, tie in public institutions to the state's capital outlay process)
3. Providing operating expenses
4. Funding the acquisition of major pieces of equipment (an imaging laboratory, for example)
5. Supporting annual awards to faculty and students
6. Covering expenses for special learning opportunities (such as travel)
7. Creating a distinguished-speakers series

Colleges and universities can always find good uses for gifts. The goal is to spend enough time with donors so that they will give amounts that make a difference and provide such gifts with only such restrictions as the institution can accommodate. If donors see that their gifts are put to good use and are making a difference, the chances that they will provide additional support in the future will be significantly enhanced.

ALLIES IN FUND-RAISING

In addition to an institution's fund-raising staff, there are volunteer and professional groups that can assist the dean in fund-raising. Volunteers who have demonstrated their commitment with personal gifts can be very helpful to a college's fund-raising efforts. Volunteers of substantial financial means are often well connected and can provide access to others with the ability to give. The fact that they believe in the institution for which they are seeking support makes a powerful statement to other potential donors. The same passion that led to their gift can often move others in the same way.

Many institutions make use of external advisory councils or boards of visitors. Sometimes these bodies are strictly for the purpose of helping with fund-raising. More commonly, they are established for a wider range of support activities, of which fund-raising is only one. In the typical case, deans' councils contribute annually to the college, help with the university's legislative agenda (if the university is a public institution), assist on certain occasions with the recruitment of students, host activities that extend the reach of the college and showcase its programs, and provide introductions and access where no acquaintance or relationship exists. Some places call these bodies "advisory councils," but a wise dean once said that it is best to avoid that designation unless one really wants advice from the council.

When looking for partners in fund-raising, the dean should not ignore other elements of his or her institution. One might think that each unit is in competition with every other unit, but sometimes two or more departments can collaborate for their mutual benefit. An example that plays out in many institutions is raising scholarship monies for music students. A dean of performing arts would want such scholarship support for music students, as would the marching band for a subset of those same students. In such a case the two parties can work together to raise scholarship money for the students they share. The collaboration may well lead to funding for more scholarships than would have been possible if each party worked alone.

For deans, several points are important to remember when it comes to development. First, fund-raising is an important part of the deanship; the cultivation of donors is a necessity. After living frugally as a faculty member, many new deans are uncomfortable with the "wining and dining" aspects of their new job. The process of cultivation requires the expense of entertainment; one must spend money to raise money. Second, the word "cultivation" was probably selected by fund-raising experts to emphasize that, as in raising crops, much work must occur and time must pass before the harvest. One should not expect immediate results. In fact, the success enjoyed (or not) by a dean in fund-raising is going to be due in some part to work done (or a lack of it) by his or her predecessor. Likewise, much of the time devoted to development by a dean will result in successes by his or her successor. It takes time to cultivate donors and move them toward the commitment of a gift. The new dean must build on the foundation established by his or her predecessor(s), bringing some donors to the point of making a major gift and beginning the cultivation process with others. The long-term success of a college in attracting private gifts will depend significantly on the commitment of a succession of deans and the continuity of leadership from one dean to another.

CHAPTER 9

Research and Creative Activities

Significant amounts of faculty time are devoted to research and creative activities. The place of research varies according to institution type, but virtually all four-year colleges and universities expect faculty members to engage in original work and share the results in appropriate outlets. It is not uncommon for faculty members, especially those in research universities, to spend the majority of their time pursuing their research and creative interests. They often accomplish this by working extended hours on evenings and weekends. The most productive scholars accomplish an incredible amount of work in the time they have available for such activities. Unfortunately, other faculty members with just as much time accomplish almost nothing. The research and creative activities of faculty have a significant bearing on the institution's academic reputation. Faculty productivity in this area is so essential that the dean must be well versed in the issues surrounding research.

SUPPORTING RESEARCH

The institution's mission will determine the place of research, but the dean must work to facilitate research in ways that are consistent with that mission. There are many ways in which research and creative activities can be supported and encouraged. There are also many choices a dean must make that will influence the extent to which the faculty is capable of creativity and discovery. The following sections identify many of the critical issues.

The Use of Faculty Time

The use of faculty time tends to be governed by two variables. One is the workload expectation of the institution; the other is the workload norm of similar disciplines at peer institutions. The mix of time allocated to teaching, research, and service varies depending on the relative influence of these two variables.

In some institutions there is a fixed teaching load for all faculty; the remaining time is allocated between research and service (including administrative duties and responsibilities). When the typical teaching load is four classes per term, there is little time left for research and creative endeavors. When faculty members are teaching an average of one to two classes per term, they have much more time for noninstructional activities.

The optimal condition for a dean is to have no fixed or required teaching load. In this case the dean can work with chairs to optimize the integration of faculty responsibilities and institutional needs. Assignments can vary among individuals and for an individual over time. Faculty responsibilities can be assigned in such a way that abilities and interests can be matched with needs, and the evaluation process can focus more on the quality of the work and less on the type of work in which the individual has engaged. Institutions have been looking for ways to think more flexibly about the faculty role. One approach that has received wide attention was offered by Boyer, who was influential in helping colleges and universities develop an expanded view of scholarship.[1]

Buyouts and Released Time

Some faculty members seek to be relieved of formal teaching responsibilities. While such arrangements can be tolerated for short terms, there are few sound justifications for allowing such a condition to continue for a prolonged period. Instruction is at the heart of every institution's mission, and teaching must remain unequivocally a central function of the tenured faculty. Even when faculty members have external funds to "buy out" some of their time, the occasions when doing so is approved should be limited. Unless on a leave of some sort, when faculty members have no formal teaching assignment they should be interacting with students as mentors, advisors, and teachers in less formal settings, some of which might be credit bearing. (Such activities are often recorded as independent study, reading and conference, thesis, or dissertation hours.)

The phrase "released time" is widely used on university campuses, and it tends to refer to time away from teaching that is available for research (or other activities). Released time is highly sought after by some faculty, because they see it as having fewer things that they must do (typically classroom teaching) and of having more time for what they want to do (typically research and creative endeavors). In many cases there are no consequences for such arrangements, but to avoid abuses of time set aside for research, such changes in responsibility should be accompanied by changes in evaluations. The paragraph below presents the logic underlying this argument.

Let's say that the typical academic-year load for faculty members is 40 percent teaching, 40 percent research, and 20 percent service and that the instruction expectation for someone with 40 percent of his or her time allocated to instruction is four classes per academic year. In this case each class taught equates to 10 percent of the annual load. If an individual in this setting has what is typically called a "two-course release" for research, his or her mix of responsibilities would be 20 percent teaching, 60 percent research, and 20 percent service. These percentages add up to 100 percent, so the individual has not been released from a portion of his or her work; rather, the job continues to be full-time, but the mix of responsibilities is different. Carrying this to its logical conclusion, such an individual, with 60 percent time allocated to research and creative activities, should be expected to produce 1.5 times as much as an individual with 40 percent of time allocated to research. If the volume of work is appropriate for the time allocated to an area of activity, attention can turn to the quality of the work produced. Looking at things in this way is fair to all parties. It is patently unfair to grant departures from the norm and then not make analogous adjustments to the evaluation.

Start-Up

When faculty members are hired, the offers made to them typically cover one-time costs of items that will be essential for the faculty member's work. At the least, this usually includes a personal computer, printer, and software for professional use. In the sciences, medicine, and engineering, start-up typically outfits and equips a laboratory to support the research activities of the faculty member. The cost for such facilities can run from $100,000 to over $500,000, depending on the type of research. Other forms of start-up can include temporary research support in the form of technicians or graduate students, modest operating funds, special access to travel monies, summer salary support, and instrument time on major national facilities.

Start-up in other areas is more modest and takes different forms. In the humanities, the package may include a computer and printer, publication support, reduced teaching, the time of a research assistant, and travel to professional meetings. In the case of artists and musicians, the package can take yet different forms and can be quite expensive. The annual hiring survey conducted by CCAS provides complete information on the contents of hiring packages at reporting institutions in the arts, humanities, social sciences, and natural sciences.

The way in which start-up costs are borne varies by institution. In some cases the department must cover the expense. In other cases the college or university covers start-up costs. More often than not there is some sharing of costs by the department, college, and university. With rapidly escalating start-up costs, it is not uncommon for recruitment at some institutions to be limited not by faculty positions but by the ability to fund the start-up requirements of new hires.

Small Grants Programs

In addition to monies dedicated to newly hired faculty, colleges (or universities) often have competitive internal grant programs. Such programs provide seed money to young investigators who lack external funding. In some cases the goal is to help the funded individual become more competitive for external funding; where there is little external money available (such as in the humanities), the goal is to allow the faculty member simply to conduct his or her research. Small grants programs can be general or targeted. Targeted programs typically support only one type of expenditure, such as international travel or a summer stipend. General small grants usually feature somewhat larger awards and allow the applicant to submit a budget covering a wide range of items. In all cases there is a "deliverable" of some form. At the least a final report must be submitted if the individual expects to have any future applications favorably reviewed.

Sabbatical Leaves

Many institutions have sabbatical leave privileges for which one can be considered after a fixed period of service, usually seven years. Such leaves take many forms, but a typical arrangement allows an individual to be away at 100 percent salary for one academic term or at 67 percent salary for the entire academic year. Such leaves can be very useful in building multi-institutional research activities and in broadening and deepening a faculty member's research capability. There are other good reasons for taking sabbatical leaves, but the enhancement of one's research productivity is the prime benefit.

External Grant-Matching Requirements

It is not uncommon for funding agencies to encourage or require an institution to match portions of a grant application. For example, a million-dollar grant (i.e., direct costs, those monies spent directly on the project) might feature a major piece of equipment with a total cost of $400,000. It would not be unusual for the funding agency to ask the institution to provide a 50 percent match toward the purchase of the equipment. If the grant were funded under such an arrangement the funded institution would be expected to pay $200,000. Commitment to a generous match will not cause a noncompetitive proposal to be funded; however, a higher level of institutional support may spell the difference by which one of two otherwise equivalent applications is chosen for funding (this occurs most frequently on very large center or facility grants). Faculty members sometimes ask for a match even when the funding agency does not require it; this is sometimes called "buying an award." In truth, the quality of the proposed science is what matters most, and so an institution match (when not required) just reduces the agency's award and reduces what is available to support the research of others within the institution.

Bridge Funding

In universities with large programs of research it is not uncommon for research groups having expired grants to come to the dean for temporary support to keep the work on track and the team together until new external funding arrives. This is called "bridge funding." There are many reasons for gaps in funding. Some are caused by federal funding delays. Some result when agencies fail to adhere to their printed funding calendars. It is not uncommon for funding to fall through on a grant that the group expected to be supported. On occasion the principal investigators are not conscientious in meeting renewal deadlines. Whatever the reason—and the dean should find out—there is a group at the door in need of bridge funding.

One can never be sure that the anticipated funding will ever materialize; therefore, it is best to make a commitment that will carry the group only until the new funding arrives, if it comes in the next cycle of awards.

An open-ended commitment to support a group removes the incentive to compete for external monies. Failure to attract new external money may signal that the group is no longer competitive. In this case the college's money should be directed elsewhere.

Safety-Net Funding

When a university has extremely valuable, perhaps not easily replaceable, individuals supported in whole or in part by external funds and the flow of such funds is unpredictable, safety-net funding is sometimes arranged. In this case the individuals responsible for seeking external support are required to be diligent in their attempts to secure support for the individual, but the college agrees to make up the difference in funding whenever the external monies are inadequate to cover the full salary and benefits of the employee. Highly valued technical people can sometimes be retained only if such safety net funding is ensured. For key people it is money well spent.

Special Initiatives

There will be times when research activities have special significance or show unusual promise. They may connect the university with strategic partners, or they might hold great potential for commercial development. In such cases many institutions offer "incubator" or "strategic initiative" grants. These might be available through an office of research or the university's foundation. Supplemental funding provided at just the right time can put selected projects on a fast track. If the university acquires an equity interest in some new technology supported in this way, it could well recover its investment once the venture becomes profitable and produces a stream of unrestricted revenue.

Cost Centers

Many fields in the sciences, engineering, music, theatre, and the performing arts are extremely expensive. It is not unusual, therefore, for a university's large support facilities to be made available to many users on a cost basis. A good example would be a surface characterization laboratory, which provides imagery of the arrangement of atoms on the surface of solid materials. The many faculty members, "post docs," and students pursuing research that involves the structural and functional properties of materials would use the facility on a fee basis. The fees would be placed into an account out of which the expenses of the facility would be paid. The idea is not to generate a profit but to cover the cost of operating the facility.

INDIRECT COST RECOVERY

Most agencies and some foundations will pay for indirect costs incurred in carrying out funded research. The total funding a university receives in these cases is the sum of direct and indirect costs. The direct costs are those incurred in carrying out the research; indirect costs represent the expenses incurred in administering such grants. An audit of administrative support determines the indirect cost rate. The most common method of calculating indirect costs is to take some percentage of the direct costs less monies spent on equipment purchases. For example, if a university's indirect cost rate is 50 percent, the indirect costs for a grant with a total direct cost of $250,000, of which $50,000 is equipment, would be $100,000 (50 percent of $200,000). The full award would be $350,000 ($250,000 direct and $100,000 indirect).

The recovery of indirect costs is handled in a variety of ways. In most cases the individuals involved in the administrative handling of grants and contracts are paid from various fund sources. At some institutions indirect cost–recovery monies are used to pay these administrative costs. At some state schools, the employees involved in grant and contract administration are paid out of the authorized budget, and all indirect cost monies are deposited in the state treasury. At other institutions the employees involved in administering grants and contracts are paid out of the authorized budget, and the indirect cost monies that are recovered are placed in a local account. In that case, the university then uses these monies in many ways. They might be used to cover the renovation of research space or for start-up. Frequently some portion of these monies is directed to the library. Small grant programs are often funded out of such accounts. Such monies can also be used to fund strategic initiatives or to retire bonds on research buildings.

In cases where the indirect cost funds are kept by the university and placed in a local account, it is not uncommon to distribute some portion of the funds back along the path of the original proposal. Distribution schemes vary greatly from place to place. As an example of how indirect cost funds might be distributed, consider an instance where 78 percent of the indirect costs recovered (ICR) is retained centrally for the purposes described above (true indirect expenses for the support of research), 10 percent is returned to the college from which the proposal originated,

10 percent is returned to the department, and 2 percent is returned to the principal investigator(s) of the project. If the project has multiple principal investigators and crosses unit lines, the allocation of ICR monies is prorated according to where the direct costs are charged. Such funds can provide an invaluable source of flexible financial support to a college and its units.

INTERDISCIPLINARY CENTERS AND INSTITUTES

Most colleges and universities continue to be organized into departments that house traditional disciplines. This arrangement is useful for many things, but not for the facilitation of interdisciplinary integrative research and teaching. That is unfortunate, because many of the most interesting questions and a significant percentage of the federal research budget (represented by the National Science Foundation, the National Institutes of Health, the Department of Energy, the Department of Defense, the Department of Agriculture, and the National Aeronautics and Space Administration) focus on applied problems that are inherently interdisciplinary and integrative in nature. Colleges and universities have addressed this problem by creating centers and institutes.

In the typical case such units neither serve as tenure homes for faculty nor offer degree programs. They exist primarily to facilitate faculty interaction and student learning of an interdisciplinary nature. Such units are typically reviewed periodically to determine if they should be continued. (These periodic evaluations are sometimes called "sunset reviews," because a unit found not to be facilitating interdisciplinary work faces the prospect of being disestablished.)

All sorts of centers and institutes exist on university campuses. Thematic centers are very common, such as in Latin American studies, Asian studies, or African American studies. Others might focus on narrow topics or regions. Some examples might be a Center for Southwestern Studies or an Institute for the Study of Texan Cultures.

Some centers and institutes cut across traditional subject areas to focus on a particular era or question, or on some subset of the human population. Examples here might be a Center for Medieval and Renaissance Studies, an Institute of Human Origins, or a Women's Studies Center.

In the sciences such centers focus on almost anything imaginable, from specialized techniques that can be applied to the study of questions in many disciplines to specific diseases or disorders, to research that occurs on a specific scale of matter. Examples here might be a Center for High-

Resolution Microscopy, a Cancer Research Institute, or a Center for Nanotechnology.

In truth, the possibilities are almost limitless. A review of university catalogs will reveal the existence of centers and institutes dedicated to almost everything conceivable. The question for a dean to consider is: How does one facilitate the work of centers and institutes? Many colleges and universities struggle with this question, but the following points seem to appear frequently with regard to the work of interdisciplinary units (IUs).

1. The quality of the work produced under the auspices of the IU depends on the quality of the individuals drawn from existing units to participate in it.

2. The IU must have strong leadership by an individual who is both respected for his or her work in the area and capable of attracting faculty members to work together in teams.

3. The IU must have a significant budget that provides support for interdisciplinary work that would not occur if the IU did not exist.

4. Credit for participation in the work of IUs must not detract from the accomplishments of the units that serve as tenure homes for faculty members involved in the effort. Departments will discourage faculty participation if their productivity measures (such as grant dollars per faculty member) suffer because of research time split between the department and the IU.

5. Where faculty positions are placed in IUs, it is not uncommon for perceptions to emerge that faculty members housed within the IU are favored over those elsewhere. In extreme cases such IUs end up operating like an independent department and lose all ability to attract faculty participation from other units.

6. Allocatable space and unique facilities or assets provide IUs a strong draw for faculty participation. To the extent that these assets are lacking, significant faculty participation will be handicapped.

7. IUs should be reviewed periodically to see if their accomplishments justify their cost. Criteria that are typically used in such reviews include:

   What has been accomplished that would not have been accomplished if the IU did not exist? (Included here would be publications, grants, special events held, faculty exchanges supported, collections built, major breakthroughs or discoveries made, and significant collaborative efforts facilitated.)

   Is there a future for continued work in the research areas covered by the IU? (One could imagine an IU focused on vacuum tubes not being relevant for today's world.)

Does the IU provide students intellectual opportunities that would not exist without the IU?

Interdisciplinary centers often report to the dean, but in some colleges and universities they report to a vice president for research or some other higher-level official. The dean's knowledge of support going to college activities is usually best when the interdisciplinary units in which his or her faculty work report to the college and not some higher-level administrator. When the reporting lines are mixed, the investments in interdisciplinary activities often fail to maximize accomplishments unless the administrators involved are in good communication and work together.

In an academic world organized by traditional academic disciplines, the existence of centers and institutes greatly expands the scope of activities whereby credible work can be accomplished. In addition to formally organized interdisciplinary units, many colleges and universities have mechanisms to encourage all sorts of interdisciplinary activity of a less formal nature. Someone once made the astute observation, "Life is interdisciplinary." Such work is obviously important for both faculty and students. It is therefore important for the dean to encourage and support activities that build the connectedness of faculty members in the various disciplines and to encourage integrative work in both research and instruction.

SHOWCASING RESEARCH

Not long ago it was considered unseemly for colleges and universities to engage in self-promotion. Academics believed they were doing good work, and American society did not question its investment in higher education. Those conditions have eroded since the 1960s, which probably represented the high point of state and federal support of higher education. This change in public attitude has elevated the importance for colleges and universities of calling attention to the many good things that occur under their auspices. Many of the most compelling stories to be told emanate from the realm of discovery. Deans should be alert to opportunities to connect the public with interesting aspects of research.

Community Enrichment Programs

In every community there are individuals who seek intellectual nourishment of the sort that university faculty members can provide. Programs are offered under a variety of names such as "journeys of the mind," "great conversations," "adventures in learning," or "Saturday scholars." Typically, these thematic offerings are made available for a modest fee and do not generate academic credit. The topics selected should match areas popular with the intellectual public with faculty members who can address public audiences in an engaging way. Some examples of topics offered at the author's university are:

1. Immortality
2. Vengeance and the rights of crime victims
3. Origins (a series on the origins of the universe, life, early civilization, and of human origins through evolution)
4. The interaction of religions and national identities
5. Islam and the world: past, present, and future
6. The art of impressionists (includes a trip to Paris)
7. The search for evidence of life on Mars

Programs such as these not only enrich the lives of community members but show the college or university in a favorable light and often lead the university to new donors. These events can be college events or university events featuring college faculty. Deans should identify those faculty members who communicate most effectively with public audiences (the best storytellers) and work with the university to offer on a regular schedule events that showcase the work of the faculty.

Thematic Outreach Activities

Is the university a large, impersonal place known for large buildings and unfriendliness to visitors? Except at athletic or performing arts events, most members of the public find large universities pretty intimidating. Parking is usually a problem, and the location of things that might be interesting to the public is not well known. A growing number of institutions address this problem by holding annual events to attract families to campus. Many colleges and universities hold special daylong events once a year for the sole purpose of building the public interest in the work of the university. The focus of such activities might be garden walks, science and discovery, art and artists, or any other theme in which the public will be interested. Undergraduate students are placed at strategic points across campus to direct people. Advertisements and maps are distributed to schools and placed in newspapers. Faculty members put together special exhibits geared to the interests of young people. Hands-on experiences are featured wherever possible. Events such as this pay many dividends and are well worth the effort.

Special Events

Occasionally a special opportunity will come along for connecting the public to the university in favorable ways. An example on the author's campus occurred when a faculty member in the geological sciences was approached about hosting an international dinosaur event. For a modest investment, the university would be able to exhibit a huge collection of dinosaur fossils and host a symposium. A window in the calendar was found when the university's activity center would be available for about twenty consecutive days (so the massive exhibit could be left in place for the entire period), and the event was scheduled. The event occupied the equivalent of more than two gymnasium floors and featured dinosaurs large and small, exhibited both in fossil and robotic form. The largest came from China and was almost ninety feet long from head to tail. Over eighty thousand people attended the exhibit over a two-week period. Schoolchildren, families, and adults who had never been to the campus were drawn by this event and left with a very favorable impression. Such opportunities do not come along often, but when they do they should be exploited.

Documentaries

With the explosion of cable television, the demand for educational programming and documentaries has increased dramatically. In addition to public television, specialty channels in need of programming include *The Discovery Channel*, *The Learning Channel*, *The History Channel*, and *The Weather Channel* (to name a few). If the university has its own educational channel, its availability should be exploited to showcase the work of faculty. It is also worthwhile to develop programming ideas that feature faculty work (where one's faculty members are credibly numbered among the nation's leaders) and promote those ideas with those who produce such documentaries, in New York and Los Angeles. Successes do not come often here, but it is always wonderful to have one's faculty featured in the national media.

Printed Materials

In addition to regular alumni publications, many colleges and universities have special research magazines. Such publications are typically published quarterly, are extremely well done, and are mailed to people important to the university. Deans should work with chairs, members of their staffs, and the research office or news bureau to develop story ideas for these publications. This represents another important way for the research and teaching of the college to be showcased to an important external audience.

EXPANDING THE IMPACT OF RESEARCH

Thomas Jefferson described the work of universities as "unfettered inquiry." Research and creative endeavors need no justification beyond seeking to know or producing original works, but their impact can be expanded in several desirable ways. Deans should take steps to do so.

Involving Undergraduate Students

At many colleges and universities, great researchers may teach lower-division general education and upper-division major classes, but undergraduates are seldom given the chance to participate in the act of discovery. With the possible exception of small and highly selective institutions, it is impractical for a university to provide a research experience for every undergraduate and probably unwise to try. There is a segment of the undergraduate student body on every campus, however, that should be exposed to such opportunities. When serious undergraduate students spend time with faculty as they engage in their research and creative activities, the result can be transformative. An ancient proverb states: "The mind is a fire to be lighted, not a vessel to be filled." Participating in work at the frontiers of a discipline, helping create new knowledge, and seeing things for the first time present special learning moments that should be exploited. Deans should therefore to find ways to extend the impact of research by increasing the involvement of undergraduates with faculty engaged in the process of discovery.

Economic Development

It is popular to say that we are entering an age of a new economy, a knowledge-based economy where new wealth is created by new technology that is inspired by new ideas. Universities are seen as important drivers of economic development, because they foster the generation of new ideas. This may sound great, but in truth most universities are not oriented toward the conversion of ideas to new wealth-producing industries. There are many reasons for this. Many areas of inquiry are not likely to lead to useful applications. Even in areas where new ideas and discoveries might lead to product development, university patenting and licensing policies are often obstacles. Finally, the typical faculty member does not know how to go about moving from making a discovery to starting a business. Even if a faculty member wants to try to start up a company, his or her colleagues generally discourage such activity.

These obstacles are significant, but many are being removed. Some states have earmarked monies for research in specific areas that hold promise for stimulating economic development. Many universities are changing their intellectual property, patenting, and licensing policies to facilitate the exploitation of discoveries. A few institutions have worked with their communities to improve discoverers' access to service providers. These providers typically include (1) experts to evaluate the feasibility of developing a commercially viable product or service from the discovery, (2) advisors to help in writing a business plan, and (3) access to business support (legal, accounting, advertising, venture capital, financial, real estate, architectural, human resources, consulting, and community services). In the absence of these changes in policy and forms of help, there is little chance that faculty members with ideas/discoveries that might hold promise for new products or services will be able to form successful companies that contribute to wealth creation.

As the commercialization of research by universities grows, deans will be exposed to some terms that have not been commonly used in academe. Several of the more basic terms and their definitions are provided below.

Intellectual Property, or IP

The phrase "intellectual property" traditional dealt primarily with literary and artistic works protected by copyright. In more current usage, the phrase also includes intangible products of the intellect of inventors, such as designs and concepts, inventions, new technologies, software, and genetically engineered microorganisms that are licensable or patentable.

Venture Capital, or VC

Sometimes also referred to as "risk capital," VC is money committed at considerable risk by investors to support an undertaking that has the potential for extraordinary profitability. In the past, most public colleges and universities could not take equity positions in scientists' discoveries that might be commercialized and become profitable. It is now becoming common for institutions of all types to put up venture capital for promising discoveries.

Licensing

A license grants formal permission to do something. If a college or university holds a patent on an invention, other parties are legally excluded from making, offering for sale, or selling the protected item without first obtaining a license from the institution (as holder of the patent). The terms of licenses vary, but they usually include a fixed initial financial commitment—it may be paid in installments or in a lump sum—and a percentage of any profits that are derived from the sale of the licensed product.

Royalties

Royalties represent a share of proceeds paid to the owner of a right, such as a holder of a patent or copyright. Some colleges and universities generate a significant portion of their annual operating expenses from royalties, but most institutions currently receive almost no royalty income.

It seems clear that the future will hold an expanded role for universities as drivers of the new economy. The cautions covered in this section are not meant to be discouraging. Rather, they are offered to guide the dean in helping his or her institution (1) create a policy environment that is more conducive to the generation of profits from discoveries, and (2) work with the local entrepreneurial community to facilitate faculty access to the necessary resources.

Research Foundations and Incubators

Another approach to the exploitation of ideas and discoveries is the use of research foundations unconnected with the university and "incubators" that nurture new ventures through the critical early years. Foundations can invest in and receive profits from companies that spin off from university discoveries. (In many states, public institutions cannot hold ownership in such companies, although federal restrictions on such ownership were removed by the Bayh-Dole Act of 1980.) Being at arm's length from the university, such foundations can facilitate the development of newly formed companies and collect monies should the venture become profitable. Money thus generated can be used to support more entrepreneurial efforts or be funneled back to the university.

Incubators provide somewhat sheltered and supportive environments for new ventures in their early years. They typically provide space, funding, and support services. At some point the new venture has to move out into the real world or be abandoned. Probably only a small percentage of ventures that start in an incubator survive to become thriving companies. However, some of the companies that eventually flourish would not have survived without the support they received in the early critical years.

Faculty research is important to deans in all institutions of higher learning. At many universities, research productivity is the primary factor by which tenure and promotion decisions are made. For deans in major research institutions, program rankings, external funding, and faculty productivity occupy a place of even greater importance. Successful deans seek to facilitate, promote, publicize, leverage, and exploit, for economic and instructional benefit, the research and creative activities of the faculty. The pursuit of ideas is fundamental to university life; therefore, deans should be attentive to the many factors that will require their attention in this important area.

NOTE

1. E. L. Boyer, *Scholarship Reconsidered* (Princeton, N.J.: Carnegie Foundation for the Advancement of Teaching, 1990).

CHAPTER 10

The Life of the College

At the most basic level, a college is merely an organizational necessity—the university must be broken into coherent units to be managed effectively. At some institutions a college is little more than this—a place where permissions are sought, approvals are granted or denied, and differences are adjudicated. There is little energy or excitement if that is all there is to the life of a college. It is the dean's job to develop a sense of community among the often disparate elements that make up a college.

There are many things a dean can do to help a college to be more viable, more significant, and more complete. Many of those things have been covered in other chapters; these events offered by a college give special meaning to many of its activities. One of the dean's roles is to be the master of ceremonies at such events. The importance of events in the life of the college warrants a chapter devoted to this topic.

Events serve many purposes. Some are offered as part of the college's development and fund-raising efforts; some are part of more general efforts at outreach. Some events honor faculty, staff, students, or alumni. Other events celebrate student accomplishments. Events can serve to thank individuals for their efforts and to develop a sense of stewardship and teamwork. Events can also be hosted that bring the college to a regional or national stage. Each event serves one or more purposes, and each enriches the life of the college.

What kinds of events do colleges typically offer? What are some examples of such events? What is their purpose? The following sections describe a rich set of events that bring attention, meaning, and purpose to many of the college's activities.

DEVELOPMENT EVENTS

Significant gifts to the college need to be recognized in appropriate ways. When a gift leads to the construction of a new facility, for example, it is customary to hold a dedication. Such events normally involve the donors, appropriate university officials, and guests. There is generally a program and a reception, as well as, often, a more private lunch or dinner hosted by the dean for the donor and a few special guests.

When the gift is an endowment, it is traditional to have a lunch or dinner. The university typically presents an attractive memento to the donor to commemorate the gift. If individuals supported by (or to be supported by) the endowments are available, they are normally present as well. Following the meal there is a small program to make the awards and tell the story of the gift.

REACHING OUT TO THE COMMUNITY

When the college "takes its show on the road" or invites friends and sponsors to the campus for special events meant to connect to the broader community, it is offering outreach events. These can take many forms or be called by a variety of names, such as "Meet the Author," "The XXX Memorial Lecture," "The International Wine Tasting Festival," "The XXX Archaeological Tour," "The XXX Institute Grand Opening," "The [college] Leadership Breakfast" (for local CEOs who are graduates of the college), "The Launch of XXX" (say, an interplanetary mission), "The XXX Reception and Exhibition," or "The Saturday Scholars Program." In each case external friends and potential friends are invited to university events. Sometimes these events are planned specifically for the purpose of outreach; in other cases the activity would occur with or without an outreach component. If the event is an exciting one, such as to mark the launch of a spacecraft that will carry the university's instruments to another planet, the dean would be remiss not to bring members of the public into the excitement of university research.

COLLEGE EVENTS

All of the events described in this chapter are college events, but many serve narrow purposes. Some events represent annual collegiate activities that are part of a tradition. Examples of events offered by colleges at various universities are graduation convocations, homecoming alumni gatherings, holiday receptions, annual distinguished-graduate leadership forums, a student awards convocation, emeriti faculty luncheons, faculty/staff socials, welcome dinners/receptions for new faculty, dinners for student national award winners, annual promotion and tenure dinners. This may seem like a lot of events, yet each serves a valuable purpose, and each contributes to the strength of the college. These events celebrate the many forms of success that are achieved by the students, faculty, staff, and graduates of the college. They remind us why we do what we do and why it is important.

STUDENT EVENTS

Some of the events mentioned above focus on students (the graduation and awards convocations), but other events might be offered that serve student interests. Included here are fairly narrowly focused awards events (such as creative writing awards), student career days, private time with visiting dignitaries, and welcomes for students and their parents as they arrive on campus at the beginning of the fall semester. These events serve a variety of purposes. Some acknowledge student achievement, some bring students together with potential employers, and some give students a chance to be in a seminar setting with famous individuals who have come to campus to deliver major public lectures but are willing to spend time in a classroom talking with students. Undergraduate research symposia, at which students make poster presentations, are becoming more popular at universities that encourage research as part of the undergraduate experience.

Parents especially appreciate events that welcome their students to campus. If the campus calendar permits such an event, each department ought to prepare an exhibit. The dean can make welcoming remarks, respond to questions from parents or students, and invite everyone to a reception where the exhibits can be viewed and representatives of each department make themselves available to answer more specific questions. Events such as these are remembered by students and create a favorable impression of the college.

FACULTY EVENTS

When it comes to faculty loyalties, many university administrators assert that a faculty member's first loyalty is (not necessarily should be) to his or her profession, next to the department, then to the college or university. What makes a faculty member feel that he or she is part of the college? Participation in college activities and events is helpful in this regard. Some of the college events identified above are oriented toward faculty (the new faculty and faculty promotion dinners), but there are other events a college might consider providing for faculty. Many campuses have orientation events, receptions, and even fully paid statewide tours for new faculty. Lunches scheduled well into the academic year can help the dean discover (as discussed in an earlier chapter) what it is like for new faculty to adjust to their new setting. Faculty members also appreciate receptions that recognize service milestones and retirements. Most colleges also give annual awards for teaching, mentoring, research, service, advising, and other activities. These awards should be given at an event that is consistent in tone with the significance of these accomplishments.

ADMINISTRATIVE EVENTS

If the dean hopes to develop a sense of camaraderie among members of his or her staff and the many chairs and directors who make up the college's administrative team, he or she should arrange special events for this group and their spouses, partners, or guests. Some deans have an annual holiday dinner, in December. Others have an event at the end of the academic year. The idea is to recognize the importance of the service provided by members of the team and to thank their spouses and partners for making the sacrifices demanded of those who are close to individuals holding leadership appointments.

Another common event is an annual administrative retreat. Typically the daytime portion of such event includes only the chairs, directors, and members of the dean's staff, but dinner in the evening includes spouses and partners. These events lead to closer acquaintances that often result in new and lasting professional friendships. Over time, the sense of family that develops among chairs and directors can play an important role in instilling concern for the greater good of the college. It is only when this deeper sense of responsibility is developed that chairs and directors are able to operate at the highest levels of effectiveness.

STAFF EVENTS

Colleges and universities are hierarchies, of which members of the staff are often forgotten and unappreciated members. The dean has to take steps to ensure that this is not the case. Events for staff can serve to remind members of the college of the importance of the support staff. There is a nationally observed "Secretaries Day," which should be observed even though few members of a university's staff are now called "secretaries." Many colleges and universities have leadership academies and other staff development programs. Milestones of service and promotion need to be recognized and celebrated.

Employee recognition receptions held during normal work hours are always appreciated by members of the staff (assuming they are allowed to attend). These events can occur during the holidays or in conjunction with ceremonies that recognize milestones of service and retirement. Appreciation receptions and luncheons are appropriate, as are special events for award winners. Deans should encourage their chairs and directors to nominate deserving members of their staffs for awards given out by the university. Some administrators are very inattentive to such opportunities and need to be reminded of their importance.

HOSTING EVENTS THAT DRAW PEOPLE FROM ELSEWHERE

Occasions arise for the college to host events to be attended by individuals from elsewhere. These opportunities fall into two broad categories: academic events and other special events. In a typical year a number of faculty members approach the dean to see if the college will host or co-host an academic meeting to be held either on campus or at a nearby hotel/conference center. The attraction of such activities is that they provide a wonderful chance to showcase the campus to academics from elsewhere. With so much attention being given to reputation and opinion surveys, it never hurts to have faculty members from other institutions as guests among whom a favorable impression might be created.

In deciding whether or not to host (or co-host) such events the dean should gather some information. It is good to know what previous institutions have hosted the event. A call to the deans of colleges where several of the most recent took place will be useful. Ask to see the budgets of the past few meetings and the proposed budget for the meeting that the college is being asked to host. Review those budgets to see if the costs seem reasonable and appropriate and to learn how the monies to be committed by the college are to be used. If the organizers plan to use the money for a reception featuring alcohol, the college may have to use precious private monies. It is also good to know if the meeting represents the major annual event of an academic professional organization or is a special meeting to be held once. When the dean has a good sense of cost and potential benefits, he or she can make a decision.

A word of caution is in order. Word will get out if the college hosts such an event, and others within the college will be emboldened to make similar requests. This represents another case where guiding principles are very useful in ensuring that such requests are handled in an equitable manner. After fielding several such requests the dean should have a good feel for the kinds of principles that make sense. Put the principles in writing and make them generally available to units in the college. These will help faculty members appreciate the college's approach to handling such requests and will filter out those that exceed the boundary conditions.

Each dean will have to select principles that fit his or her situation. Items that might serve as the basis for principles will differ greatly from place to place. Some of these variables include the budgetary health of the college, the attractiveness of the campus as a location for meetings, the restrictions on monies that might be used, and likelihood that those seeking support will be effective hosts.

The second type of event—"other special events"—that can attract individuals from elsewhere can take many forms. Several examples from the author's experience are described below. In each case there was a compelling college interest that warranted the commitment of time and resources.

Meetings of College Deans

It is common for deans (representing similar colleges) from members of athletic conferences or states or regions to gather annually at a hosting institution. Sometimes such meetings are held at the same location (the Big Ten deans meet in Chicago), but often the meetings rotate among participating institutions (the Pac Ten deans operate this way). In cases where the meetings rotate among campuses, an institution's turn to host the event will come up on a regular cycle. These events provide the chance to for the host institution to show off its highlights. As in the case of academic events, these opportunities can pay dividends in how people rate your campus on opinion surveys of reputation.

Other Target-of-Opportunity Meetings

There are national professional groups that like to meet on college campuses. One such group is the Council for the Advancement of Science Writing (the professional development arm of the National Association of Science Writers), which annually meets on one of this country's university campuses. How often does a college have a chance to have the science writers from the nation's leading newspapers and magazine periodicals as its guests? As in the other examples cited above, if a college manages to be chosen to host such a meeting, it has an unparalleled opportunity to get national exposure for its faculty, research, students, and programs.

There are many other attractive targets for the dean seeking to raise the visibility of his or her college by hosting events. The author's institution hosted such activities as the Southeast Asian Studies Summer Institute, the National Ethnic Studies Association, and the Medieval and Renaissance Studies Conference. The latter meeting was initiated by faculty of the college and became a very popular annual event.

Hosting events requires staff time and can involve significant expense. Events should therefore have a purpose, and the benefits should match or exceed the cost. If choosing between (a) doing many events poorly or on a tight budget and (b) doing a smaller number of events with class, one should always err toward the latter, hosting only as many events as one can afford to carry off in a first-class fashion. Events that are lacking in taste, sincerity, or quality can do more harm than good.

A new dean will inherit a package of events that have been put on by the college. The dean should review the events, determine their purpose, try to assess if they have been effective, and discover if they are important to institutional traditions. He or she must determine what the budget will allow and then plan to hold as many high-quality events as can be afforded. They will add significantly to the life of the college.

CHAPTER 11

Other Aspects of the Deanship

The preceding chapters have identified some of the major areas of responsibility facing the college dean. This chapter gives attention to some of the many other aspects of the job. Included here are some thoughts about new activities that deans are taking on in the colleges they lead, and about relationships with peers and supervisors. Also included are the special topics of strategic planning, facilities, and space. Each section provides an overview and offers insights on how the dean can achieve maximum effectiveness.

NEW AREAS OF CONCERN FOR DEANS

The nature of college deanships altered little during much of the twentieth century, but there are many who believe that the dean's portfolio is now changing in significant ways. Clearly, the addition of fund-raising responsibilities has significantly altered the deanship in recent years, especially in public colleges and universities. Several other trends are emerging and influencing the portfolios of some deans.

External Councils

It has been common for professional schools to have friends groups, often called "advisory groups" or "dean's councils." Institutions with friends groups are moving away from the use of the word "advisory," because such councils infer from it that part of their role is to give advice, when in fact such advice might not be welcome. Nonetheless, the creation of dean's councils for colleges of all types is now much more common than was once the case.

What is the purpose of such councils, and how do they work? Typically, the council is created with a number of outcomes in mind. Some of the more common goals include:

1. Raising money for scholarships or discretionary use (this money comes from annual membership fees, which range from five hundred dollars a year upward)
2. Building advocacy groups to be used with legislatures, donors, and others who might be helpful to the college
3. Connecting to community, business, and professional leaders and increasing their familiarity with the college (this allows them to speak with knowledge and authority about the college and thus to serve as ambassadors)
4. Developing a core of volunteers to help with the recruitment of talented students (council members are often very effective recruiters)
5. Providing access to potential donors with whom the college has no direct connection
6. Helping with such special projects as raising funds for a new wing of a building or a new mediated-learning laboratory
7. Providing a vehicle for building a network of influential individuals who will benefit from knowing one another

Dean's councils can and do serve many other purposes. At their best they can be very helpful to the dean and his or her college; at their worst such councils can take the dean's time and accomplish little good. In forming such councils it is important to (a) be clear about the purposes for which they are being formed, (b) have a leadership structure (with rules for turnover) for the group, and (c) have specific projects in which the members can be engaged. It is also important to plan a series of programs that help council members become acquainted with the college, its faculty, and its students. If these basic organizational elements are addressed, there is an excellent chance that the dean's council will make a positive difference. The dean's life, however, will have become more complex, since such a group requires attention if it is going to be effective.

Media Relations

Universities have offices that handle media relations, but colleges typically have not had personnel of their own dedicated to this area. This is changing, especially in the larger universities. There are vast differences between having one's own media relations person and relying on the university's news bureau. A typical news bureau must cover the entire university and divide its time between developing releases on what it determines are potentially interesting or important informative stories and crafting institutional responses during periodic crises. News bureau staff do not have time to become well acquainted with students and faculty; they have neither the time nor the inclination to develop stories with certain goals or messages in mind; they seldom develop a good feel for which news outlets might be interested in specific stories; and they have no sense of the value of seeking national attention for the work of the faculty.

A media relations specialist hired directly by and for a college can overcome all of the shortcomings of the typical university news bureau. In the author's experience, the addition of a specialist in the college dramatically increases the media's coverage of college activities, brings far greater national attention to new discoveries and breakthroughs by the faculty, greatly enhances success in getting stories out that carry messages one wants conveyed, and improves the faculty's sophistication in dealing with the media.

It is an unpleasant fact of academic life that colleges must be more aggressive than was once necessary in telling their stories. If a dean wishes to increase media coverage of the many wonderful things that are occurring in his or her college, adding a specialist to the dean's staff will make a dramatic difference. It will also create one more demand on the dean's time. If circumstances allow, however, this is time well spent.

University-Industry Liaison

As noted in chapter 9, on research, it has become common for universities to embark on special initiatives intended to promote research that holds promise for stimulating economic development. This, of course, is more easily said than done. One never knows with any degree of certainty which lines of inquiry are most promising. Also, the cultures of universities and business could hardly be more different. Further, as we have noted, university licensing, patenting, and intellectual property policies often create insurmountable barriers to potential faculty entrepreneurs. Clearly, universities, as we saw, have much to learn when it comes to being drivers of the new economy.

One step that some colleges are taking is to hire individuals to bridge the gap between the university and business or industry. Such an individual is often called an "industrial liaison." For such a position one typically hopes to attract an individual who has spent significant time in the business sector, preferably with some experience in research and development, licensing and patenting, product development, and management. Such an individual can learn about the university and become acquainted with the research directions being pursued. The individual can help connect faculty with ideas, discoveries, breakthroughs, and new technologies to companies or investors who might wish to purchase rights or enter a partnership with discoverers so that the ideas can be pushed toward new product development.

As in the examples above, adding such an individual to the dean's staff means one more person to supervise and an expanded set of activities to be encouraged. A few successes here, however, would more than cover the time and expense invested. If the college is engaged in research of the sort that may lead to exploitable discoveries, the dean may wish to add this new position to the staff, while providing the individual chosen with a clear set of expectations (to be used for accountability and performance assessment).

FACILITIES AND SPACE

A university president once remarked, "Every university in the country has less space than its peers!" One would be hard-pressed to find any department or college in any university that believes it had adequate space. External visitors conducting unit reviews for accreditation or general evaluation almost always observe that space is heavily utilized and recommend that more space be assigned to the unit. There are few deans who serve their term without dealing with issues pertaining to space.

Policies on the assignment of space vary from campus to campus. At some institutions all space is "university" space and is assigned by a central coordinator. Some places have mixed models, wherein office and laboratory space are "owned and controlled" by departments but classrooms are controlled and scheduled centrally. A small number of colleges and universities are highly decentralized, with all space controlled by individual academic units.

Unless the dean thinks about space in a comprehensive way, he or she will be left trying to make decisions on an ad hoc basis, with little knowledge about general conditions regarding the use of space under his or her span of control. A better approach is to have the college's space-utilization practices studied, so that a basic understanding can be developed about how decisions are made and space is currently allocated. Such reviews normally reveal a state of chaos. Some space decisions will have been based on historical precedent, some on seniority, some on productivity, some on good timing, some on friendships, some on intimidation, some on safety, some on useful adjacencies, and the rest on dozens of other rational and irrational bases. Some units will be relatively space rich and others space poor. Some will have new space; some will be housed in old space in need of repair. Some departments will have single, 250-square-foot offices for faculty, while others can provide only shared, 180-square-foot offices. Some units will have student, staff, and faculty lounges and generous, comfortable public space; other units will be housed in "temporary" portable buildings (temporary more accurately describes the expected life of the building than the length of the residency). The inequities will be vast and not easily addressed.

Once informed about space, the dean should take at least two proactive steps. First, he or she should develop some principles to guide the allocation and assignment of space, in consultation with the chairs, directors, and faculty leadership of the college. (An example of such a set of guidelines is provided in appendix I.) Once approved, these guidelines will provide the basis for a more uniform management space, an improvement in space utilization, and a decrease in squabbles over space assignments.

Second, the dean should meet with those on campus who develop the capital development plan to learn what projects are in the building queue or are being considered for the college. The dean should work with these officers to ensure that the college's needs are understood and that the college's projects are given the highest possible priority. It is by taking these two proactive steps that the short-term and long-term space issues of a college are best addressed.

MANAGEMENT TRENDS

The dean may find it distasteful to think of him- or herself as a manager, but a significant portion of the dean's leadership task is effective management. There are hundreds of books about management, but few of them are based on the unique environment of higher education. Watching highly effective deans, however, reveals certain valuable habits, practices, and approaches. The most obvious and basic things have been identified in earlier sections; the items that appear below are neither as fundamental or universal, but they are important.

Move Quickly to Seize Opportunities

Most colleges have plans and priorities. These are useful in bringing order and direction. One can be almost certain, however, that unexpected opportunities will present themselves. The dean is then faced with a choice: pass up the opportunity because it was not part of the plan or find a way to seize the opportunity. What should the dean do? Special opportunities come along infrequently. Every effort should be made to exploit them.

Perhaps a faculty member of great distinction contacts one of your unit heads and expresses an interest in joining your university. Hire him/her! Perhaps you have advertised a position and have three wonderful protected-class members as finalists. Hire all of them! Perhaps you learn that a famous institute is looking for a new home. Move it and all of its personnel to your college! The author was faced with each of these opportunities, exploited each one, and never regretted any.

Keep Your Best Even as You Try to Attract the Best

Colleges and universities fill new positions by conducting national searches with the goal of attracting the very best individual available. There is nothing wrong with this approach, but it is interesting to observe that far more energy goes into trying to attract new talent than goes into retaining the best faculty already employed. As noted toward the end of chapter 6, on faculty, all institutions have faculty members who are impossible to replace—the "difference makers." A dean should know who these individuals are and work with chairs to do what is necessary to keep them with the university. Other institutions know these individuals and will recruit them. Take proactive steps to retain them.

Excellence Should Be Your Standard

In times of tight budgets, colleges and universities are often forced to settle for suboptimal arrangements. Perhaps class sizes have to be increased. It may be necessary to reduce the number of laboratory sessions required to fulfill hands-on experience objectives. Additional classes may have to be taught by part-time faculty associates. Field trips may have to be canceled. Each of these steps erodes quality. An institution sometimes carelessly finds a new equilibrium, losing sight of the fact that backsliding has occurred. The dean should always be in contact with peer institutions, identifying benchmarks of excellence and working to reach or exceed those benchmarks of excellence. Adequacy may be acceptable to some, but for a college with any ambition, excellence should be the goal.

Do Not Forget Your Basic Mission

It may seem hard to imagine, but institutions are sometimes so focused on new issues that they are inattentive to their core activities. This is analogous to putting new windows in a home but ignoring the foundation. Colleges and universities are constantly faced with new issues. New efforts at outreach, mediated instruction, distance learning, and research focused on economic development are trendy now, but other ideas will come along to replace them. The core activity of the university is discovery and learning through the pursuit of ideas. Even as the dean urges attention to new initiatives, he or she should remember the college's core functions and competencies and take steps to see that they continue to be both honored and nurtured.

The dean should never take for granted that faculty members understand this. If the dean announces a new initiative to encourage the use of technology in instruction without reinforcing the enduring value of proven approaches, some people will think that the only forms of teaching that will be rewarded in the future are those featuring technology. Unless this is what the dean actually seeks, encouragement of new approaches must always be accompanied by the reinforcement of traditional approaches that are good.

Reshape or Evolve Rather than Eliminate

Periods of budgetary hardship and constraint lead many institutions to conduct painful exercises that lead to the elimination of whole sets of things. (These are sometimes referred to as "vertical cuts.") When faced with the same difficulty, other institutions take every opportunistic cut that is presented and then make up the difference in what is needed to meet the reduced budget by applying an across-the-board budget reduction. (These are often referred to as "horizontal cuts.") Which is better? More often than not, vertical cuts lead to great despair and little permanent savings. In the typical case a decision is made to eliminate (for example) the School of Journalism, the Department of Family Resources, and the marching band. The institution is inundated with angry letters from alums, crucified in the local media, and taken to task by important friends (legislators, business leaders, donors, and professionals) who have some connection to the groups to be eliminated. When an institution waivers on its decision, the campus becomes distrustful and cynical. Eliminating the least central or important programs or activities often seems to present an easy way out of a budget reduction problem, but it is seldom the best solution.

A far better strategy—one that is seldom adopted by novices—is to start by making every cut for which opportunity arises. This means not filling vacant positions, even if they occur in high-priority areas. It may mean deferring maintenance or not opening a new building (which would incur new operating costs). It will also mean reducing all budgets by some amount. Everyone suffers a little, but no entire programs are threatened with elimination and no one loses his or her job. The university's priorities are not revealed by what is cut; the reductions are blind to priorities. The university's priorities are revealed instead by where the university reinvests when better times return.

Seasoned administrators know that the second strategy is better and usually take this approach if possible. They think of the choice of methods as analogous to an individual trying to lose weight—he or she can diet (losing a little weight everywhere) or cut off an arm. This is not a difficult choice. The process of trimming the university by making opportunistic cuts, making the necessary across-the-board reduction, and then adding back to priority areas when budgets improve is a way to reshape the university. In this way budget adversity may allow changes to be made that would be more difficult to accomplish in better times. There may be things that are outdated, no longer relevant and not worth remodeling; they should be eliminated no matter what the state of the budget. For difficult budget times, however, the lesson for deans is simple: reshape rather than eliminate.

Invest in Technology for the Right Reasons

Universities have become heavily invested in technology, but they often make decisions based on false assumptions. The higher education investment in technology is already staggering, and it is growing. A significant portion of the initial investment at many institutions was made with the expectation that new technology would change the scalability rules for instruction, resulting in wonderful new efficiencies. It turns out that distance-learning technology produces decent completion rates for credit coursework only when things that are inherently not scalable are provided, such as regular interaction with a faculty member, regular assignments and feedback, the opportunity to interact with classmates, and a method of testing that provides proof of identity of the individual doing the work. Despite the investment of hundreds of millions of dollars and years of study, technology has been able only to improve the quality of instruction, usually at a higher cost. Technology has not led to the hoped-for advances in instructional efficiency.

Connectivity, communication, and the quality of instruction all have been improved by technology. New approaches to instruction and new possibilities for learning have been made possible because of technology. Many campus-based students enjoy taking part of their coursework through distance technology, and campuses have extended their reach by using a variety of media to take coursework to place-bound and time-limited individuals.

Deans should watch the trends here, because this area is still new and changing rapidly. Investments should be made based on what one knows can be accomplished through new technology, not on what people imagine can be done. Paying attention to the difference will reshape how money is spent and will result in savings over what would be spent in a less attentive mode.

Be Responsive in Appropriate Ways

Colleges and universities exist to fulfill a societal need. To the extent that academic institutions are appropriately responsive to those needs, they will be appreciated and supported. A college or university that is inattentive to the demand for its services is asking for difficulty. In an area when accountability is always under question, a university should strive to provide appropriate services in ways that cause it to be seen as indispensable. This does not mean responding to every demand or meeting every need. Colleges and universities are equipped to do certain things but are ill suited for many other things. The dean must encourage and provide incentives for faculty to give attention to those things that are basic to its mission and for which the institution is well suited. If the university is responding fully to the community's needs with which its services and competencies are congruent, it will indeed be seen as indispensable.

Form Partnerships and Alliances

The world of work is becoming a more collaborative place. Higher education has been slow to pick up on this trend, although governing boards and legislators have been forcing change in this area. There are dozens of ways to collaborate with other organizations. Some colleges and universities package their distance-learning offerings together. Others bundle emerging, related technologies to make them more attractive for development by corporations. In urban areas, institutions of higher learning cooperate in trying to find positions for both members of dual-career academic pairs. Public and private institutions sometimes work together to help address specific local problems, such as teacher or nurse shortages. Partnerships and alliances are becoming more common in higher education. Deans should be attentive to opportunities to partner with other groups, for the benefit of all.

Protect Existing Competitive Advantages and Develop New Ones

What makes one's institution attractive to students? Where is the college most competitive for research funding? Which employers are most attracted to your graduates? Each institution will have areas of advantage and areas of disadvantage. Deans should work to protect and exploit any area of advantage and to develop new ones. Perhaps an honors program makes the institution especially attractive to high-achieving students. Perhaps being located in what is known to be a great college town draws many students. The presence of unique facilities and a special collection of faculty expertise may make competitiveness for federal funds greater than that of other schools.

Sometimes the dean can see a new opportunity developing and take steps to exploit it. A good example from the author's experience came a few years ago when a new research program was announced by a federal agency. The request for proposals (RFP) indicated that five universities would be selected to be the "founding" institutions to head this new research effort. In business, companies like to develop a new product and have 100 percent of the market initially; they have the lead, with market share to lose. This is far better than getting to something late, when others have 100 percent of the market, and trying to break in for some small share of the existing market. The following is a similar case, but in an area that has significant research funding.

The university already had some strength in the area and additional strengths in related areas, but it was clear that to be competitive for one of the coveted places as a founding institution, we needed to be stronger. After careful study, two extremely talented individuals were hired into the research group, one from UCLA and one from the Jet Propulsion Laboratory. With these new additions, the college was selected to be one of the five founding university members of the group. This particular story illustrates both the importance of exploiting competitive advantages and of taking advantage of opportunities, even if they are nowhere in the strategic plan.

Be on the Lookout for New Revenues and Potential Savings

Colleges and universities seem always to be struggling with their budgets. This may be because there are always ways that quality can be enhanced. There are two approaches to the budget: (a) use whatever resources are available to do as much as is possible, or (b) look for ways to achieve savings and generate new revenues, thereby stretching what is possible by increasing the pool or resources and using it more wisely. As higher education evolves there are always opportunities for savings or for reallocating existing resources in better ways. Some large universities tax every college a certain small percentage each year (1 to 2 percent is common), requiring that an amount of money equal to this proportion of their base be returned to a central pool for reinvestment. This allows a university to continually reshape itself by investing in new ideas.

Savings can also be realized by changes in the support needs of faculty. A good example from the last decade of the twentieth century is the conversion to PC use. The use of word-processing software and e-mail by faculty members themselves significantly reduced the need for many traditional forms of clerical and secretarial support. Often positions can be left vacant when someone retires or resigns. Alternatively, staff needs can be reviewed using a "blank slate" approach, asking how one might staff an office if there were no history. If the ideal staffing is substantially different from the current arrangement, perhaps a formal reorganization is in order. At many institutions, employees filling positions that are no longer needed can be released through reorganization (although more typically they are reassigned to positions for which they are better suited).

Finding new revenue streams is more challenging. Some deans have been successful in generating new monies by changing the way they operate their summer sessions. At some colleges and universities, teaching in the summer is a "perk," and assignments are given based on seniority. This practice typically produces low-enrollment classes taught by expensive faculty and seldom produces any profit. By changing policies to increase class sizes (and thereby revenue generation) and by restricting costs, a large college can annually generate as much as a million dollars in profits. Such monies typically go into a local fund to be used by the college for discretionary uses.

Other sources of new revenue include such things as distance education, royalties on patents, fees on licenses, event ticket sales, and funds raised from private sources. Increasing sponsored research helps, but the impact is usually more limited, since the monies are targeted and certain deliverables must be produced. (As noted in chapter 9, indirect cost monies generated by research can sometimes be used for general purposes, depending on how the costs of research administration are actually covered.)

LEGAL MATTERS

Higher-education organizations operate within a framework of federal and state laws and constitutional provisions, executive orders, governing board guidelines, and campus-specific policies and procedures. It is important for anyone assuming a deanship to become familiar with the legal and procedural environment as it pertains to the operation of an academic unit. A national meeting for university administrators that is especially helpful on aspects of law that apply to higher education is the Law and Higher Education conference sponsored by the Stetson College of Law and held each February in Clearwater Beach, Florida.

Decanal professional organizations will also provide a session or two on specific legal issues as part of their annual meetings. Such organizations will also, on occasion, offer a special seminar for deans and the law.

The office of general counsel on one's campus will also have materials useful to the dean and to other administrators. Typically, some of this information will be universal in its application, and some will be specific to one's state, university system, and campus.

One could write an entire book on the legal aspects of university administration. This section attempts to acquaint the reader with those points of law and policy that are most critical for deans. The discussion serves as an overview and as a guide for directing additional study. It is not meant to serve as an exhaustive treatment of any of the topics addressed.

Employment Law

Employment law is probably the legal area of greatest concern for the academic dean. Typically, over 80 percent of a college budget is devoted to personnel. The employment of the college workforce, therefore, is a major activity for the dean and other members of his or her administrative team. The major areas of employment law are these.

Contracts

Included here are written contracts, letters of offer, notices of appointment, and other written documents that are seen in the eyes of the law as legally binding contracts. Have the university's legal office review any document containing contract provisions about which there is any uncertainty. Most colleges and universities have model letters with language that must appear in letters of offer.

Policies

The provisions contained in policy and procedure manuals create contract rights for the employee and the employer. Such manuals should be referenced regularly and applied consistently.

Due Process

Due process is protected by the Fourteenth Amendment to the U.S. Constitution and applies in cases such as termination, demotion, and suspension where the removal of a property right may occur. In the typical case the university must show "good cause" for such action, must provide "notice" of a hearing to consider the action, and must hold a "hearing" that follows the norms of the institution. Due-process requirements apply to all employees who serve under work arrangements that anticipate continued employment (and thus constitute a "property right").

Progressive Discipline

This concept goes by different names, but in most personnel systems, members of the support staff who are not performing in a satisfactory manner must undergo "progressive" discipline before termination, suspension, or demotion proceedings can be initiated. Progressive discipline involves first documenting shortcomings with the employee, initially verbally through counseling by the supervisor (with a note to the file) and subsequently with written reprimands. The process varies from organization to organization and in union environments is often handled in a more structured manner. The purposes of progressive discipline are: (a) to ensure that the employee has clear information about the areas of substandard performance and what it takes to make the performance acceptable, and that they are provided with time to work on the shortcomings; and (b) to document the nature of the performance deficiencies so "due cause" can be shown if additional steps must be taken.

Whistle-Blower Protection

This protection is extended to employees who inform a supervisor of a violation of law, mismanagement or gross waste of funds, or abuse of authority by another employee of the institution. Whistle-blower protection means that the person is not to be retaliated against. Claims for such protection have become common on university campuses. Two critical questions are typically asked. First, if the employs suffers some adverse action, was it in retaliation for "blowing the whistle" with respect to an activity covered by the protection, or was it a result of nonrelated and coincidental factors? (It is not uncommon for an employee who sees harmful action coming his or her way—even if such action is warranted—to "blow the whistle" on something as a tactic in responding to the threat.) A second, more basic question is, "Was what was reported by the whistle blower something that is covered by the protection?" (Perhaps only a minor deviation from a policy or procedure has been reported. This may not confer whistle-blower protection.)

Affirmative Action Preferences

Court cases continue to shift what is permissible in acting affirmatively to achieve greater diversity. There are both federal and state aspects to issues of equal opportunity and affirmative action. (A comprehensive table showing the basis in law for federal provisions is provided in appendix J.) The provisions apply to the employment of members of protected classes and to the student admission and scholarship decisions.

Injury, Illness, and Leaves of Absence

Each state and institution has unique policies regarding sick leave, health-related leave, family leave, extended leave, compassionate transfer of leave, workers' compensation, alternative duty assignments, sabbatical leave, maternity leave, leaves with and without pay, and leaves covered by the state and federal laws. The requirements and interactions of five major categories of federal and state laws affect a university's leave policies and practices: the federal Family and Medical Leave Act (FMLA); state family and medical leave acts; the federal Americans with Disabilities Act of 1990 (ADA); state workers' compensation statutes; and miscellaneous federal legislation such as military service and jury-duty leave laws. The dean should review institutional policies regarding injury, illness, and leaves of absence so as to enforce existing laws and policies.

Conflicts of Interest

It is always good practice to avoid conflicts of interest in decision making. State laws govern deans in state colleges and universities; therefore, violation of conflict-of-interest rules may result in criminal prosecution. Each state employee is responsible for compliance with conflict of interest rules. Compliance typically features three requirements: the individual must be aware of the conflicts of interest requirements of state law, recognize situations where conflicts of interest exist, and take the required action in each situation featuring a conflict of interest. The normal action is to declare the conflict and recuse oneself, taking no part in the decision in question.

Employees and Students with Disabilities

Colleges and universities are subject to the provisions of the Rehabilitation Act of 1973 (Section 504) and the ADA. The general provisions of the acts specify, "No individual with a disability shall, by reason of such disability, be excluded from participation in or be denied the benefits of the services, programs or activities of a public entity, or be subjected to discrimination by any such entity." In the academic areas of the university, these guidelines refer to such activities as classroom instruction, academic advising, testing, field experiences, and access to materials required by instructors. It is the responsibility of a student to inform the university of any disabling condition if the student requests some modification that will allow participation. It is the university's responsibility to make reasonable accommodation for the student, although never lowering academic standards. Colleges and universities have elaborate procedures for handling the special challenges facing students with disabilities. The dean should be acquainted with such procedures and ensure that they are followed by the faculty and staff.

Political Activity

State-funded institutions must take care to ensure that its employees engage only in political activities that are permissible. Generally, a simple way to distinguish permissible activities from prohibited ones is to refrain from engaging in political activity on university time or with university resources or property. Political activities should be conducted on one's personal time and with one's own resources. University stationery and e-mail accounts should never be used for political activity.

Public Records

State-funded institutions are subject to the public records laws of their state. Such laws typically require that certain records be established and maintained. These laws also define what records fall under the definition of "public records" and provide ground rules for the retention and inspection of such records. One should learn what sorts of records are subject to review under the laws of his or her state. At a time when much correspondence occurs by e-mail, it is especially important to understand how such records can be used.

Student Records

Federal law allows students to access their educational records and limits the access of others to those records. The law is called the Family Educational Rights and Privacy Act (FERPA), or the Buckley Amendment. Records can be in any medium (such as electronic files, handwritten notes, paper files, e-mail, video- and audiotapes, microfilm, or microfiche). Colleges and universities typically establish processes for and limits on such activities as posting grades, handling requests for educational records by parents, public records requests, subpoenas, and disclosures.

Deans are often caught in a dilemma when a parent-financed student fails to give accurate information to the parent, who does not have access to the student's records. In an actual case the author was contacted late in the spring semester by an irate father (calling from halfway across the country) who could not imagine why we were keeping his daughter from graduating when she was in good standing and lacked only one credit hour of a foreign language to be eligible for graduation. A check of the records revealed that the student had not been enrolled for the past two years and was almost sixty credit hours short of graduation. She had been enjoying a two-year, parent-financed vacation, living just off campus in a private apartment.

What was the dean to do? The parent was called and told that he and his daughter needed to talk, because his understanding of the circumstances was not consistent with the facts. The father called back several days later to apologize, saying that he would never have called if he had known that his daughter was actually fifteen credits short of what was required for graduation! The student had told her gullible father yet another story.

UNRESOLVED ISSUES

At least three of the legal issues being tackled by colleges and universities are being driven not by law but by technology. In these cases an attempt is made to adopt reasonable policies that simultaneously protect the institution and serve employees and students. The first of these is determining permissible personal uses for institutionally purchased computers and Web access. The second is making provision for students to gain access to electronic materials and services that are integral to a class. The third has to do with copyright and ownership of materials developed by faculty using university technology and support systems. Policies among institutions vary widely in these three areas. The dean, however, is responsible for ensuring that whatever policies are currently in force are adhered to in the college.

This chapter may seem to consist of odds and ends, but that impression could not be further from the truth. Rather, the topics reviewed here reinforce the complexity of the dean's role and the reality that university administration is a complex, constantly evolving responsibility. The wise dean knows that he or she must keep learning to keep up and remain effective.

CHAPTER 12

Concluding Thoughts

Individuals serving as deans have a lot to learn before they can be fully effective. Time spent as a faculty member is invaluable in attending to the academic aspects of a deanship. A dean's administrative assignment, however, will require skills, abilities, and interests that are quite different from those of a faculty member. A deanship features new responsibilities, new relationships, new issues to be addressed, new perspectives, and the need for new knowledge and understanding. This book has been written to provide insight into the many aspects of academic leadership at the level of college dean.

A few messages bear repeating for emphasis. This book is not organized around a theoretical base, and it is not meant to be a "how to do it" book of prescriptions. This is a book that conveys ideas, perspectives, principles, and practices that worked at a specific time in a specific setting. This information will help the new dean come to his or her position better prepared to face the challenges of academic leadership. In each aspect of the job, he or she will be able to build from a stronger platform of basic information and ideas. The new dean will be better able to imagine the possibilities that are presented and will be more strongly positioned to act on them. Those actions will be appropriate for his or her institution at this time and place, not carbon copies drawn from this book or elsewhere.

The first line of this book observed that chance favors the prepared mind. This book should have prepared the reader's mind for effective academic leadership. Like the landscape photographs of Ansel Adams, the beauty of the progress produced by the rich mix of talent and opportunity of a college will be both pleasing to the eye and satisfying to the heart.

Best wishes for an enjoyable and productive deanship.

APPENDIX A:
Sample Administrative Retreat: Substantive Program Elements[1]

DEPARTMENT EVALUATION

(The dean served as discussion leader.)

How do departments compare? What are some outstanding examples of excellence in creating a quality learning environment, moving programs to national prominence, and being responsive to institutional needs? How can annual reports serve to inform and guide progress? What incentives might be appropriate to encourage change? Are there useful guidelines for choosing among conflicting priorities? Is the evaluation of individual faculty attentive to unit-level goals? What is the chair's role in enhancing department performance?

CHAIRS' CLINIC: LEADERSHIP CHALLENGES AS CHAIR

(Three chairs served as panelists.)

Students believe they are "customers" and expect to be satisfied. Each search for a new faculty member seems to involve a trailing partner. Departments are polarized on many issues. There is too little space, and there are too many needs for additional space. Deadlines blur as the upper administration asks for one report after another. A key secretary is out indefinitely due to an illness. Welcome to life as chair. Come prepared to pose questions to your administrative colleagues. Learn how others handle similar problems.

EVALUATION AND PLANNING DIRECTIONS

(Three chairs served as panelists.)

Each year more faculty and chair time seems to be devoted to program review, assessment, strategic planning, capital campaign planning and numerous commissions, task forces and ad hoc committee study efforts. What is the product of all these activities? Are recommendations ever implemented? What limits the usefulness of external advice? What outcome measures illustrate the unique advantages of a research university? How far into the future is it useful to plan? Is the legislative budget reform and reauthorization initiative another time sink? How can effort and benefits in evaluation and planning be kept in balance? What aspects of planning are most useful to units? What priorities should be centerpieces of college planning in the next several years?

A LIBERAL EDUCATION IN THE INFORMATION AGE

(Three chairs served as panelists.)

Historically, a liberal arts education was expected to develop habits of the mind that would allow an individual to think clearly, gather information reliably, and express him- or herself persuasively. The ways of knowing were developed through exposure to classical thought. The arts of understanding thereby acquired (the arts of inquiry, resolution, interpretation, evaluation, and communication) were seen as nonutilitarian, in that they contributed little to one's ability to do manual tasks.

In modern times, a liberal education serves a dual purpose: the development of cultural literacy and the development of habits of the mind that will allow an individual to move through a career and through life with ease and dignity.

Ironically, in the information age, skills that were formerly seen as nonutilitarian provide the best preparation one can receive for a majority of the upper level jobs in the world of work. Companies continue to hire specialists for special needs (accounts for accounting, engineers for engineering), but most positions in the world today are for nonspecialists. Employers need employees who have breadth and can learn, who can communicate effectively in writing and orally, who can adapt to the changing needs of life and work, who are capable of critical evaluation and reasoned thought, and who can work effectively with others. Education in the liberal arts provides an intellectual range and orientation that best prepares individuals for life and the world of work.

This sounds great, but do our programs deliver graduates with the knowledge, orientation, and skills we claim to deliver? Should exposure to the fine arts be required? Why isn't a course in speech/communication part of the B.A.? Access to information will occur increasingly by electronic means; are our graduates technologically literate? What changes in our current B.A./B.S. seem appropriate?

CONVERSATION WITH THE PROVOST

(The provost attended this session and led the discussion.)

National, state, local, and campus issues will be discussed in a wide-ranging conversation with the provost. What federal actions will affect higher education? Will state support for higher education grow, diminish, or remain stable? Are we headed for an era of greater legislative intrusiveness? Given the current makeup of the governing board, are significant policy swings expected to push the state universities in new directions? What is the status of capital campaign planning? Are new campuses going to be built using main campus resources? What agenda items will command campus attention next year? The provost will discuss these issues and respond to your questions.

CHAIR'S CLINIC: PERSONNEL

(Three chairs served as panelists.)

The department chair, being the one with line authority at the operational level, is usually the first administrative official to learn about difficult personnel matters. Education is a human enterprise; the interaction of students, staff, faculty, and administrators produces a myriad of problems in need of attention. If handled successfully in early stages by the chair, time-consuming reviews, grievances, lawsuits, and unwanted publicity can be avoided. If left unattended or poorly handled, personnel problems can take nasty and unpredictable turns. Learn from your colleagues as they react with first impressions and then join in the discussion of some actual (but disguised) cases from the college.

POST-TENURE REVIEW: ISSUES PERTAINING TO PROFESSIONAL DEVELOPMENT AND PERFORMANCE CONTRACTING

(The three panelists were individuals from the employee assistance program, the equal opportunity and affirmative action offices, and the office of general counsel.)

As we enter a new era of post-tenure review, honest evaluation and formal intervention will be required in all cases of less-than-satisfactory performance. How does one deal with unproductive faculty without being charged with unlawful discrimination, retaliation, violating academic freedom, ADA noncompliance, mean-spiritedness, or whatever else might come to the mind of the nonperforming faculty member? Panel members will offer preliminary observations about the use of professional development agreements and performance contracts and then respond to questions and discuss the problems encountered in actual cases.

ESTABLISHING A HEALTHY DEPARTMENT CLIMATE FOR STUDENTS

(The dean served as discussion leader.)

The Office of University Evaluation has been conducting exit interviews of graduating seniors. These students represent our successes and thus probably hold the most favorable views about us. What do these students say about the quality of instruction and advising, about the concern of faculty for students, about opportunities for interaction with faculty, about course availability? The survey instrument captures student opinions in a variety of areas pertaining to student academic life. What can be learned from units exhibiting the highest levels of student satisfaction?

INSTITUTIONAL PERFORMANCE AS SEEN BY PERFORMANCE MEASURES USED BY THE GOVERNING BOARD

(The discussion was led by the executive associate dean.)

The university's strategy in responding to concerns over the use of faculty time (and the threat of mandated teaching loads) has been to ask that authority for determining the distribution of faculty effort be left to the university. The result of this strategy has been a commitment to progress on a number of indicators of institutional performance (productivity). Two measures of particular concern are graduation rate and access of students to tenure track faculty. What is revealed by a three-year retrospective look at unit performance on these measures? What can be done to improve the college profile on these performance indicators?

NEW CHALLENGES IN THE RECRUITMENT AND RETENTION OF FACULTY

(Three chairs served as panelists.)

Over the past twenty-five years the recruitment and retention of faculty was not highly competitive, because (a) most institutions were "tenured in" with faculty members hired in the 1960s, (b) higher education was in a period of general retrenchment, with little new hiring, and (c) there were many more Ph.D.s being produced than there were vacancies in higher education to fill. Things are changing. The recruitment of new faculty is becoming much more competitive and costly. Efforts to retain faculty being courted by other institutions have created new tensions within units and greater challenges for the institution as counter offers are constructed. How do chairs view current practices? What are some useful counter-offer strategies? Are there preemptive steps that might be taken to retain our most marketable faculty? What are the implications for unit morale if new faculty or faculty retained through counter offers enjoy a better standard of living than their peers? Should the university consider different policies and practices when it comes to recruiting and retaining faculty? These and other issues will be reviewed by the panelists and then discussed by all participants.

CASE STUDIES: THE PERILS OF PERSONNEL

(The session was led by the executive associate dean. Four case studies were provided to attendees several days before the retreat, to be read prior to the retreat.)

A faculty member wants to change his workload distribution for the previous year a day before annual performance reviews are conducted. The dean wants your unit to look at a potential partner accommodation appointment. You have a star faculty member who is making increasing demands for special consideration. It is rumored that a senior colleague is getting overly interested in some of the female graduate students. It is just another day in the life of a chair! Real (but disguised) cases will be discussed with the purpose of helping all chairs get ideas for dealing with difficult personnel cases.

STATE OF THE UNITS IN THE COLLEGE: INSTITUTIONAL DATA

(The dean led the discussion.)

There is a growing body of institutional data that describe the departments and programs of the university. The provost makes budget decisions using these data. They are used by the graduate college in program reviews, and they inform college decisions about unit performance in response to institutional needs. Data from the graduating senior survey, the department profile, and the allocation of personnel will be reviewed. There will be things in these reports to make units simultaneously proud and humble, elated and angry, boastful and shamed. These data are almost certainly flawed in nettlesome ways, but they should cause each unit to reflect on what they suggest about achievements and challenges.

UNIT PLANNING IN UNCERTAIN TIMES

(Three chairs led small discussion groups.)

Higher education exists in a broader environment featuring mixed signals, uncertain budgets, changing expectations, and increased com-petition from for-profit educational enterprises. The mixed signals seem to cause institutional attention to jump from undergraduate edu-cation to sponsored research, to teaching loads, to community out-reach, to fund-raising, and so on. Budgets seem meager, unpredictable, and unrealistic in terms of ambitions. Roles and rewards for faculty seem to be changing, but with reluctance and worry on the part of institutions. Enrollments are threatened because of "path of least re-sistance" degree offerings on campus and in the marketplace. How do units craft functional strategic plans in such a sea of change? In the early part of this session, retreat participants will divide into subgroups, each led by a discussion leader. The groups will reconvene in the latter part of the session for a group discussion about planning in a period of uncertainty.

GAINING ACCESS TO CAPITAL CAMPAIGN RICHES

(The session was led by the College's senior development officer; three chairs served as panelists.)

The university is in the last two years of a five-year capital campaign that will raise over five hundred million dollars. These monies will pro-vide support for scores of endowed chairs and professorships, hundreds of scholarships and fellowships, and numerous other forms of program en-hancement. A question that is often asked is: How does a department get its hands on some of these resources? The answer is: You'll have to wait to hear from our panelists and senior development officer. Three Admin-istrative Council members who have been involved with aspects of friend raising, fund-raising, and program enhancement as a result of the capital campaign will discuss their experiences. The senior development officer will provide insight into the development process, highlighting important steps for a department to take if it wants to be on the receiving end of major gifts.

RESPONDING TO THE UNIVERSITY'S NEW STUDENT MIX

(Three chairs served as panelists.)

The university is attracting greater numbers of freshmen (the freshman entry-class size has tripled in ten years) and far greater numbers of high-achieving students. While the notion of student as consumer has caused marginal students to be more "noisy" about being satisfied, the expectations about class quality and opportunities for deeper enjoyment have grown with the swelling population of high-achieving students. Are we providing quality offerings that challenge our best and brightest students? Can we offer as many undergraduate research experiences as are needed? If trends continue, there will be between five and six hundred National Merit Scholars on the campus in two years. How can departments simultaneously deal with the increased numbers of freshmen and with the heightened expectations for quality held by the strongest undergraduates?

CASE STUDIES: ADMINISTRATIVE PROBLEM SOLVING

(The discussion was led by the executive associate dean. Four case studies were distributed prior to the retreat, to be read before the retreat.)

Four case studies (all loosely based on actual incidents) serve collectively as a basis for discussing approaches chairs might take to address various personnel issues. The cases touch on the chair's authority and bylaws, maternity leave and issues of accommodation, contested performance evaluations, and the chair's role in influencing faculty morale. As a chair, one never knows what the day will bring. Inevitably, difficult personnel issues will emerge. The purpose of the session is to gain insights about how chairs from diverse units would approach and deal with some difficult personnel issues.

TELLING OUR STORY: BUILDING PUBLIC AWARENESS OF THE UNIVERSITY'S STRENGTHS AND SUCCESSES

(The panelists included the college's director of media relations, a producer of television documentaries, and the university's director of research publications.)

When state universities were widely viewed by most Americans as important to the common good, efforts aimed at getting publicity for campus activities were almost unseemly. In more recent times, public support for higher education has decreased, and the importance of favorable publicity has become much more significant. How can the college be more effective in "getting the word out" about its strengths and successes? What are the best vehicles for different messages and audiences? What are some strategies for successfully marketing your department? How can the college exploit "big" stories with the media? What should one expect in working with the mass media? This session is intended to help chairs get answers to these questions and learn how to be more effective in getting favorable publicity for their units.

IMPROVING FACULTY RETENTION: CURRENT STRATEGIES AND LIMITATIONS

(Three chairs served as panelists.)

After nearly a quarter-century of limited recruitment, the academic marketplace has moved to a new level of competitiveness for the best faculty. The recruitment of new faculty is featuring escalating salaries and a variety of "perks" unheard of in the recent past. Partner accommodation for academic professional couples is a frequent complication. Preemptive offers and counteroffers are necessary to retain top faculty. Recruitment packages for academic "stars" can be extraordinary. Relief from normal teaching is commonly offered, but this runs at cross-purposes to goals of undergraduate education. What are chairs doing to attract and retain academic talent? What is the morale cost of successful recruitment and retention when those who are more and less marketable have different standards of living? Are salary compression and inversion problems? What university policies and practices are undermining our ability to retain faculty? Should they be changed? This session is meant to help chairs better understand the challenges and perils of a more competitive academic marketplace.

ISSUES IN GRADUATE EDUCATION

(Three chairs served as panelists.)

The university's graduate education programs are under pressure from all directions. Stipends are low, and the number of waivers of out-of-state tuition has been reduced. There are few graduate fellowships, and state-funded research assistantships are being phased out. As our academic reputation grows, the students we compete for are receiving offers from stronger institutions. The work expectations for teaching assistants remain high. Graduate-student militance is growing nationally. How should the college respond to these challenges? What steps should chairs take to protect and strengthen their graduate education programs?

SPACE UTILIZATION: GUIDELINES FOR MANAGING
A CRUCIAL RESOURCE

(Discussion led by the associate dean responsible for facilities management.)

The quality and quantity of space available to a department has a direct impact on its ability to operate effectively. The acquisition of new (or additional) space is an agonizingly slow process. The renovation of existing space is expensive, and the approval chain is long and complex. Internal reallocation of existing space is normally resisted and occurs at a political cost to the chair. What authority does the chair enjoy in assigning (or reassigning) space? What universal guidelines might be established to help chairs make the difficult decisions necessary to utilize existing space fully?

ENHANCING THE CAMPUS ENVIRONMENT:
WHAT CAN DEPARTMENTS DO?

(Discussion led by the associate dean responsible for academic affairs.)

In the past few years here and elsewhere, attempts to advance cultural diversity on campus have generated much activity among both faculty and student bodies. Given the manifestly rising racial and ethnic tensions on campus, do you believe the Faculty Senate–mandated cultural diversity awareness course requirement is an appropriate or inappropriate response? Do you believe such a requirement or newly proposed regulations inhibit legitimate expressions of thought on issues that relate to race, ethnicity, religion, gender, or other group identity? How can the stated university goal of promoting awareness and appreciation of cultural diversity in our society and among our students be best accomplished while protecting principles of academic freedom?

LEADERSHIP AMONG PEERS: NORMS OF BEHAVIOR FROM
DIFFERENT PERSPECTIVES

(Three chairs served as panelists.)

The chair, the faculty, and the dean may view what constitutes effective leadership quite differently. Three "seasoned" chairs provide their observations and perspectives on leadership in four areas: practices of consultation with the faculty, the chair's role in mentoring, balancing the need for departmental advocacy with the expectation of an institutional perspective as part of a broader administrative team, and strategies for dealing with difficult people.

EVOLVING FACULTY RESPONSIBILITIES:
IMPLICATIONS FOR PROMOTION AND TENURE

(Three chairs served as panelists.)

American universities have been renewing their commitment to undergraduate education and engaging in new and varied outreach activities; the responsibility to deliver on these growing promises falls to faculty. The evaluation and weighting of contributions to student learning and community enrichment (campus, local, and professional communities) is undergoing change, with portfolios revealing a greater emphasis on responsiveness to institutional needs. Complexity is introduced by a number of conditions, most significantly that the institution's national reputation is driven primarily by the quality of the faculty as judged by leadership in research and graduate education. Also, the university's policies suggest that items other than academic performance can be significant in tenure decisions. Three chairs will provide their thoughts and lead a discussion of the changing (or constant) criteria for promotion and tenure.

CRAFTING FUNCTIONAL FACULTY WORK PLANS

(Three chairs served as panelists.)

A fundamental concept imbedded in post-tenure review is the expectation that chairs/directors develop a prospective work plan for each faculty member and that if the faculty member carries it out, his/her performance will be evaluated as satisfactory or better and the dean's audit will find the faculty member's responsibilities to have been a full and "appropriate" workload. ("Appropriate" has been defined as relating to "kind, amount, and quality.") What mixes of things represent a full load? How general or specific should the statements be? Are there implications for tenure denials that are reviewed by the Committee on Academic Freedom and Tenure if specific modest goals have been set and met each year leading up to the negative tenure decision? How does the chair deal with the faculty member who will not sign the workload plan or who refuses to teach an assigned course? Is there a way to use the plan to address problems of faculty who disrupt and interfere with the work of others? Distrusted faculty members are never elected to committees; should service expectations be reduced for such individuals? Can work plans be used in ways that revitalize faculty? The panelists will provide personal perspectives and lead a discussion about these issues.

PROTECTING ONE'S RESEARCH TIME AS CHAIR

(Three chairs served as panelists.)

For most individuals, service as chair or director represents a temporary diversion from the full-time academic life that precedes and follows the stint in administration. The university and the individuals chosen to be chair hope and expect that career scholarly achievement will not be permanently impaired by the distractions of administration. For many, this is the case. For others, especially those who serve extended terms, remaining active as a scholar is difficult, and faculty life becomes "boring." Administrative life, however, is punctuated with interruptions and deadlines. Attending to the needs of others often takes precedence over one's own research and creative endeavors. How do successful chair-scholars protect their calendars? How do they find the blocks of time needed for major projects and travel? Can access to graduate students be maintained? These problems and strategies for dealing with them will be discussed by three experienced chairs, who will then respond to questions and participate in an extended conversation by the entire group.

NOTE

1. These sessions were approximately one and one-half hours in length and were used as a professional development tool for improving the talent of chairs and directors.

APPENDIX B:
Chair Administrative Evaluation Form

These questions can be used with a scale using verbal anchors ranging from "strongly agree" to "strongly disagree." The evaluation can be conducted by department faculty and by members of the dean's staff.

LEADERSHIP

1. Works with faculty to establish objectives and strategies to move the unit forward.
2. Works with the community to generate additional support for the established objectives and strategies of the unit.
3. Communicates to appropriate administrators the unit's needs, objectives, strategies, and problems.
4. Involves faculty in the shared governance of the unit.
5. Makes the needed decisions to further the unit toward achievement of its objectives.
6. Continues to develop as a recognized scholar.
7. Overall, this chair is a good leader.

SUPPORT FOR FACULTY

8. Establishes and follows procedures for recognizing and rewarding faculty accomplishments.
9. Conducts faculty evaluations in a meaningful and supportive manner.

10. Provides leadership and support for an environment that allows faculty members to realize their potential.

11. Works to prevent dissension within the unit and to provide a collegial atmosphere.

12. Supports a program that assists new faculty to develop as teachers and scholars.

13. Overall, this chair does a good job in supporting faculty.

MANAGEMENT

14. Demonstrates commitment to affirmative action and cultural diversity.

15. Follows established procedures for allocating resources such as travel and research monies.

16. Does a good job of hiring and supervising staff.

17. Provides concise information about policies, procedures, and professional opportunities.

18. Efficiently manages scheduling, committee assignments, recruitment procedures, etc.

19. Supports teaching, mentoring, and other programs that enhance the student experience.

20. Overall, this chair does a good job of management.

APPENDIX C:
Faculty Recruitment Ethics Statement

THE ETHICS OF RECRUITMENT AND FACULTY APPOINTMENT

A statement adopted by the Council of Colleges of Arts and Sciences in November 1992 was jointly adopted by the American Association of University Professors in June 1993.

PROLOGUE

The standards which follow are intended to apply to the recruitment and appointment of faculty members in most colleges and universities. These standards are directed to administrators and faculty members in the belief that they will promote the identification and selection of qualified candidates through a process which promotes candor and effective communication among those who are engaged in recruitment. The standards are offered not as rules to serve every situation, but with the expectation that they will provide a foundation for appropriate practices. The spirit of openness and shared responsibility which these standards are intended to convey are consistent with affirmative action as well as other guiding principles in the recruitment of faculty.

I. The Announcement of a Faculty Position

A. Prior to the announcement of a faculty vacancy, there should be agreement among all responsible parties on each major element of the position (e.g., rank, salary, and eligibility for tenure), how the position relates to the department's (or equivalent unit's) likely needs for the future, the expectations concerning the professional work of the faculty member(s) being recruited, and the resources that will be provided to help the faculty member(s) meet those expectations.

B. An institution that announces a search should be genuinely engaged in an open process of recruitment for that position. Descriptions of vacant positions should be published and distributed as widely as possible to reach all potential candidates. The procedure established for reviewing applicants and for selecting final candidates should be consistent with the institution's announced criteria and commitment to a fair and open search.

C. All announcements for faculty positions should be clear concerning rank, the length of the appointment, whether the position is with tenure or carries eligibility for tenure, whether the availability of the position is contingent upon funding or other conditions, teaching and research expectations, and requisite experience and credentials. Criteria and procedures for reappointment, promotion, and tenure at the institution, as well as other relevant information, should be made available to all interested candidates upon request.

D. Interested candidates should have at least thirty days from the first appearance of the announcement to submit their application.

II. Confidentiality, Interviews, and the Final Decision

A. Institutions should respect the confidentiality of candidates for faculty positions. The institution may contact references, including persons who are not identified by the candidate, but it should exercise discretion when doing so. An institution should not make public the names of candidates without having given the candidate the opportunity to withdraw from the search.

B. Those who participate in the interview should avoid any discriminatory treatment of candidates. All communications with the candidates concerning the position should be consistent with the information stated in the announcement for the position.

C. Candidates for faculty positions should disclose in a timely fashion conditions that might materially bear upon the institution's decision to offer the appointment (for example, requirements for research funds, unusual moving costs, a delayed starting date, or the intention to retain an affiliation at the institution with which the candidate is currently associated).

D. If candidates request information about the progress of the search and the status of their candidacy, they should be given the information.

E. The institution's decision about which candidate will be offered the position should be consistent with the criteria for the position and the duties as stated in the announcement of the vacancy. If the selection of the final candidates will be based on significant changes in the criteria for the position or the duties as stated in the original announcement, the institution should start a new search.

III. The Offer and the Acceptance

A. The institution may wish to provide informal notification to the successful candidate of its intention to offer an appointment, but the formal offer itself should be an unequivocal letter offering appointment signed by the responsible institutional officer. "Oral offers" and "oral acceptances" should not be considered binding, but communications between the successful candidate and those representing the institution should be frank and accurate, for significant decisions are likely to be based on these exchanges. The written offer of appointment should be given to the candidate within ten days of the institution's having conveyed an intention to make the offer; a candidate should be informed promptly if the offer is not to be forthcoming within ten days.

B. The terms of an offer to an individual should be consistent with the announcement of the position. Each of the following should be stated clearly in the letter offering an appointment: (a) the initial rank; (b) the length of the appointment; (c) conditions of renewal; (d) the salary and benefits; (e) the duties of the position; (f) as applicable, whether the appointment is with tenure, the amount of credit toward tenure for prior service, and the maximum length of the probationary period; (g) as applicable, the institution's "startup" commitments for the appointment (for example, equipment and laboratory space); (h) the date when the appointment begins and the date when the candidate is expected to report; (i) the date by which the candidate's response to the offer is expected, which should not be less than two weeks from receipt of the offer; and (j) details of institutional policies and regulations that bear upon the appointment. Specific information on other relevant matters also should be conveyed in writing to the prospective appointee.

C. An offer of appointment to a faculty member serving at another institution should be made no later than May 1, consistent with the faculty member's obligation to resign, in order to accept other employment, no later than May 15. It is recognized that, in special cases, it might be appropriate to make an offer after May 1, but in such cases there should be an agreement by all concerned parties.

D. The acceptance of a position is a candidate's written affirmative and unconditional response sent by the candidate to the institution no later than the date stated in the offer of appointment. If the candidate wishes to accept the offer contingent upon conditions, those conditions should be specified and communicated promptly in writing to the institution which is offering the position.

E. If the candidate intends to retain an affiliation with his or her current institution, that circumstance should be brought promptly to the attention of the current institution and the recruiting institution.

F. Individuals who accept an appointment should arrive at the institution in sufficient time to prepare for their duties and to participate in orientation programs.

APPENDIX D:
Policy on Partner Accommodation

This policy statement outlines what can be expected by academic pairs when one member applies for a position with the university.

POLICY ON PARTNER ACCOMMODATION

The college recognizes the importance of accommodating dual-career academic couples. Increasingly, such accommodation is necessary in order for departments to be successful in their recruitment efforts. Because dual-career partnerships typically involve employment needs or opportunities across units, college-level policy is required. The following guidelines characterize the role of the college and the procedures it will follow in support of a domestic partner accompanying a successful candidate for a tenure-track faculty position.

- The college's willingness to entertain requests for partner employment is a matter of public record. Thus, all short-listed candidates for faculty positions will be informed, in a like manner, of the procedures involved in a potential partner hire.
- While the college will facilitate placement of an accompanying partner (budgetary conditions permitting), it will in no way curtail the departmental prerogative (as exercised through the chair) to make decisions on hiring. If an accompanying partner does not have the credentials or sufficient promise to be compatible in the unit in which a position is sought, no employment will be pursued.

- Any offer of employment within any unit in the college will be contingent on the candidate's qualifications and on the availability of resources. The academic unit must systematically review an accompanying partner, like any candidate for any faculty position. A recommendation on whether or not to hire will be made by the chair/director of the academic unit after consultation (as determined by unit bylaws) with the voting members of the unit.

PROCEDURES

1. Every candidate for an on-campus interview for a faculty position in one of the college's units, at the time an invitation for the interview is extended, will be informed that she or he should feel free to discuss partner needs without risk of potential bias. (Search committees, following established equal opportunity policy, will not consider partner needs in arriving at hiring decisions.)

2. When a candidate who has been offered a position seeks a faculty appointment within the college for an accompanying partner, the chair of the department recommending the original offer will request a copy of the partner's c.v. and other relevant credentials. The chair will then forward the materials to the dean.

3. If the budgetary situation permits, the dean will forward the credentials to the relevant college unit. The unit will then review the credentials, possibly requesting further information and a more complete dossier.

4. If there is sufficient interest in the unit in which the accompanying partner would seek employment, then a regular interview process may ensue.

5. After the interview process is completed, the chair/director will forward a recommendation to the dean. The recommendation may be either for or against an appointment to a regular position, or the recommendation may be for an alternatively characterized position. The dean will then make a decision on whether or not to support an appointment (which must further be approved by the provost) based on the unit's recommendation and budgetary considerations.

6. When a candidate who has been offered a position seeks a faculty appointment outside the college for her/his partner, the dean (after being informed of the request by the chair) will forward a copy of the partner's credentials to the dean/vice president of the relevant college, school, or other university unit for consideration under the policies governing that other unit.

APPENDIX E:
Performance Evaluation Review Guidelines

These guidelines are used to regulate the process of seeking a review of an annual performance evaluation that the recipient believes is incorrect.

PERFORMANCE EVALUATION REVIEW GUIDELINES

In the college, the Performance Evaluation Review process is undertaken only after a faculty member has appealed his/her performance evaluation and salary adjustment at the department level and not obtained relief.

According to the trustees' "next higher level" policy, a College Performance Evaluation Review is the final appeal of the departmental performance evaluation. Therefore, it is essential that the appellant's case be presented clearly and convincingly, be based on specific grounds, and include all relevant facts. The appellant should provide supporting documents in as far as possible; if documents are unattainable, their nature and probable location should be given.

An appeal to the Performance Evaluation Review Committee should include:

1. A brief description of how the appellant's performance was evaluated within the department, including a summary of the steps taken by the appellant within the department to appeal the evaluation

2. A specific appeal of this performance evaluation, based on one of the Grounds for Appeal listed below, with supporting evidence

3. A request for redress, stating what the appellant feels the performance
   evaluation should have been and what adjustment is requested

Grounds for an appeal fall in one of two categories: either procedural irregularity or formal inadequacy. The appellant should appeal on the grounds of *procedural irregularity* if it is claimed that established departmental performance evaluation procedures were not applied fairly.

In appealing on these grounds, the appellant should describe the departmental procedures and demonstrate as clearly and convincingly as possible the nature of the unfairness. In general, procedures that have been applied in a discriminatory, negligent, inconsistent, or unreasonable manner would be considered to have been applied unfairly.

The appellant should appeal on the grounds of *formal inadequacy* if established performance review guidelines are in conflict with Regents or University principles and guidelines for performance evaluation procedures.

ASPECTS OF THE REVIEW

The first level of appeal is in the department. Departments have been requested to establish an appeal process. At a minimum, appeals must have been brought to the attention of the department chair, who following appropriate consultation, provides the appellant with a written response (decision).

If a faculty member has appealed his or her performance evaluation and salary adjustment at the departmental level and not obtained relief, the individual may request a review of his or her salary adjustment at the next highest administrative level (the college). The review of these appeals will be conducted by the CLAS Committee of Review, which will make a recommendation to the dean regarding each case referred to the college committee. The dean's decision is final.

GRIEVANCE OF FAILURE TO FOLLOW UNIVERSITY POLICIES AND PROCEDURES

An individual may grieve a deviation from board policies and procedures to the appropriate grievance committee. Grievances based on discrimination are to be referred to the Office of Affirmative Action and Equal Employment.

APPENDIX F:
Supplemental Review Policy

This policy statement serves to guide reviews conducted outside the faculty member's tenure home, most typically in support of an interdisciplinary program.

1. The primary locus of all reviews will be the tenure home (primary unit) of the candidate. The chair or director will be responsible for ensuring that the guidelines are followed.

2. Any faculty member or academic professional who has affiliated status in a unit beyond the tenure home (secondary unit), or whose work plan involves academic service (teaching, research, or committee work) in a secondary unit, may request supplemental review. Requests must be made in the spring of the year prior to probationary, tenure/continuing status, or promotion reviews.

3. A faculty member or academic professional who requests supplemental review may choose one of two options, to be reviewed internal to the secondary unit, or to have commentary solicited from supplemental external referees.

4. An internal supplemental review will require a letter from the line officer of the secondary unit and a letter from the relevant review committee (if the secondary unit is a department or instructional program).

5. An external supplemental review will require a minimum of six external letters rather than the customary four letters. The additional two letters will be expected to focus on the candidate's teaching, research, or service efforts made in support of the secondary unit. The chair or director of the primary unit will solicit additional names from

the candidate as well as the chair or director of the secondary unit. All letters will be solicited by the primary unit and those pertaining to work in support of the secondary unit will be available to its review committee and line officer during the review process. Deadlines for submission of external letters must be set so as to allow sufficient time for review by the two units. The authors of external letters must be informed about who will see their responses.

6. Materials assembled by the secondary unit, including the letters from the review committee (if relevant) and the line officer, will be sent to the primary unit (date due) to be included in the normal review process as conducted by the primary unit committee and line officer (due to the college by the beginning of [date]).

7. Any unit with lines must have a review committee constituted in accordance with its bylaws. The composition of the review committee must be consistent with provisions in the academic affairs manual.

8. In both the primary and secondary units the reviews by the review committee and the line officer must be handled independently. All participants must sign the letter from the review committee.

9. All reports and letters from the secondary unit must be a part of the review process.

10. All faculty and academic professionals who engage in significant teaching, research, or service in support of a secondary unit, when being considered in the review process, must be given the option of requesting or declining supplemental review as described above.

APPENDIX G:
Professional Guidelines for the Evaluation of Academic Deans

CCAS STATEMENT ON PROFESSIONAL GUIDELINES FOR THE EVALUATION OF ACADEMIC DEANS

INTRODUCTION

The quality, character, and reputation of an academic institution are determined largely by the people (faculty, students, administrators, staff, and friends) brought together to realize its educational mission, and by the organizational success it enjoys in achieving that mission. Next to decisions about the hiring, tenure, and promotion of faculty, which give academic definition to an institution, the most important personnel actions taken in colleges and universities are those involving administrative leadership. The quality of academic life and the level of institutional effectiveness depend upon sound management by chairs, directors, deans, and vice presidents. It is, therefore, important for academic organizations to operate in a professional manner regarding the evaluation of academic administrators. This statement is directed at the evaluation of college deans; it offers advice on two basic elements of professional practice: establishment of policies and common courtesies.

POLICIES: A BASIC ELEMENT OF SOUND PRACTICE

Organizations establish policies to bring clarity and standardization to their internal practices. Sound policies ensure that principles rather than personalities are the basis for action, thereby eliminating ad hoc decision making on appointments, evaluation reviews, reappointments, extensions, nonrenewals, and dismissals for cause. Sound policies allow for change that is handled fairly and according to stated procedures and rules. The existence of sound policies brings order and predictability to, and builds confidence in, actions pertaining to administrative leadership. There are two aspects that are foundational to sound practice when it comes to the evaluation of administrators: the existence of an accurate position description and the reliance on standardized evaluation processes.

Position Description. At a minimum, institutional policy should include a generic written description for each academic administrative position. The description should include the duties and responsibilities of the position, the authority vested in or delegated to the individual holding the position, the appointment period, and the conditions for renewal or extension, including decision rules for cases in which formal voting is featured.

Standardized Evaluation Practices. There should be clarity and consistency on all aspects of the administrative evaluation or review of deans. An institution's policies on the review of academic administrators should be congruent with the following principles:

1. The scope and mechanics of all evaluations of administrative performance should be known, codified, and exist as an aspect of institutional policy. (CCAS recommends that evaluation policies feature provision for broad input from a variety of venues, rather than being limited to a single source and instrument.)

2. Those individuals asked to provide input should be well informed about the requirements of the position and the job-related accomplishments (or lack thereof).

3. Reviews should occur on a known, regular cycle. (Where possible, CCAS recommends a review period of no fewer than three years, with five years as the preferred period. This provides the time needed to begin to observe the changes and results of actions taken at the college level.)

4. The collection, statistical treatment, and conclusions drawn from evaluative data should be handled with the same rigor and objectivity that would be viewed as sound practice in research.

5. Successful administrative evaluations feature an appropriate balance between (a) the right of the college's members to have input that is appropriately confidential and access to summary results that are disseminated in a timely way, and (b) the right of the dean being evaluated to

receive appropriate summary data and to enjoy the same level of privacy normally associated with other related personnel actions in the institution.

ADMINISTRATIVE COURTESIES

Academic officers to whom deans report should extend a number of basic courtesies when it comes to evaluation and the use of results as they pertain to the administrative appointment. The dean should expect that his/her supervising academic officer will:

1. start the evaluation process by alerting the dean about its nature, purpose, and timetable for completion;
2. use the evaluation results as a tool for providing constructive feedback and advice;
3. provide an opportunity for the dean to respond to the results of the evaluation;
4. give the dean reasonable time to deal with any deficiencies;
5. develop a final written evaluation statement that considers all appropriate forms of evidence and serves as the basis for decisions about salary adjustment, extension, or nonrenewal;
6. provide appropriate conditions for a return to a faculty appointment (once the administrative term has been completed) that will facilitate the resumption of normal faculty life. Considerations here include administrative leave with pay, favorable action on a sabbatical leave request (where available), and a salary reversion tied to appropriate benchmarks; and
7. afford due process in any contested personnel action.

When an institution adheres to the guidelines described above it provides a sound foundation for constructive evaluation, and creates conditions under which the benefits of healthy administrative relationships can be realized. The Council of Colleges of Arts and Sciences and its members endorse these guidelines for use in all institutions of higher education.

APPENDIX H:
Policy on Salary Support for the Recipients of Fellowships

POLICY ON SALARY SUPPORT FOR RECIPIENTS OF FELLOWSHIPS IN THE HUMANITIES AND SOCIAL SCIENCES

Faculty in the humanities and social sciences often receive distinguished fellowship opportunities and are unable to accept such awards because the award is far less than the salary. Stipulations of the award generally preclude teaching during the award year. In an effort to ensure that faculty can accept such fellowship awards without suffering large financial loss, the following guidelines will be followed.

1. The total supplement may never exceed 50 percent of the faculty member's salary during the year of the fellowship.
2. The faculty member's department must agree to replacement of the individual by course section and not by the hiring of a full-time replacement.
3. Commitment to these guidelines will be made at the time of fellowship application.

APPENDIX I:
Principles Governing Space Resources

PRINCIPLES GOVERNING SPACE RESOURCES

1. Space is an essential and frequently program-constraining resource that must be effectively managed to enable departments/centers to meet their immediate and long-term goals.

2. Chairs/directors have the authority and responsibility to manage the space resources under departmental/center jurisdiction. This includes the authority for reassignment and reallocation of space among faculty, staff, and programs.

3. Chairs/directors may appoint space committees to assist in planning and to provide advice on the modification and management of space resources.

4. Faculty/staff/programs are granted occupancy or custody of space, but these assignments are not in perpetuity. Review of space utilization should be performed annually.

5. Space assignments to faculty/staff/programs should be based on acceptable standards or operating practices that will enable the department to reach its goals by making full and efficient use of assigned space.

6. Criteria to be used in assigning/allocating space to faculty/staff/programs should include, but not be limited to, consideration of the following items:

   special or unique requirements related to teaching/service assignments or activities,

   special or unique requirements of the research area,

productivity of faculty/staff/program as indicated by:

a. number of supported post-doctoral associates and technicians,

b. number of participating graduate and undergraduate students,

c. amount of extramural funds obtained (and the proportion of the work to be conducted on campus), and

d. number of publications/presentations generated.

7. Chairs/directors have the authority and responsibility to recommend a change in function, modification, or renovation of existing space under their jurisdiction.

8. Chairs/directors may request use or assignment of space outside their jurisdiction that clearly would assist the department/center in meeting its goals and that (a) has been identified as being available for bid, or (b) is underutilized by other departments.

9. Chairs/directors have the responsibility (and obligation) to plan for and seek authorization for new construction if it is essential to achieving approved goals. Justification requires demonstrated needs based on university-approved guidelines.

APPENDIX J:
Equal Opportunity and Affirmative Action in Higher Education

I. Equal Opportunity is freedom from certain forms of discrimination that have been deemed to be illegal. Decisions in higher education—and elsewhere—require discrimination, but such actions must rely on appropriate discriminating measures. The forms of discrimination that are prohibited are reviewed in outline form below.

    A. *Civil Rights Act of 1964* (as amended)

        1. *Title VI*. Prohibits discrimination on the basis of race, color, or national origin, in programs or activities that receive federal funds.

        2. *Title VII*. Prohibits discrimination on the basis of sex, color, national origin, or religion, in employment.

        3. *Title IX*. (Amendments of 1972) Prohibits discrimination on the basis of sex, in education programs and activities.

    B. *Executive Order 11246* prohibits discrimination on the basis of sex, color, national origin, or religion, in employment.

    C. *Rehabilitation Act of 1973, Section 794* (as amended), prohibits discrimination on the basis of disabilities, in programs, and in activities.

    D. *Vietnam Era Veterans Readjustment Assistance Act of 1974* prohibits discrimination in employment for special disabled veterans, veterans of the Vietnam era, and any other veterans who served on active duty during a war or in a campaign or expedition for which a campaign badge has been authorized.

    E. *Equal Pay Act of 1963* prohibits discrimination on the basis of sex, in rates of pay and benefits.

F. *Age Discrimination in Employment Act of 1967* prohibits discrimination against individuals age forty and above, in employment.

G. *Age Discrimination Act of 1975* prohibits discrimination against people of all ages, in programs or activities that receive federal funds.

H. *American with Disabilities Act of 1990* prohibits discrimination on the basis of disability, in private sector employment, in services rendered by state and local governments, in places of public accommodation, in transportation, and in telecommunication relay services.

II. Affirmative Action is a policy or program for correcting the effects of past discrimination in the employment or education of certain groups. Such programs give preference to members of protected classes when two individuals are otherwise essentially equal in their job-related qualifications. The legal basis for affirmative action is reviewed in outline form below.

A. *Executive Order 11246 of 1965* (as amended) requires affirmative action in employment and requires employers of fifty or more employees and a federal contract of fifty thousand dollars (or more) annually to have a written affirmative action plan.

B. *Rehabilitation Act of 1973, Section 793* (as amended), requires affirmative action to employ and advance in employment qualified individuals with disabilities.

C. *Vietnam Era Veterans Readjustment Assistance Act of 1974* requires affirmative action to employ and advance in employment special disabled veterans, veterans of the Vietnam era and any other veterans who served on active duty during a war or in a campaign or expedition for which a campaign badge has been authorized.

D. Court Cases Bearing on Affirmative Action

    1. *Regents of the University of California v. Bakke* struck down the use of quotas in college admissions, but held that colleges could give some consideration to race in trying to achieve diversity.

    2. *Hopwood v. Texas,* for institutions under the jurisdiction of the Fifth Federal Circuit (Texas, Louisiana, and Mississippi), prohibited the use of race in college admissions.

    3. *Grutter v. Bollinger* held that the consideration of race and ethnicity in admissions serves a compelling government interest. The Court ruled that colleges may use race-conscious admissions policies, so long as they consider applicants as individuals and do not automatically give some edge to protected class members. The Court further held that efforts at maintaining a "critical mass" of protected class members did not amount to using an illegal quota, if the institution did not have a fixed number of students in mind. Those writing the

majority opinion noted the importance of having an admissions policy that was "flexible enough to ensure that each applicant is evaluated as an individual and not in a way that makes race or ethnicity the defining feature of the application."

4. *Gratz v. Bollinger* held that policies that treat whole groups of applicants differently based solely on their race are impermissible.

E. State Laws and Executive Orders

1. *Ballot measures* in California and Washington State have outlawed affirmative action in university admissions.

2. *An executive order* issued in 1999 by the governor, prohibited the use of affirmative action and required race-neutral admissions in the state colleges and universities of Florida.

III. Reasonable Accommodation refers to the requirement of employers to make modifications to a job application process, the work environment, or the ability of qualified applicants and employees with disabilities to enjoy equal benefits and privileges of employment as are enjoyed by similarly situated employees without disabilities, unless such action creates an undo hardship for the employer. Reasonable accommodation may include such actions as making existing facilities available, job restructuring, part-time or modified work schedules, acquiring or modifying equipment, changing tests, training materials or policies, providing qualified readers or interpreters, and reassignment to a vacant position. The legal bases for these requirements are the *Rehabilitation Act of 1973, Section 794* (as amended), and *Title I of the Americans with Disabilities Act of 1990.*

BIBLIOGRAPHY

Allen, G., ed. 1999. *The resource handbook for academic deans*. Washington, D.C.: American Conference on Academic Deans.

Austin, M. J., F. L. Ahearn, and R. A. English, eds. 1997. *The professional school dean: Meeting the leadership challenges*. New Directions in Higher Education. No. 98. San Francisco: Jossey-Bass.

Boc, D. C. 2003. *Universities in the marketplace: The commercialization of higher education*. Princeton, N.J.: Princeton University Press.

Boyer, E. L. 1990. *Scholarship reconsidered*. Princeton, N.J.: Carnegie Foundation for the Advancement of Teaching.

Bright, D. F., and M. P. Richards. 2001. *The academic deanship: Individual careers and institutional roles*. San Francisco: Jossey-Bass.

Diamond, R. M., and B. E. Adam. 1995. *The disciplines speak*. Washington, D.C.: American Association for Higher Education.

Employee Assistant Program (EAP) and EAP Core Technology. 2002. Arlington, Va.: Employee Assistance Professional Association.

Fogg, P. 2003. Academic therapists. *The Chronicle of Higher Education* 49(28): A12–A13.

Herlihy, P. A., M. Attridge, and S. P. Turner. 2002. The integration of employee assistance and work/life programs. *EAPA exchange* 32(1): 10–12.

Keller, G. 1983. *Academic strategy: The management revolution in American higher education*. Baltimore: Johns Hopkins University Press.

Kerr, C. 2001. *The gold and the blue*. Vol. 1. *Academic triumphs*. Berkeley: University of California Press.

Krahenbuhl, G. S. 2003. Are we preparing institutional difference makers? *Quest* 55: 25–29.

———. 1998. Faculty work: Integrating responsibilities and institutional needs. *Change* 30: 18–25.

Martin, J. (pseudonym). 1988. *To rise above principle: The memoirs of an unreconstructed dean*. Urbana: University of Illinois Press.

Middaugh, M. F. 2000. *Understanding faculty productivity: Standards and benchmarks for colleges and universities*. San Francisco: Jossey-Bass.

Nedwek, B. P., ed. 1997. *Doing academic planning: Effective tools for decision making*. Ann Arbor, Mich.: Society for College and University Planning.

Rameley, J. 1984. Challenges for deans. *CCAS Newsletter* 16(1): 1–3.

Rosovsky, H. 1990. *The university: An owner's manual.* New York: W. W. Norton.

Seldin, P. 1988. *Evaluating and developing administrative performance*. San Francisco: Jossey-Bass.

Selingo, J. 2003. What Americans think about higher education. *The Chronicle of Higher Education* 49(34): A12–A17.

Tucker, A. 1984. *Chairing the academic department: Leadership among peers*. New York: American Council on Education/Macmillan.

Vellery-Radot, Rene. 2003. *The life of Pasteur*. Translated by R. L. Devonshire. Whitefish, MT: Kessinger Publishing Company.Wolverton, M., and W. H. Gmelch. 2002. *College deans: Leading from within*. Westport, Conn.: American Council on Education/Greenwood.

Wolverton, M., W. H. Gmelch, J. Montez, and C. T. Nies. 2001. *The changing nature of the academic deanship*. San Francisco: Jossey-Bass.

INDEX

About the Author

GARY S. KRAHENBUHL was Senior Vice President and Deputy Provost at Arizona State University, Tempe. He was, for eleven years, a very successful dean of the ASU College of Liberal Arts and Sciences. Dr. Krahenbuhl also served a term as president of the 570-member Council of Colleges of Arts and Sciences and served for five years as the Convener (like the President) of the Council for the Arts and Sciences in Urban Universities. Dr. Krahenbuhl is now a higher education consultant.